This Will Be Funny Later

This Will Be Funny Later

A Memoir

. . .

Jenny Pentland

HARPER

An Imprint of HarperCollinsPublishers

THIS WILL BE FUNNY LATER. Copyright © 2022 by Jennifer Pentland. All rights reserved. Printed in Canada. No part of this book may be used or reproduced in any manner whatsoever without written permission except in the case of brief quotations embodied in critical articles and reviews. For information, address HarperCollins Publishers, 195 Broadway, New York, NY 10007.

HarperCollins books may be purchased for educational, business, or sales promotional use. For information, please email the Special Markets Department at SPsales@harpercollins.com.

FIRST EDITION

Printed in Canada

Library of Congress Cataloging-in-Publication Data has been applied for.

ISBN 978-0-06-296292-8

22 23 24 25 26   FB   10 9 8 7 6 5 4 3 2 1

I dedicate this book to everyone who helped create its
contents in any way, including the assholes.
To my kids, who are the funniest, deepest, rowdiest ingrates
around, and to my husband, who gave them to me and
participates equally in their care while being my biggest ally.
To my extended family for no dull moments.
To my siblings for always shooting me a look of solidarity from
across the room right when I am about to lose my mind.
To my mom for teaching me how to find the humor in everything
and anything, which has saved my life a million times.
To my dad for supporting me always and also
for remembering all the details.
Beckie, Jen, Kate, Maneli, who have listened to me
process every thought and feeling I've ever had.
To everyone who loves me and is invested in my
happiness in any way, I love you and thank you.

This Will Be Funny Later

Introduction

My life is a sitcom. I mean, I know everyone's life is, but mine is literally. The TV show *Roseanne* was based on my family. All nine years of the original show were content-mined from actual events in the lives of the five of us. My dad, Bill, was the inspiration for Dan. My mom played Roseanne Conner, a prime time–friendly version of herself. Becky and Darlene were amalgams of my sister, Jessica, and myself. D.J. was based on my little brother, Jake. Jackie was based on my mom's sister Geraldine.

The set was decorated much like our childhood home, minus the thick thatch of seventies carpet that would have stopped the camera dollies in their tracks. The overall look of it, though, half hand-me-downs and half thrift store finds, was dead-on. The pantry was full of the processed junk of the eighties. The fridge was covered in kids' drawings layered over *National Lampoon* cartoons and was full of Velveeta cheese and other nonvegetable products. There were dishes in the sink and laundry piling up on top of the washer.

As the seasons went on and what was actually happening in our lives was increasingly rated R, a lot of things were left out, and by the end of the series, it looked like a parallel-reality version of what would have happened to us had the show never existed. Roseanne and Dan stayed married. Becky never asked for a coffin as a bed or bought meth. No paparazzi hid in the bushes of the Lanford Lunch Box awaiting Roseanne's shift to be over so they could pounce on her and her boyfriend.

No illegitimate children were found via private detective. Roseanne and Jackie never had a falling-out. D.J. never crashed the Jeep he got for his Bar Mitzvah, and Darlene was never in a mental hospital.

My mom, who was the show's creator and a head writer, attempted to close that divide in the last season by doing something bold and controversial. She had Roseanne win the lottery, which allowed her to talk about how people behave around money and success. Then, once everyone had gotten used to the new direction of Roseanne's life, she pulled the rug out from under the audience and revealed that Roseanne Conner had invented this new reality from whole cloth, that she had in fact been writing the previous twenty-one episodes in order to cope with Dan's death. It was a confession of sorts, that her happy marriage to Dan had no Disney ending, and that her writing had taken liberties with her real life, which was far more tragic. I loved that storyline. I loved that ending. It was perfect, although there is no way the show's fan base could understand the importance of it.

But I saw those episodes only much later. Only a few episodes of the show had aired before my own story took me further and further from the world of the Conners. I found myself in various institutions and placement programs separate from my family.

I resented Parallel Jenny's simple life. I couldn't watch the show without feeling angry, and then I couldn't watch it because TV was not allowed in reform school. I didn't see anything beyond the second season until I was twenty-four and a married housewife with a kid of my own, stuck at home and able to catch the reruns airing seemingly nonstop on Nickelodeon. It still made me sad sometimes to think about what I had missed, but I had a life I wanted now and my pain was dull enough that I could enjoy the truly excellent joke writing. I made an effort to catch up.

I could relate to Dan and Roseanne now more than I could to Darlene, and that freaked me out. I would have a conversation with my husband, Jeff, and then I would hear it almost verbatim from the other room, but in my mom's voice. Imagine what that does to a Jewish daughter's fear of turning into her mother.

I noted the similarities of the early seasons and my childhood, and I also noted the differences, which forced me to look back at the past that I had been ecstatic to leave behind.

Neither Becky nor Darlene had to manage a public life because of their mother's fame. There were no crash diets as they didn't struggle with their weight. They lived at home through their teen years, and when they sneaked boys into their house, the boys got to stay and become a part of the family. They suffered no PTSD or mental illness in the form of anxiety disorders. Neither of them had been indoctrinated into a cult, OD'd, or spent a year or more in a private mental health facility. They were lightweight, PG versions of us with no complicated backstories. Must be nice.

1.

Most of My Dolls Had Polio

The obstetrician was stuck in Memorial Day traffic, and the nurses in my mom's hospital room demanded that she wait for him before pushing. Thankfully, listening to the instructions is not her forte, and so she pushed. I shot out just as the doctor rushed in. He caught me inches from the floor. The cord was around my neck, and I was seconds away from brain damage. My family loves to insinuate that maybe I didn't escape that fate.

From the moment I bungee-jumped out of my mom's uterus, I was ready to have kids of my own. I had already done the hard work of growing a couple ovaries full of eggs, and I was on my way to start hunting for a sperm donor. As I grew to be a toddler and beyond, this single-minded compulsion to procreate was embarrassing in our second-wave feminist circle. It was *obviously* a result of programming—if not programming by society, then by genetics or cellular memory. Either way, I wasn't strong enough to overcome it. I was born a breeder.

My not-yet-famous mom, Roseanne Barr, her radical sister, Geraldine (whom we called Beanie), and all the friends they were making in their feminist bookstore collective (a group of "womyn" who gathered to support one another's exodus from the patriarchy), worked hard to make sure I knew I had choices. They would see me struggling to change one of my doll's diapers and say, "You know, you don't have to do that. You can go read a book or play guitar or drive a truck! Be a doctor! Anything you want!" That was a big thing in the seventies, people telling kids they could be anything they wanted. When I was first asked what I wanted to be, I said, "A shopping center! And a cow!" My bitch of a sister, Jessica, who answered that same question with "an archaeologist and a parapsychologist," loved to poke my side fat and say, "At least you attained *one* of those goals."

I would act excited to try these other things my mom and her friends spoke of just to shake them off my trail, and then I'd slink away to force-feed applesauce to a doll I'd modified with a utility knife to have an open mouth. This was before we could afford the fancy dolls that were meant to be fed. When I'd squeeze my babies' cheeks to open their lips, their heads were often full of rotten food and mold. No matter. My love was unconditional.

My mom and Beanie were challenging the programming they were exposed to back in Salt Lake City, where they had grown up in the sixties watching women have upward of ten kids for their Lord. As the only Jews in their Mormon neighborhood, they were outsiders, which is a prerequisite for noticing oppressive systems at play. From their unique perspective, they were able to question why things were the way they were, instead of just blindly falling into line. Thus began their rebellious journey into destroying these systems.

While my mom and aunt and their like-minded pals sat around talking about their part in the return of the Divine Feminine in the basement of the bookstore, I was upstairs playing in the aisles with my babies, trailing after Jessica, who was thirteen months older than me, as she searched the shelves for Nancy Drews she hadn't read yet. The store had regular used books, along with lots and lots about alternative subjects. It had works by Mary Daly, the lesbian theologian; how-to Wicca books; the inspirational series *Seth Speaks*; and *A Course in Miracles*. There was a section on mysticism and Kabbalah, and books about the Akashic records. There were zines and booklets with back-page ads for mail-order witchcraft kits featuring a black-and-white photocopy of an amulet, a mostly illegible text description, a PO box address, and an amount of cash to send along with a self-addressed, stamped envelope. You had to do a lot of work back then to put a spell on someone.

I would pick up a book here and there, especially if it seemed like it might contain some sexy stuff, but mostly I just played house. I loved hanging out with my dolls, not necessarily because I loved dolls but because I loved the maternal way I *felt* playing with them. The problem with loving to play with dolls is that everyone defaults to buying them for you as gifts. Eventually you end up with a special shelf full of creepy porcelain sprites in bonnets that you have to turn around before you go to sleep at night. Just don't forget to turn them back around in the morning and apologize.

The first doll I remember getting as a gift was Mattel's Drowsy doll. She was different because she didn't drink a bottle or wet herself. Her sole purpose was to sleep. You were supposed to tuck her in bed after supplying her requested water, story, and kisses. She had a body like Yogi Bear inside the poorly structured pink polka-dotted onesie that was the only skin holding in her stuffing guts. She was soft like a pillow, but when you hugged her you could feel a hard little heart inside her that, when you pulled a string, would make her whine for things incessantly. She'd say "Mommy, kiss me good night," and "I wanna 'nother drink of water," a strange request from someone with no mouth or urethra. She had tiny, monochromatic plastic hands sticking out the onesie cuffs, and a huge blushing head that was connected to her body via an electrical tie beneath the fabric. Her face was molded and painted in such a way as to make her look half-asleep, but the sculptors missed the mark and she looked more like a drunk aunt at Passover who was about to tell you a sexually revealing story about your uncle. Her hair was "real" rooted hair, but they had skimped where they could. When you ran your hand back over her humongous forehead, you could see the alternating rows of smooth baldness and too-big holes with clumps of polyester strings geysering out. It was like a blighted cornfield in an agricultural collapse and was styled into the same humiliating one-length bob that every kid had at the time.

Even though you had to pull the string to make her talk, you were always a smidge irritated by, and resigned to, the fact that she was bothering you again.

This level of resignation was my true goal in life. I would watch the women around me in awe as they scheduled their kids' after-school activities, planned their meals, shopped, cleaned toilets, curated closets, stacked the mail in a certain place, worked outside the home, challenged the patriarchy, multitasked, handled every aspect of menial day-to-day life, and didn't flinch.

I knew I was the kind of person who could hardly stand up without feeling overwhelmed. I would crumble underneath that pressure. The idea of being in charge of another human being seemed godlike, and to do that calmly without fear? To gracefully handle so much with no self-congratulatory attitude? To just *be*? Wow. How does one even attain that high a level of spirituality?

Drowsy doll made me feel the way I imagined the moms I admired and envied must feel. She was my favorite. She was also the first doll I remember getting new.

Most of our toys were scavenged by my dad, who had developed a skill for finding discarded treasures during his time working as a trash collector for the city's sanitation department, a job he reluctantly took after he and my mom found out they were pregnant with Jessica and needed something more stable than the basic retail jobs they had been working. They were living in a small trailer and figured it was time to start moving toward a brighter future: one with a home that didn't have an axle.

My dad had originally applied to work at the post office, but there were no open positions, so he put his name on a waiting list and took this gig in the meantime. He grew to hate the sanitation job, not because he came home stinking like a dumpster and had to disrobe before coming into the trailer, not because it was viewed as low status, and not because sometimes he'd notice a dead pet being pulled into the crusher as he dumped the cans in. He hated it because his boss had intentionally not called him off a shift the day Jessica was born. My dad had missed the birth of his first child and wasn't able to be there as a birth partner for my mom, something they were both dead set on, despite the fact that both sets of grandparents told them dads aren't supposed to be in the room or "see that." And all because his boss didn't want to be inconvenienced with finding someone to cover the rest of his shift. My dad was furious and wanted to quit, but there were now medical bills to pay and then my mom got pregnant with me just a few months later, so holding on to a job became even more important. It wasn't until a few months before I was born in May 1976 that he finally received a call that a position was available at the post office.

My parents had been living in a trailer when Jessica was born. It was the second trailer my parents owned. The first one exploded from a gas leak and would've killed them both had they not been out of town. They moved into an apartment as soon as my dad had job security, and I was born there. By the time my younger brother, Jake, came two years later, they had purchased their first home—a five-hundred-square-foot bungalow in Lakewood across from a chop shop. My favorite memories of that little house were crawling through a hole in the wall that went into my parents' closet and the time my dad mowed the six-foot-tall grass by driving our '73 Ford station wagon over it.

After a couple years, my parents had collected enough equity to trade up to a bigger house *with a basement* in a better area.

My parents were hippies who despite themselves had fallen into the American dream of capitalism: ladder-climbing, equity, property values, and trading up. This helped reinforce some oppressive gender roles: Dad with his blue-collar job sorting mail for sometimes sixteen hours a day, and Mom tending to three toddlers, at one point all in diapers at the same time. If she wasn't cooking and cleaning, she was breaking up fights between Jessica and me and craving time to be creative. She was also desperately trying to reconcile her naturally contrarian character with this safe, suburban life.

We may have been climbing the ladder, but we were still on the lower rungs. We could afford name-brand foods now, but we couldn't afford to spill them. We still had to make all our frivolous unneeded purchases, like toys, from other people's lawns. I always went for the dolls, of course, lined up in a row with their naked, twisted bodies topped with ratted hair. I didn't mind that they were wounded and in need of a little extra care. I was just the person to nurse them back to health.

Most of my dolls had polio. Some had sickle cell anemia. Some had mystery illnesses that hadn't been discovered yet. They had homemade prosthetics, stitches, eye patches, etc. Any ailment I'd ever heard of made an appearance in their medical charts at some point. I read any health-related information I could get my hands on. That's how I was able to diagnose them so accurately.

The terminally ill were hooked up to my radio for life support, the speaker wires plucked from their input and rerouted into soft nylon elbows. The little bouncing lights that flickered as sound came through the speakers monitored their heart rates and oxygen levels.

I remember my mom getting frustrated with me once because she was trying to take me and my two siblings on a walk and I was holding everyone back helping my poor injured baby walk on his homemade pencil crutches—a slow recovery, but he was doing so much better since the accident. This was the first time he had tried to use his legs, and it was exhausting for him. My family had no patience or empathy for my disabled son, and I wanted to protect him from their comments, like "Hurry up, goddamnit!" and "You're gonna get hit by a car, get out of the crosswalk!" I feared he'd lose his motivation to beat this thing if he was subjected to this kind of discouragement, so I was forced to carry him, his humiliation apparent on his face. We avoided talking and making eye contact for the rest of the walk, and when we got home, he got back into bed and never tried to walk again.

I really loved human babies, but they were harder to come by, so dolls sufficed. When a real baby was near, I hovered, volunteering to do any required nurturing tasks. I'm naturally good at kids. I have been told countless times that "my baby doesn't like anyone, but she likes you." I have been called a baby-whisperer and, more rudely, a baby-hog. I was the designated sitter at every family get-together. I worked at my bubbe's in-home day care, drawn to the kids who needed the most attention, like Negan, who had to have goat milk in a bottle three times a day. I would happily change diapers and wipe dripping noses while Jessica sat in the corner reading books and saying things like, "I refuse to be near anyone who can't talk and is covered in snot and smells like ketchup."

When I was four, I potty trained my two-year-old brother, Jake, when our mom was at her wits' end with him. He had spent the entire first eighteen months of his life in a baby swing and didn't know you were supposed to do things by yourself. I was sick of smelling shit as he'd breeze by with a load in his pants, and I was tired of repeatedly being scolded for eating all of his reward chocolate.

Knowing that Jake was the kind of kid who wouldn't walk five feet to a toilet when he could just bear down on the spot, I took his potty chair into the living room and put it right in front of the TV, where he spent most of his time craning his neck up at *He-Man*. Then I sat next to him, giving him cup after cup of water, asking every five minutes, "Do you have to pee? What about now?"

He said no, no, no, and then, finally . . . yes.

"Okay. Take your diaper off and sit down and pee in the potty. You can keep watching *He-Man*." Because this involved virtually no effort on his part, he was potty trained that very day.

Around the same time, Jake still hadn't uttered a full sentence. Then one day he toddled into the kitchen and opened his mouth. "Mom, when is Dad coming home from work?"

My mom's jaw hit the floor. All her months and months of worry that he had developmental delays, her trips to a speech therapist, her constant watching him for signs of growth . . .

"Did you hear that?! He talked!"

"He talks to me all the time," I said, shrugging. He just wasn't a chatty kid, or as we discovered years later in therapy, he just couldn't get a word in edgewise.

Jake wasn't opinionated about much, but he hated my dolls. Or more accurately, he feared for his life in their presence: the stitched-up babies; the naked, defaced Barbies with their huge tits that I sanded off to better suit the proportions of their hips, their long blond hair cut short and the leftover clumps colored black with markers. I'd paint their faces, melt their noses, and try to flatten their feet. I was going for a natural, realistic look, but they always ended up like one of Frankenstein's monsters.

Part of the reason they were so horrifying to Jake was that I kept my dolls in the dark, chilly basement of our house. This was a typical Colorado basement. Half-finished, wet, and constantly flooded, it smelled like the interior of a washing machine drain hose. The floor was concrete and cold, the windows were buried halfway below the grass of the backyard, and any paint on the walls was blistering from the moisture that leaked in, while the laundry room and water heater hissed and gulped like a couple of ghosts. In middle America, you can tell a person's station by how finished their basement is. Is it just framing and dirt? Poverty level. Concrete floor and cement board walls with no paint? Working class. Drywall? Blue collar. Paint? You're about to sell your house and move to a better neighborhood.

Before we renovated it, our basement was an alternate universe. It was magical and mysterious to me, like one of the cold moist caves in the Bible where mystics hid to channel texts. It was a safe zone. We waited out a tornado down there once, the windows cracked to relieve the pressure in the room and the corded rotary phone pulled as far as the wire would go toward the corner where we were huddled, waiting for my dad to call us to let us know he was coming home from work. We sat there for hours expecting the roof to fly off.

When we weren't hiding from acts of God, my siblings and I would draw stick men having sex on the exposed drywall (we were encouraged to express ourselves freely down here) or play a game where we would slide around in the algae-coated puddles of the inevitable winter flooding until we fell on our asses. We would then change out of our wet clothes into dry ones and do it again. We'd bring stacks of clean clothes from the laundry area next door. We played this game until we had no changes left. My dad did most of the laundry and also worked full-time, so you can imagine how much he appreciated that.

My mom and dad had talked about having five kids, but once Jake was born, Mom immediately had her tubes tied. Nothing like three kids to cure a desire for five. Since she wouldn't be breeding anymore, she could have her body back. She went on a crash diet that consisted of just one ice-cream cone and one doughnut a day, and one long walk, until she reached her goal weight of one hundred pounds. Because of her weight loss, she tied all her fat clothes up in black trash bags and put them in the basement. A year or two later, all her skinny clothes would be tied in black trash bags while the fat clothes went back into circulation. This was a never-ending cycle. Jessica and I would try on the various eccentric outfits she had collected from thrift stores: muumuus, sequins, vintage dresses, pieces of fabric she'd tie around other pieces of fabric that she'd wear as a toga. Sometimes we would throw on a feather boa and nothing else and go ride our Big Wheels around the neighborhood.

My dad had found a large couch in the trash and put it in the basement, trying to give the room a homey feel. He had a work table against the wall with all his renovation supplies and tools on it, most that he had stabbed himself clumsily with at some point while making us homemade Christmas gifts when we couldn't afford to buy new. My dad was very good at turning limitations into opportunities to be creative. My favorite was when he bought an old suitcase for each of us kids from Goodwill, screwed a piece of finished wood on, and burned our first names into in cursive. It was an art desk I could keep my supplies inside: my half crayons augmented with my mom's Mary Kay cosmetics that she tried to sell for extra income before I found and ruined her stash of products by using them as oil pastels for my art. I still have the wooden board somewhere, but the suitcase was loved apart.

Once the renovation was underway and a spare bedroom was added in the basement, the youngest of my mom's siblings, fifteen-year-old Stephanie, came to live with us for a while. Sometime around then, Beanie moved in, too. Only their brother Ben, the third of the four kids, remained in Salt Lake City.

Steph stayed in the bedroom and hardly came out. When she did, she was wearing too-big scrubs rolled at the waist and ankles. She would come upstairs, microwave some eggs, eat them with ketchup, and then say, "There goes the phone!" which would always ring a few seconds later, and then retreat back to her lair.

Before my aunts arrived to act as live-in babysitters, my mom used to drive us ninety minutes to my dad's parents' house in Colorado Springs so that she could get anything done without us at her heels. Their house had been my dad's home growing up, and I loved going to stay with them. My grandparents were down-to-earth, steadfast, stubborn, loving, patient rocks, both Taurus, like my dad, and being at their place was totally different from life at home. It was quiet and uneventful.

We visited them probably once a month when I was little. We called my grandpa Papa Woody (say it aloud—it wasn't the greatest idea for a nickname). He would come home from work, take off his work clothes, and lie in his recliner chair in his undershirt and pants, and my grandma would bring him a glass of instant Lipton tea with ice cubes that he would sip while he watched TV. My grandma would finish making dinner, always some version of red meat and potatoes. She'd get fancy and make a casserole occasionally out of canned foods. I'd crawl onto my grandpa's lap and curl up on his chest and lie there listening to the ice cubes hit the side of the glass, the gulping, the gurgling of the tea hitting his empty stomach while he waited for his dinner to be ready. I felt safe here, not like I was protected from the darkness outside, but like darkness didn't even exist. Their house was a whole other dimension.

My grandparents had been married almost fifty years. They'd mumble passive-aggressively at each other occasionally, but they were a team. My grandma was a typical American housewife of the fifties and followed most of the expected protocols of being subservient to men, doctors, and God but would make exceptions when she felt strongly about something. She had to try pretty hard to get pregnant with my dad, and then nine years later with my uncle. She had to have emergency C-sections for both, which was rare at the time. Even rarer was breast-feeding your kid. The doctors' first order of business was to tell a woman she'd be malnourishing her baby if she attempted to feed him her own milk. My grandma rolled her eyes and nursed both her babies. She knew when not to listen, and that was a quality I greatly admired.

My grandma was the only person I would let untangle my giant dreadlock. I had curly, fine hair that would rat up in the back of my head as I slept, and I would scream like a Ringwraith if anyone other than my grandma touched it. She would sit with me for an hour and gently pick through every knot, never raking or pulling it. She'd sing to me and tell me stories as she'd brush. She was patient and gentle and knew how to engage me.

She and Papa Woody were Lutherans. She became more and more involved in her church as I was growing up and was concerned for my salvation. She tried to talk my mom into baptizing us, but my mom was not raising infidels and Jews didn't require such things. Afraid I would go to hell, my grandma licked my forehead with her holy spit when no one was looking and said a prayer. My mom found out somehow and was livid, but eventually had to let it go since the only other childcare option was to lock us outside.

All moms did this in the seventies, and we loved it. We'd ride our bikes to the local park, cruising downhill at deadly speeds straight into intersections, or prank drivers with a stuffed cat we'd throw in the road as they passed. We'd sneak through the bushes trying to see inside the neighborhood's token Creepy House, run away from that one preteen boy who'd shoot you with BBs if you made eye contact with him, and tease the teens making out in their cars. We'd sneak onto the empty school campus and swing higher than we were allowed to during the week. We'd go through each other's garages looking for items to decorate our staged child weddings with. I married my across-the-street neighbor Keith (my first kiss) in a modest ceremony beneath our crab-apple tree, while his big sister Melissa acted as bridesmaid and Jessica, of course, officiated. One day, Melissa asked me if I wanted to make some money, and when I said yes, she punched me in the mouth and told me to "put those teeth under a pillow and wait for the tooth fairy." Fucking in-laws.

Aside from being half-naked and feral, we were also being raised part atheist, part Jewish, and part Wiccan, with a touch of paganism and voodoo thrown in. All these roads led to the same destination: mysticism. Mysticism has always been the only spiritual belief system that makes sense to me, as it marries all of science, quantum mechanics, the supernatural, ancient alien theory, auras, souls, reincarnation, palmistry, and astrology with ethical and practical applications. Mysticism is essentially: Everything is energy. Energy can't be created or destroyed, only transmuted. Your Higher Self is the one in charge of transmuting that energy, though, and it doesn't give a shit about nice cars or money.

Because of our beliefs, we didn't fit in. Okay, it was *one* reason we didn't fit in. We were also the only Jews, the only fat people, and the only ones who decorated for Halloween in such an alarming way that the neighborhood kids refused to come to our door for candy and fled crying. We were the only ones home on Sunday mornings. We were pretty much the Munsters, which was my favorite show, for obvious reasons. My sister would chant spells in Melissa's front yard after we'd get in a fight with her. We could be seen burying crystals in the dirt outside, and moon worshipping. Some nights, our mom would take us out to lie on the lawn and gaze at the stars. She would teach us to "cloudbust" using only intent. She would point and say, "Here comes a shooting star." Then one would shoot right across the path she'd traced with her finger. We would talk about metaphysics in ways that kids can understand and also in ways they can't, but do anyway.

It was during one of these stargazing sessions, when I was about five, that I "downloaded" (suspend your disbelief, aka fuck off. I don't like it, either) the information that my mom was going to be famous, that our lives were about to be upended and disrupted. We wouldn't be here in this tiny neighborhood for long. This was made even stranger by the fact that my mom hadn't yet started pursuing a career, though she had been working part-time as a window dresser at a local clothing boutique. A change was coming. It was going to be a violent roller coaster, and if I wanted to survive, I had better just put my arms up and scream.

I didn't know how to process this experience. How was I supposed to go to school now? How was I supposed to care about growing mealworms and solving math equations? I was going to have to tuck this experience away like a weird recurring dream that just becomes part of your subconscious, the kind where any attempt to bring it into the light of reality makes it fade and lose all clarity. Some ideas get clearer when you examine them, but the most important ones do the opposite. They wriggle out from under the microscope lens and disappear. Nobody believes they were ever even there. Not even you, who saw them with your own eyes.

What do you do with that? You try to use those same mind-over-matter techniques that control clouds to make boys like you, to manifest cakes out of thin air, to lose ten pounds overnight without effort, to win two gumballs with one quarter from the machine. You pretend nothing means what you know it means. You eat everything in sight to keep yourself too heavy to float into the ether. You fixate on the things you can control. You go to school, do your homework, take a lot of baths, put your dolls on life support, and wait.

My parents were fighting a lot. My mom's sisters were living with us at the time and had made it their mission to upgrade my dad's wokeness level. As a kid, my dad had been a bit of a reactionary and had handed out to his elementary school classmates pamphlets from the John Birch Society identifying which Hollywood actors were sympathetic to communist causes in order to warn his fellow students. It was printed in pink ink, my dad remembers, since they were called "Pinkos."

But by nature, he was progressive, and by the time he married my mom his sympathies were more with the actors than the Birchers, but he still needed to do the work of deprogramming himself from the beliefs he had been raised with. Intellectually, he wanted to help dismantle oppressive systems, but they were also benefiting him, so there was a conflict of interest. I believe he was afraid my mom would outgrow him, so he unconsciously tried to keep her from growing at all. He doubled down on his Man role, staying out late after work drinking Coors Lights with his post office buddies and talking about ladies' butts, while my mom stayed home growing more and more restless. Eventually, for sanity's sake, she took a job as a cocktail waitress at Bennigan's, an Irish pub–themed chain restaurant known for the "flair" management asked its staff to wear. It was at this job that she started cracking everyone up with her quips and wit, and her new sense of independence seemed to be straining the marriage even more.

My mom and dad were still trying to make their relationship work for us kids' sake, though. They took advantage of Beanie living with us and had her babysit while they went on dates. One night, they ended up at a comedy open-mic event and were in awe of the performances. They had an awakening that *this* was what they were both meant to do. That night, my mom added her name to the sign-up list for the next open-mic night. She and my dad and Beanie workshopped jokes all week until she had an act. At the same time my dad was working on his own act and finding places to get some time onstage.

But while my dad's jokes were mostly shock humor, my mom's jokes were mostly self-deprecating commentary on her own body. One was about her breasts being "real American"—red, white, and blue. Red from rashes, white from a lack of sun, and blue from her visible veins. The crowd loved it.

She got a great reaction at the open mic and was able to get time at the Comedy Works, the number one local comedy club. She was trying to come to terms with her recent weight loss and the way people, especially men, treated her differently according to her size. She made jokes about her body, but she was skinny and hot, and no one could process a skinny hot woman saying self-deprecating things about her body. They didn't know if they were supposed to want to fuck her or not. She was confusing them. Most men just defaulted to telling her how she could make them want to fuck her more. She didn't love this reaction and was verbal about it, throwing sharp words at them like daggers. Though some of them loved this, most couldn't take it, and she didn't last long because, as the club owner told her, she was "too angry."

She ended up mostly working in an alternative club her friend and local icon Lannie Garrett performed and emceed at, as well as doing sets at other clubs and gay bars that had a variety of entertainers, not just comedians, and could handle her rage. She refined her act at these venues until she could successfully couch her anger in nonthreatening jokes. It helped that she was also gaining her lost weight back, making her less threatening to men.

Her sisters eventually moved out. Stephanie went back to Utah to finish high school, and Beanie moved in with her girlfriend, Haddie. Haddie had a grandson my age named Dwight, so we would go over to play with him. I loved her house. It was warm and comfortable and messy and full of aunties, like ours. Haddie's daughter, Dwight's mom, would sit naked, never breaking eye contact with the TV and, except for modestly covering the nipples on her long breasts with three fingers for a couple of seconds while you walked through the room, wouldn't acknowledge you at all.

Now that my aunties were rehomed, the basement bedroom was empty and became Mom's office. It had a small closet and a built-in desk with shelves, all of which were filled with napkins and scraps of paper from various bars and comedy clubs and bookstores, where she did her actual workshopping of jokes. She didn't really spend time down there, it was just a place to store the notes. I would grab handfuls of them and lay them out on the desk to try to understand their obviously adult content: "Men think the ~~vagina~~ uterus is a tracking device," and the like.

When I was seven, I asked for this room to be my own, since Jessica and I were sharing a bedroom upstairs and this arrangement was reaching a breaking point, although not due to me. Jake had wiped a booger on Jessica's wall and she flipped out and demanded a bubble of space that no one could enter. I was her roommate and I had to go. I get it. I still peed the bed sometimes, and I had no sense of fashion. I told on her when she snuck out her window to go buy candy. I did weird things like climb to the top shelf in the closet and chew on shank bones left over from dinner. She was a control freak, and I was a Jack Russell terrier.

We fought constantly. Jessica was a thirteen-month-old baby when my parents brought me home from the hospital, though the physical limitations of her age didn't stop her from constantly trying to kill me. She'd pinch me and push me and test what PSI was needed to pop my skull. Her intellectual constraints, having a vocabulary of five words, made it hard to express the jealousy she felt at the shift of attention from her to me. I had basically just strolled in, ripped the teat out of her mouth, and sunk into my mom's warm, loving arms, all while making extended eye contact with her. I didn't displace her on purpose, but she didn't know that.

Though we were essentially the same age, we were very different. Jessica was quiet and broody, intelligent and introverted, cautious but brave. She loved to read books and test limits. When she was told no, she would quietly just go do the thing anyway. When I was told no, I would scream (like the being-murdered kind) and yell and not back down. I was overly sensitive and very, very stubborn. I was also social and extroverted. I loved playing house and drawing while Jessica read her books and studied to be an archaeologist/parapsychologist.

I liked the basement partly because it was outside of Jessica's influence. I had grown used to having her tell me what to do and think. In the basement, I could finally hear my own thoughts and pursue my own interests, and now that I was able to develop into an individual, it was time to get weird. I was having conversations with myself about philosophical ideas and God, which would turn into daydreams where I'd be at a podium trying to explain the meaning of being human as if I were an alien journalist stuck on Earth reporting back to my people at a press conference. Whatever daydreams were not about being some kind of space reporter were about humping boys and eating cake. I had very elaborate fantasies involving both, so I needed my privacy. I could be a Baby Artist–Alien Journalist–Cake Slut in peace down there, plus

I could pee my bed, take the sheets straight to the washer in the next room, and no one would have to know.

Thankfully, I finally quit peeing the bed shortly after moving rooms. Everyone had been sure it was some kind of Freudian problem, acting out, or personality disorder. Now they know that bladders just mature later in some people. Thanks, science, for once again waiting until I've suffered to come out with evidence that vindicates me. After my first solid week of not wetting the bed, I got to pick out a gift. My mom took me to the local superstore and I picked, you guessed it, a doll. I chose him for his realistic, pained expression. He had a crying face that, in hindsight, looked like Kuato from *Total Recall*. I brought him home and I loved him along with my other underdog babies. I was proud of my son, whom I named Toby, and when my dad got home from work that night I wrapped him in a blanket and presented him to his grandfather. My dad audibly gasped at seeing Toby's wrinkled, contorted face and shouted "That is the *ugliest* doll I have ever seen!" I cried for two days. My dad apologized, but the damage was done and, not long after that, Toby was struck with a debilitating autoimmune disease.

After Louie Anderson and Dennis Miller saw my mom performing at Lannie's club, they told her to look them up when she came to Los Angeles. Louie helped my mom get a Monday night showcase at the Comedy Store on Hollywood Boulevard in Los Angeles. This was a big deal since being offered a spot there meant she had finally mastered her delivery. She was told that if she ever wanted to really "make it," she needed to move permanently to LA.

So she did.

She packed up a few of her things and left within the month. She would go ahead of us, and if everything worked out, she would find a house and we would join her then. If it didn't, she'd come back to Denver and keep trying. Our dad would have to care for us and continue to work while she was gone. He didn't want to quit his job at the post office until he knew there was a future elsewhere. For the last few months of the school year, we were what was known as latchkey kids: kids with single working parents or two working parents who got home from school before their parents got home from work. Latchkey kids were generally pitied. They were considered victims of the times, the times being when moms were allowed to leave the house and pursue a career and the poor kids were given a door key on a cord to wear around their necks (hence the name).

Jessica wore our key because she was the oldest, but under her shirt, so we wouldn't be targeted by predators. She'd wait for Jake and me by the school gate, and we'd all walk home together. In the two hours a day we were alone, many chemicals were mixed, matches played with, snack foods invented, like peanut butter microwaved and rolled into bite-size balls that were then rolled in sugar. Sugar was eaten off spoons, drawers gone through, makeup abused. Butterfingers were stolen from our dad's work lunch stash. Somehow, we managed to survive and gain only a few pounds.

When school was over, my mom sent for us. She wanted us to spend our summer break with her. Those few months were the longest we had been away from her, and we all really missed one another.

My dad loaded up our Mazda hatchback with everything we would need for the summer, and we kids were crammed strategically into the leftover space so that Jessica and I couldn't reach each other's hair or faces. Because of the limited room, we were each allowed to bring only one toy. It was like Sophie's choice to pick one favorite doll, but at the last minute I chose the handmade knock-off Cabbage Patch my mom had bought when we couldn't afford real ones. Her name was Goldie. She looked enough like a real Cabbage Patch, except her head was cloth instead of plastic and she was obviously missing the Xavier Roberts signature on her butt, though she did have a very nicely sewn authentic crack. She had yarn hair in two pigtails, which distinguished her from Jessica's doll, Roxy, who had her yarn hair in a single high ponytail. Jessica never played with dolls, so Roxy looked newer than Goldie, who was a shade of filth seen only in pirate movies. Jessica wanted to bring her whole book collection but had to pare it down to just a few Sweet Valley Highs, and there was no room for Roxy. I was devastated that the sisters were to be forcibly separated, and I screamed and wailed inconsolably until I was allowed to bring her, too. Jake quietly pocketed two metal Transformer toys and wedged into the car, and Beanie drove us out to Santa Monica, where we'd all live in a one-bedroom apartment my mom's friend from the Denver comedy clubs had sublet to us.

It was just a fun vacation for us, but for my mom it was something much bigger. She had known since she was a toddler that she was destined for something great, and that path was being laid out right before her eyes, one plank at a time. These were not some slow-traveling, transient, king-of-the-road-type train tracks, though. They were the rollercoaster kind.

2.
Hi, Fat!

We were the only kids in that Santa Monica apartment complex where we were subletting. Jessica, just eight, stayed inside reading. I don't even remember her presence in this phase of our lives; she was suddenly invisible. I missed her. I missed my dad and grandparents. I missed my school, the yard, our terrible neighbors. Jake would get bored with my doll playing and would sit quietly in his own world repeatedly changing his little yellow Transformer from a Volkswagen Bug into a robot.

Jessica didn't ever want to play with dolls no matter how many times I tried to trick her into it, but I was able to rope Jake in by occasionally letting our knock-off Cabbage Patch kids, Roxy and Goldie, play out a war/soldier scenario. Without other kids to play with, I spent most of my time sitting on the concrete stairs that led from the first-floor apartment to the busy street below. As far as people watching goes, it was five stars.

The area we were in was still, at the time, an affordable beach town. It was populated mostly by older people who had retired to small, manageable square footages once their kids were out of the house or a spouse had died, or young, fit types who were constantly cruising for a sweaty fuck under the guise of a workout. I would watch people in tight

Lycra bodysuits halfway up their asses jog by. Some casually sauntered along with a boom box on their shoulder blasting their own personal soundtrack. There were a lot of cyclists, too. These were either triathlete types or people with DUIs, and it was very easy to tell the difference. The people who drove by were either young, coked-up professionals with underage actresses in the passenger seat, families from the Midwest doing the Disneyland vacation thing, or production assistants trying to balance twenty coffees on their laps in their Honda Civics.

I was in awe of Los Angeles. The unfamiliar birdsong, the Santa Ana winds, the snails that left trails over the evergreen ivy bushes outside every apartment block, and then, later, their empty shells. The street-smart wildlife: squirrels that waited until the absolute last second before getting out of the way of your car tire, crows that intentionally dropped food in the crosswalks for cars to run over and crack open, feral cats that lived outside every convenience store and didn't even acknowledge your drive-by petting. The smell of the sea-level sun and the low cloud of fossil fuel that hung at my ankles.

The culture was completely unlike suburban white Denver, where the neighbors would lock their doors when my parents' Black friends came over or would sit at their windows staring as we played with the Black kids out front.

No two people looked alike here. It seemed as though one representative from every village on Earth had moved to Los Angeles to share their customs with one another. There was a sense of solidarity in difference, and I felt like I fit in here in ways I didn't know were possible. I could've easily blended in wearing only a feather boa here. We weren't freaks anymore.

We jumped right in and spent our days exploring the apartment complex, the streets outside of it, and the beaches nearby. We tried to decode the graffiti on every wall and decipher the rantings of the mentally ill homeless people who seemed to be everywhere. There was a thin line between them and the eccentric artists who were *choosing* to be transient to be closer to whatever god they were exploring at that moment. It would take me years to figure out that there was no figuring out where that line was.

The days were hot and humid, making the smog from the endless cars stick to everything. Over the course of the summer, Roxy's and Goldie's beige Lycra faces turned gray. They smelled of asphalt, sweat, and ocean—like everything else here—one exception being the very rich in their cartoonishly expensive cars. *They* smelled like ambergris. There was nothing more glamorous in the eighties than slathering yourself in the waste of a giant sea creature. These people cruised past, always looking straight ahead through their mirrored Wayfarer Ray-Bans. They wore animal prints and clown makeup. Their hair ratted out of the top of their convertibles. For a population so enslaved to their images, there was also a deep sense of freedom in the air, the freedom of anything being possible at any moment.

I first met Max while sitting on the stairs watching the world cruise by. He was an eighty-year-old Jewish man with a little waddle. He walked past me daily, and I always smiled at him and then looked down at my feet as a sign of respect, pretending not to notice he was winded and struggling to climb the few small stairs. He always smiled back, then looked away to show that he was not going to shame me for sticking out like a sore chubby thumb, for seeming lonely, for playing barefoot with a dirty doll all day, for having no friends and seemingly no parents. One morning when he was walking by, instead of our usual silent exchange, he said, "Hi, Dimples."

"I don't have dimples." I figured this was a grandpa joke and the punch line was coming. I hoped it wasn't about my weight.

"You *do*! They're in the creases of your cheeks! Look!"

He pulled out a compact mirror from inside his baggy pocket and handed it to me. I opened it and looked. I could see his face in the mirror behind me, smiling and pointing, and I broke eye contact with him and looked at my own face.

"Smile."

I did the Pentland smile, a forced and fake grin that basically looks like a toddler shitting its diaper. We've ruined countless family and school photos with it, but it's compulsive, we can't help it.

"Not *that* kind of smile." He grimaced.

Max was blunt. A kind old man, kind enough to tell the truth. Being made fun of gently like that always makes me laugh, and I did.

"*There!* See them now, Dimples?"

I did! I had dimples! I never knew. I laughed and closed the compact to hand back to him. I had never seen them. *How can I have a face that has things I don't know about it?* I was truly flabbergasted. He thought it was funny that I was so shocked. He said, "See you later, Dimples," and started up the stairs again. I told him he forgot his mirror and he told me to keep it and make sure every day that my dimples were still there. For the next two months he brought me daily gifts from his walks. Once, he gave me three red balloons that were bobbing around like a drunken Cerberus. They were printed with the name of the local used-car lot, and their ribbons were shredded by whatever means he had used to rip them away from their intended signpost.

"These were not easy to get, Dimples," he said, and handed them to me as he walked past my place on the stairs and disappeared into his apartment. This continued all summer until I went back to Denver and never saw him again. I would like him to know that I still love him and think about these small gestures of kindness during lonely times.

I spent my days on those apartment stairs and my nights in the greenroom at the Comedy Store, being babysat by whichever comic was on after my mom. There was a small opening in the wall from which you could look out and see the stage below, and we would lean through and watch our mom making everyone laugh. We were proud of her and proud to be hers.

We loved the kitchen staff there, who would let us have endless sodas and snacks. Everyone looked out for us, but in a cynical, coked-up-comic sort of way. Beanie would head down to the audience and watch my mom perform so she could properly critique her for next time. We'd stay in the greenroom long enough for Beanie to know we were safe, then sneak down to the kitchen for our soda and snacks. It was during one of these performances that a scout for Johnny Carson saw my mom's act. He immediately approached her afterward and invited her on the show.

She was overwhelmed and shocked, but mostly elated. She was watching the ocean for a perfect wave to surf, and this one was the most promising yet. All the things she wanted and had been trying for were starting to unfold. She needed to buckle down without distraction, so she had our dad come get us and drive us back to Denver in time for school to start. We weren't going to be in the audience for this one. We would have to watch her Carson appearance on TV like everyone else.

My dad is a meticulous planner and had our road trip back to Denver mapped out by the hour. We would leave Los Angeles early Friday morning and stop in Salt Lake City, where my mom's parents, Bubbe Helen and Grandpa Jerry, lived. My dad had flawlessly orchestrated our arrival so that we could eat dinner, watch my mom's first-ever appearance on *The Tonight Show*, sleep, fill up on love and sugar (which for my bubbe were the same thing), and then head back to Denver to do all our school shopping Sunday and start the new year Monday.

We arrived at Bubbe's right on schedule, which, with three young kids, is usually an impossible feat, but my dad was so good at planning that he had made allowances both for bathroom trips and to pull over to threaten Jessica and me into submission. The living room was already crowded with family and friends. The kids sat cross-legged on the shag carpeting while everyone else brought chairs from the large dining room table. My grandpa took the most comfortable chair in the place because, after all, he was the man of the house. My bubbe took up the rear of the room so she could nervously go in and out of the kitchen, grabbing snacks to tuck into the slackened jaws of family who were too entranced by the TV to fight her. Once, she even gave a dog diabetes.

We turned the TV on and waited for the show to start. We sat through Johnny Carson's introduction, all of us nervous for my mom. Finally, there she was, appearing from behind those iconic curtains. She walked to her mark, stopped, looked around at the crowd, and opened her mouth.

"Oh, hi. I've been married for thirteen years and lemme tell you it's a thrill to be out of the house . . ."

She'd practiced these jokes at home, her voice bouncing around the acoustics of our little kitchen. But now her delivery was organized and perfected. Coming through the speakers of a modern television, she sounded . . . different, like when you first hear yourself on a recording and refuse to believe that voice is *yours*.

Watching her giggle at her own jokes made me giddy. Seeing her on a screen and hearing the audience's laughter made me realize that my mom was not just my mom, but a separate, individual entity. Before this, she was "Mom," "honey," "sis," "Rosie," or "Mrs. Pentland." This was the first time I had heard her called "Roseanne Barr." My parents had agreed that it was smart to use her maiden name instead of her married name to protect our privacy.

Her set was only about three minutes long. After she was done, Carson called her over to the desk, a prestigious invitation bestowed upon only a handful of debut comics, but my mom panicked and ran offstage.

We turned off the TV and the whole room sighed with relief (including the couch), as the adults started milling about, weighing in on what they had just witnessed.

"She did great!" my bubbe said, but because this was her daughter, and everything her kids did was great, we waited to hear what everyone else thought.

"She killed!" my dad said, starting to use the comedy-club-speak he was picking up.

As everyone competed to be the one to perfectly tear apart and explain what they'd seen, I noticed the language in the room change from "She did great," to "I would've done it *this* way . . ." It was the beginning of a time when family and friends—people we'd known all our lives— would suddenly begin to look at us differently, like a bunch of office workers greeting the news of a colleague's promotion with gritted smiles and barely concealed envy. I felt an unnamable tingle in my stomach. The premonition on the lawn was coming true, and I wasn't ready.

The rest of the road trip felt strange. I vacillated between wanting to scream out the window to passing cars that my mom was famous and pining for my old simple life when my mom would blast Pat Benatar and dance in our little living room while my dad was working at the post office. I did my best to find the positivity and joy in the situation, and to figure out how to use it to my advantage. I pictured myself telling my new classmates about my summer in Los Angeles with the dangerous riffraff on the streets, the neighbors who gave you a new gift every day, the ocean, evenings hanging out in a comedy club and drinking endless Diet Cokes, and all the dirty jokes I got to hear.

When we got to Kmart, the school supply section had been picked clean, and my dad did his best to throw together three backpacks full of Number 2 pencils, erasers, rulers, crayons, and glue. We stopped at

King Soopers on the way home and bought every processed thing they had for a week of meals. Our diets weren't great to begin with since we were the children and grandchildren of postwar families who lived on leftover bunker cans and Great Depression food substitutes. Healthy meant fed. It didn't matter if the calories you consumed were from vegetables or ambrosia salad (don't google it), as long as you ate three meals a day. And now, with my dad single parenting, any nods toward healthy eating went out the window.

All the clothes at Kmart had been picked clean, too. Everyone had already bought their new outfits to wear the first day back to school (the second day back, everyone looked like shit again), and there was nothing left for my second-grade debut. I would once again have to put together an ensemble from hand-me-downs mixed with whatever from the previous year that still fit.

My adventurous summer had made my return to Denver feel nostalgic, and I thought back to my first day of kindergarten two years ago, when I had brushed down my numerous cowlicks and put on my favorite brown dress with the white lacy trim my mom had made me from scraps and a curtain. When Jessica had attended kindergarten a year ahead of me, I had spent every morning watching her disappear into the big mysterious world inside the school grounds. She'd reappear later in the day with colored drawings and origami animals and glitter-covered holiday crafts we were too poor to make at home with our broken crayons and dried-up glue sticks. I couldn't wait to go, too.

I vividly remember the feeling of walking into the classroom for my first day and seeing the endless shelves full of things to do above a whole town of playhouses and soft things to sit on while reading. As a kid, nothing is your size. You're always accommodating the world, but in kindergarten the tiny tables and chairs and safety scissors accommodate you. What an amazing turn of events! There's also no smell like a kindergarten classroom: leaky lunch boxes and year-old pee in the carpets; rubber cement and disinfectant; sweaty running shoes mixed with the teaching assistant's Avon perfume; fresh paper and old library books; orange Dial liquid soap and general, comforting filth. It was heavenly. We even had our own separate playground just for our class so we didn't have to fight other grades to get a turn on the swings.

It was on that jungle gym that I noticed a boy named Matt staring at me. Matt had a face like he'd Scotch-taped the tip of his nose to his forehead, taking his upper lip with it. He already had his adult front teeth, which fully bucked out in the cold Denver air. As the weeks went by, Matt seemed to be paying more and more attention to me and doing everything he could to be near me during recess. This made me uncomfortable because I was finally enjoying some autonomy outside of my loud house and overbearing family. I was "kindergarten Jenny" now, a woman of the world. I didn't want my newfound freedoms encroached upon by anyone, especially a boy.

Suddenly, I couldn't lose myself in a game of playing house, because I was aware of being watched. My response was to stick my tongue out and roll my eyes, or kick at him when he dared walk past me on the swings. This only made him more ardent, which made me more combative. In the last week of kindergarten, he had tried to kiss me and I screamed, *"Ewwwwwwww! You're disgusting!"* so everyone in class would hear, and he was so embarrassed that he cried. I felt bad for the way I acted, but I had to save face and pretend I didn't care.

Starting first grade, I would be forced to wake to the cruel reality of life. I had assumed the year would be like kindergarten, but with better art supplies and cooler books. Maybe the dolls would be made of china, not plastic. The scissors would have sharp tips. The glue would be the dangerous-smelling, good kind. The paper might be canvas! I was excited to get to the next phase of crafts. I couldn't wait. But here's the thing: kindergarten is the catfish grade. It is a trick to get you to put your name on a register somewhere so the US census can keep track of you. It is entrapment, indoctrination into barely survivable indentured servitude to prepare you for your lifelong unpaid internship as a cog in the machine. In first grade, there are no more free juice boxes. No napping among friends. No more gentle sweet talk in your ear. No one telling you that your scrawls are beautiful because art is subjective. No crayons. No glue. No tiny tables. The books have no pictures in them. There are a lot of numbers in the math books where illustrated animals used to be: $2 + 2 = 4$ instead of cute cat and cute cat make . . . *double cute cats.* I loved school, but this was not school. It was something new and horrifying.

But I still had Matt. I continued to catch him staring at me, but he didn't approach me anymore. Strangely, I missed him but was too ashamed to talk to him after the way I had treated him. We became mostly indifferent to each other, or so I thought, and first grade ended without any resolution. Maybe next year we would reconcile and could be friends.

I had spent that summer thinking about Matt's longing gaze while playing make-believe in the Santa Monica apartment, and started having feelings for the version of him I'd invented to be my husband. As summer came to an end, I realized I couldn't wait to see him again.

With this anticipation in mind, I found last year's wardrobe staples and tried them on in different combinations to create a perfect second-grade outfit. The strange thing was, all my clothes had apparently shrunk in the dry basement heat over the summer. Things that had comfortably fit me just months ago were now very rudely pulling against my arms and thighs. The zipper on my favorite orange corduroy pants stopped halfway up then groaned and stumbled backward tooth by tooth. The weirdest part was they hadn't shrunk in length at all. Maybe I would learn about this scientific anomaly this year. I might not know who to blame yet, but it most certainly was not me or my extremely bad diet. I chose an ensemble that mostly fit and was ready to meet my fate.

I walked into school and scanned the crowd for familiar faces, and even though I saw plenty, everything felt so different after the summer's experiences.

And then I saw Matt. He looked older, maybe even handsome. His facial feature ratio had evened out, too, with his front two teeth no longer as prominent now that other adult teeth flanked them. He was wearing new clothes and had clearly showered. His hair had grown longer and now fell in his eyes a little when he looked down at his paper as he aced all his math problems. The tables had definitely turned. Now it was me who couldn't stop looking at Matt, willing him to return my gaze.

What did a girl have to do to get some goddamn eye contact around here?

I lived in a home very open about sexuality and had always been told I might fall in love with a girl or a boy or no one at all. I could get married, but better yet, I could stay single. I could have kids either way.

Or not. There was no pressure or expectation of cis heterosexuality, yet here I was, dying for male attention. What a waste.

As soon as I could walk my mom had had to buy a leash to keep me from wandering off with literally any old man I saw. I would get excited at the sight of gray hair, pointing and yelling, "Ol' man! Ol' man!" Then I'd toddle over and try to sit on his lap. Where she saw potential pedophiles, I saw manly grandpas.

This unfortunate aspect of my personality had me fixated on Matt's strange new behavior. I began to wonder if maybe I'd crossed a line that could never be uncrossed. Maybe he hated me. No, I could turn this around. Surely there was a way to show him how nice I was now, how much I'd grown (internally, as a person) over the summer.

One day, he asked for the boy's hall pass to go to the bathroom. This was my chance. I waited a few strategic minutes and asked for the girls' pass, calculating when he'd be heading back to the classroom. As I rounded the corner, there he was. Now it was just the two of us (and the overwhelming scent of Pine-Sol from a recent mopping). When we passed each other, it would be impossible for us not to make eye contact. He'd see my change of heart, know how humble I had grown, and fall in love with me all over again. As he headed toward me, he kept his eyes on his feet, so I stepped harder to get his attention. Then, radiating the Midwestern female super-niceness I'd picked up like an accent, I said in my sweetest, most submissive voice, "Hi, Matt."

He looked up and we locked eyes.

"Hi, Fat."

He said it casually and smoothly, as though it were my true name. The devastation was total; it felt like an actual fist. I continued to walk to the bathroom despite having the wind knocked out of me. I had never really thought about my weight before. Until now, my body had been a very functional piece of equipment I had the pleasure of operating. I had never considered its aesthetic value. That didn't matter for bike riding or doll playing or fighting with a sibling. My body was here to do a job, and it was very efficient at it. It was my best friend, following me everywhere and premeditating all my needs. Now I wondered if I had misjudged it. Maybe it had an agenda I didn't know about. Maybe it was a bully more than a friend. I went into the bathroom and looked at myself in the mirror.

Matt was right. I was fat. That's why he wasn't interested in me anymore. How could he be? I was gross. I was embarrassed that I had never noticed how unattractive I was. How could I have not seen it? The sadness I had felt minutes ago turned to anger at myself for not knowing I was a beast. When I was sufficiently angry and therefore unable to feel hurt, I blew my nose and headed back to class, where I spent the remainder of the day trying to shake the humiliation. I stared at my classmate Michelle's weird 3D birthmark that looked like a pink pencil eraser sticking out from right between her eyes. I imagined it popping or it being ripped off on the playground and got sick to my stomach. I looked out the window. I wandered like a zombie into the cafeteria for lunch, but I didn't want to eat. I was never going to eat again. I was going to starve myself and get skinny like Tammy, the hot, popular girl. She was an idiot, but she looked like a Twizzler, and that's what mattered most.

The only thing more humiliating than being humiliated is everyone knowing that you're humiliated, so I continued to go through the motions of a regular day. I opened my lunch box so no one would suspect that I was dying from internal injuries. Inside was a smashed peanut butter and jelly on white bread, a granola bar, and a pudding cup. I glared at my lunch, angry at it. Food was the reason I was fat, and it had betrayed me. But also it looked really good, and it wasn't the pudding's fault that Matt was an asshole. I shouldn't take my anger out on it; it looked so creamy and delicious and chocolatey. Okay, I was going to eat the pudding, and then just get really good at math. Better than Matt.

I wished my mom was home to tell about my shitty day. She would have told me that Matt was an idiot, that he didn't deserve my attention. She would've called him an imp and I would have laughed and felt better. My mom was great at defending our honor and talking us back from the brink. One time our ten-year-old neighbor hit Jake, who was six. When my mom confronted his mom, she did nothing. My mom saw the boy in his yard later and said, "Don't *ever* put your hands on one of my kids again!" to which he responded, "You're fat," to which she growled sociopathically at him, "Yes, I am. And if you touch my kids again, I will *sit on you* and *snap* you in half like a potato chip." He didn't bother us after that.

She wasn't here, though. It was just me and my latchkey siblings, so instead of talking about my shitty day, I stole a Butterfinger out of my dad's secret stash, ate it, then stuffed the wrapper in a hole in the bathroom drywall where the doorknob had gone through it. This was where I always hid evidence of my pantry raiding. It really was genius. No one would suspect this hiding spot. It was too random. Not having wrappers in the trash basically made my crime invisible. Most of the time, the stolen snacks went unnoticed, but occasionally my dad would have been saving something for his work lunch and would be livid that it was gone. He knew it was me, but he couldn't prove it without the wrapper. It was the equivalent of not being able to prosecute a known killer because you didn't have a body. My dad didn't have time for a full investigation, what with his being a single parent while my mom was away in Los Angeles.

After *The Tonight Show*, my mom had to get a manager to deal with all her scheduling and the offers that came in. She hired a man named Herbie Nanas. We immediately named him "Goes-ba" because one of our favorite movies series was *Herbie: The Love Bug* and there was one called *Herbie Goes Bananas*: Herbie Goes-Ba Nanas. We were very clever.

Herbie had big plans for her, and demanded she fully commit to living in LA. Sometime around Halloween, we were told we'd be moving permanently, too, during the Thanksgiving break. In the previous months, her fame had been growing into something bigger. The teachers started making comments to us. "I saw your mom on TV. She's funny. Is she funny at home? What's she like? Is it weird having a famous mom? Are you guys really Jewishes?" And on and on.

None of the kids at school back in Denver had seen my mom on TV because they weren't allowed to stay up that late, but even they had heard about her secondhand, and had questions of their own. "My mom said your mom is famous. How come you dress like that if your mom is rich? My dad said your mom is fat but she's funny so it's okay." Every time the sting of the last comment had worn off and I had returned to my corduroy-coated chub-armor, another zinger would come.

Parents were now telling their kids to invite me to parties and sleepovers so they could hold me hostage and ask me the same questions the teachers were asking me, but the kids weren't even our friends and I didn't want to go to their houses at all. That is, until Harmony asked me. Harmony was my real friend and had been since before any of this fame stuff had happened. She was bossy, which made me feel at ease. I didn't have to make decisions when I played with her. I could just follow along and enjoy myself.

Harmony's family was like mine, big and loud, and like ours they didn't fit into suburban, white Denver. They were blunt, food-centric, and hedonistic. Their house and cars were always full of extended family, and aunties picked her up from school as often, if not more often, than her mom. Harmony's mom was gorgeous. She blasted Prince at all hours of the day, not surprising since all his songs seemed to be about her. She had long black hair, brown skin, and a big attitude that she stuffed into tiny, sexy outfits. She was nothing like the other moms. I felt like I'd be okay there and accepted the invitation.

This was my first sleepover. I was still kind of nervous about peeing the bed even though I hadn't for months, and I had been exhibiting signs of separation anxiety, probably because of my mom's absence, like bad dreams and stomachaches. I was nervous but also excited at the prospect of having a friend outside the schoolyard, a house I could walk to and go inside of on Saturdays, a door to knock on to get invited in for cookies, access to another person's toys and dolls. And snacks! I showed up to the sleepover with my own sleeping bag and nothing else. They thought I was being polite, but I was actually just bringing my own linens to pee on, which actually *is* courteous, I suppose.

Harmony gave me and the two other girls she had invited a tour of her house. It was exactly as an early-eighties, Prince-obsessed young mom's multigenerational small fifties home should be. She ended the tour in her room, which was huge compared to my basement alcove. There was a life-size Pink Panther doll on her bed, and it was surrounded by other dolls. Her room was covered in toys. It was palatial that way. We had been playing in her room for a couple hours when a preteen girl came in. She moved slowly and spoke inaudibly, her tongue too thick for her mouth. Her limbs weren't completely in control and swung around her when she moved. She had on black sweats and a T-shirt. Harmony demanded that she leave. Our curiosity was obvious, so she started to explain. "That's my cousin. She's a freak. She has twelve toes. I can't stand her."

My heart dropped and I felt sick. I saw in her cousin's eyes that she understood and was hurt by the comments as she turned and left the room. I started tearing up and was embarrassed. To regain composure, I got up to go to the bathroom, which happened to be off the room the cousin had retreated to. She was sitting on a couch just staring. I went and sat next to her and tried talking to her. I asked her name and how old she was and what she liked to do and struggled hard to understand her answers. I thought I better get back to the bedroom, but I couldn't bring myself to leave her alone. Eventually Harmony and the other girls came to find me.

When she saw me with her cousin, Harmony's face scrunched up and she angrily left the room. A few minutes later, she came back in and told me she had a present for me. She was holding a piece of paper flat on her palm. She extended her hand and I craned my neck to see what it was. Something didn't feel right about her tone. I wondered if there was a slur witten on it. The page was blank and I was relieved—until I felt the page smash into my face. Harmony turned her wrist to rub the paper into my nose and when she pulled it away, I saw a glint of moisture and my face was wet. I could smell spit. I jumped up and ran to the bathroom. The girls ran away giggling, and I washed my face with soap several times and waited until the laughing stopped, and then for a long time after. I went out into the room and grabbed the push-button phone with its long tangled coiled cord, and dragged it into the bathroom with me. The cousin had gone from the couch and the girls were silent. Everyone was asleep. I called my dad and asked him to come get me and he did.

I don't remember if I told my dad what happened or if I just said I didn't want to be there anymore. I just remember that he came and got me when I asked, and that I never wanted to be away from my family again.

Between Matt and Harmony and the adults' increasingly intrusive behavior, I couldn't wait to get out of here. I was done. I had never felt like I fit in here, though I had made a significant effort when I thought Denver would be my life forever. I thought that I would marry my high school boyfriend and have several kids all named something like Tyler. I tried to sell myself the idea that this was the ultimate reward. Now I could let go of that pretense. I could let myself want more. I wanted my mom. I wanted a new start and anonymity. I wanted the filth of Los Angeles baked into my exposed skin by the constant sun. I wanted endless sodas at the Comedy Store.

November 1984 came and we started packing, organizing our clothes and toys, choosing what to leave behind and what to take. I chose Roxy and Goldie, naturally. They would go in my suitcase. Some of my other dolls and toys were staying behind with my dad to be packed up in a moving truck after he sold our house and wrapped up our lives in Denver. This meant he was coming, too, and not staying behind like he had last summer. This meant this move was for real. We emptied our lockers and said goodbye to all the teachers and kids and neighbors. They seemed extra disappointed to see us go now that we were Somebody.

Beanie flew out to collect us, and we did the drive from Denver to LA once again. After two days crammed into our little Mazda with our luggage, we were thrilled to arrive at our new home, a one-bedroom apartment in Hollywood. My mom and Beanie would share the bedroom, and the three of us would line up in sleeping bags on the living room floor. I still have mine somewhere in storage, a purple cotton thing with a yellow lining, not intentionally the Lakers colors, but fitting. They weren't like the thick Coleman bags we used when we went camping in Colorado; they were lightweight for our new climate. We'd struggle to fall asleep and toss and turn, bumping into each other and barking "Watch out!" Even though we knew the sleeping arrangements were temporary, that didn't make them any more comfortable.

The first item on the agenda was to go down to the local school and sign up. The plan was that we would start immediately and get our new lives underway with minimal interruption. There was just one problem: my mom hadn't anticipated that California had different vaccination requirements for school than Colorado. Since we weren't up to date, there was a waiting period that meant we couldn't start until January.

So in the six short weeks that we lived in that apartment, with my dad a thousand miles away, my mom busy creating an entire career out of thin air, no school, no friends to play with, no toys besides Roxy and Goldie, I would have to entertain myself.

My adventures usually consisted of finding a weird piece of garbage and pretending it was a clue to a hidden treasure, or a hidden message from a hostage in another apartment, a young kid who needed my wits to save her. Sometimes they involved being a spy and listening outside the windows of other tenants, reverse engineering their origin stories from their phone conversations. Sometimes they were snooping through their carport parking spots looking for clues as to their *real* identity, the one they were hiding from everyone while pretending to live a normal life. I was able to talk Jake into coming on some of these adventures with me, but Jessica refused to do anything other than read books indoors.

Our landlord was especially interesting because he had a thick accent and dressed so much better than all the tenants. He had a Mercedes-Benz and his own single-car garage in the building, which he usually locked, except for one day when he did not lock it and I talked Jake into exploring it with me. I wanted to see what this guy was really up to. There was a set of cabinets above the hood of his car and I opened them to see what was inside. He was doing a great job of pretending to be a landlord. He had tools and plumbing supplies, brass numbers for the apartment doors, and dirty rags. He also had a few cans of spray paint.

Given that I was allowed to draw on the walls at home, it was no surprise that as soon as I saw those cans of spray paint, I had the idea to do a piece that would improve the plain white wall of the garage. What should I draw? How about a giant ironically unironic happy face? I was Banksy before no one was Banksy. Hey, maybe I still am. My installation still needed work, so I added "hi" and then went about cleaning up.

Jake and I went back to playing in the courtyard. About an hour later, we saw the landlord making an angry beeline toward us and we froze. He came up and took hold of Jake by the arm and started scolding him and then he turned to me and started yelling. I pretended not to know what he was upset about and I grabbed Jake and we ran to our apartment. The landlord didn't follow. Instead he went back to his own apartment. I barged into ours and told my mom that the landlord had grabbed Jake by the arm and she and Beanie lost it. They picked up a kitchen knife for self-defense, stormed over to his apartment, and threw open his door. My mom and Beanie both yelled at him, "Don't you ever put a *hand* on my children!" He tried to explain to her what had happened with the spray paint, but all she cared about was his touching us. He was yelling now, too, about how all our family did was yell and how he was sick of hearing us kids (me) screaming.

My mom countered. "We've had to sit here and listen to you *beg* to be let back into your girlfriend's apartment every night for months: '*Ohhh Chrissy, Chrisssy, pleeeaase, I love you, Chrissy! Please!*' So fuck you!"

We weren't about to wait around for an eviction notice, so my mom asked around to see if there was anywhere else we could stay. Mitzi Shore, who owned the Comedy Store, also owned a condo building in La Jolla where she would sometimes stay, or put up struggling comics. There was a Comedy Store in La Jolla, too, and it was a perfect place to hone your act for the Hollywood Comedy Store. We stayed in Mitzi's personal unit for a week or so until we could find something else back in LA.

We scrambled and found a house to rent near the school we were going to attend. My dad came out to help us get immunized at the free clinic in downtown Los Angeles where we waited eight hours to be seen. We were moving up, but not having-health-insurance moving up. Not yet.

Jake freaked out so badly when he saw the MMR needle coming toward him that he punched the nurse and screamed like he was being murdered. I was sitting outside the office watching all the kids who were going next turn white with fear at hearing him. Several of them started crying and clinging to their moms. I wanted to tell them not to worry, Jake was just a big baby, but it wouldn't have helped.

All three of us got enough shots to be up-to-date, and then we were finally allowed to go to school. We started right after winter break.

When I asked my dad if he remembered when we started at our new school, here's what he said: "I flew from Denver to LA to take you three to the free clinic for immunizations. First day of school was Monday, January 6th. I flew back to Denver to finish the move, and came back January 25th to unload our meager furniture. I know because I had the waterbed set up by the time the Challenger exploded on January 28th."

Thank God for my dad's genius-level IQ, perfect memory, and ability to accurately recall everything that happened at a specific time, *and* tie it all into whatever personal, local, or global tragedy was taking place. It's very OG (Original Goth). Too bad he couldn't do all that *and* keep us on a diet.

3.

Bye, Fat!

Herbie "Goes-ba" Nanas pretty quickly booked my mom on a nationwide tour as the opening act for the sultry, swarthy, sexy Latino singer Julio Iglesias. Although it might seem a little strange to have a comic open for a crooner, their fan bases were the same: horny, oppressed housewives.

We were finally enrolled in school, freshly full of injected viruses and ready to join modern society, when my mom left for her tour. She would be gone six weeks at a time and come home long enough to see that we had gained yet another five pounds each from eating pizza and fast food every day with our busy stay-at-home dad. You can leave one parent in charge of three kids, but don't be cruel and expect that they also feed them.

Before leaving for the next leg of her tour, she'd put us all on a crash diet. She'd hang new rules on the fridge, rewrite the chore list, make a schedule for us to follow, and throw away all our junk food. She'd buy into the fad diet of the moment, and we would follow it until she left again. We went through every single one. The absolute worst was Nutrisystem, whose idea of a sweet-tooth fixer was a tiny pump mouth spray of flavored saccharine. I still imagine the peanut-butter-and-jelly-flavored spray when I'm on the precipice of vomiting but need a push.

My dad would do his best to keep us on these diets for several days. Then the pizzas would slowly start being ordered again, and fast food would be brought home once a week, until it was once a day.

One of the fad programs we followed was the Rice Diet. The logic was as follows: most of the world exists on rice, and aside from the fact that these people were starving to death with swollen tummies, sunken eyes, and no immune system or energy to stand, they were *thin*. The diet was one serving of rice for breakfast, one for lunch and four ounces of white-meat chicken and rice for dinner. If it was organic brown rice or another kind of supergrain, this diet would probably be fine short-term for someone who is trying to fit into a wedding dress. However, we were pubescent kids trying to grow. And this was no organic supergrain, this was eighties rice: Minute Rice. Minute Rice is white rice that has been cooked and dehydrated. It was astronaut food. Not even. It was gimmick food.

I would eat my rice cereal breakfast and head to school, where I would beg for snacks from friends or eat off other people's discarded lunch trays. I'd steal change from home and go to the candy truck after school. I'd climb to the highest shelves of our pantry, where my dad would put the granola bars and grab-and-go foods, thinking I couldn't possibly get my large butt up there. Lard finds a way.

On top of our weight gain at home, the constant unpredictable schedule and moving, driving, writing, and working meant that our parents needed help during school breaks, so they would drive us the eighteen hours to Utah and drop us at Bubbe's house/feedlot, where I was sure to gain a quick twenty pounds even during a weekend stay.

My bubbe couldn't help it. She is the daughter of a Holocaust survivor and fed us like it was a personal fuck-you to Hitler, like every bite was a proclamation that we were alive to eat whatever the fuck we wanted to. Eating was our victory dance. Breakfast could be an entire sleeve of graham crackers and a liter of whole milk. Each. Lunch, a sandwich, a granola bar, soda, a candy bar, cheese—pepper jack (counted as a vegetable)—and Fruit Roll-Ups, which constituted a serving of fruit. Snacks were more cheese, juice, and crackers. I would pull up to the YMCA camp Bubbe enrolled me in with a large brown grocery bag full of food, positive everyone was laughing at the fat girl and her giant sack lunch. I just wanted to hide. I didn't know anyone here, and I wasn't in the mood to make new friends. Friends were disappointing. I just wanted to be home. My separation anxiety was getting unbearable at this point, and I spent every day of camp crying in the corner of the dark, air-conditioned game room with my sack of food until it was time to be picked up.

A favorite snack of mine was granulated sugar. It got right to the point. No prepping, no cooking, no cleanup. Putting a giant spoonful of dry sugar into your mouth feels unnatural, though. You have to be careful not to breathe in, as you might fill your lungs and asphyxiate, and then everyone would be proven right about your eating disorder and that would be all they'd talk about at your funeral and you'd be too dead to tell them to fuck off and mind their own fat businesses. (My family likes to tell the story about how, as a toddler, when I saw my sister get a mouthful of sugar to cure her hiccups, I faked my own by saying the word "hiccup" over and over. It worked once on account of being cute, but the next hour of trying was all in vain.)

As I grew older and more discerning, my snack preference was butter right off the dish. Sometimes I'd take just a fingerful. Before I was more experienced, I'd take a bite off the stick, but the problem with biting butter is forensics. You might leave imprints of your teeth behind, evidence that it was you and not your sibling who was responsible for this. All three of us relied on the plausible deniability afforded by having multiple suspects. At one point, my parents stopped trying too hard to figure out who was the individual perp for a given crime and would just distribute the force of their punishment to us all, sparing us the full weight of individual consequences.

After my affair with plain butter had run its course, my new love was peanut butter. What other protein-rich, premasticated, raw food can you finger straight into your face? Maybe there are other options, but I don't need to know about them. Between sugar, butter, and peanut butter, no other foods are necessary.

During one of our weight-loss attempts, I think it was the Grapefruit Diet, all the food was removed from our house except a few items: whole grain bread, some SnackWell's Devil's Food Cookie Cakes, nonfat milk, fat-free margarine, and natural peanut butter. The first commercially available natural peanut butter was Laura Scudder's, and she must have been a psychopath. The bottom three quarters of the jar was filled with peanut cement that you couldn't even stab your sharpest knife into, and the top quarter was just pure oil to the brim. You were supposed to mix it, but few people have that kind of stamina. The thing that made it healthy is that, by the time you were done stirring, the cardio workout made it a net-zero-calorie food. These benefits were undermined by the physical therapy needed to overcome Scudder's-induced carpal tunnel.

All these foods were kept in the fridge. Why? Because they were safe in there. Safe from me. The fridge had a large heavy-gauge chain wrapped around it that was woven through the door handle. It was held in place with a hefty stainless-steel padlock. The key was hidden for the short time it took me to find it, and after that, it was in my dad's possession at all times.

It wasn't long before I realized that, in order for my dad to close the padlock, he needed both hands on the actual mechanism, which meant the chain would have some slack in it from the way the door handle bulged right at his reach level. If I were to wiggle the chain up so it was level all around, I could open the fridge enough to work my nine-year-old arm in. If I did it right, the pressure from my arm being inside would hold the chain taut enough that I could let go, drop to my knees, wiggle my arm down to the door shelf, keeping the pressure on so the chain wouldn't slide down, grab the jar of peanut butter, and use my thumb and middle finger to twist the cap off. I would carefully dig my finger into the peanut cement, let the wad drip its excess oil back into the jar, and then bring my hand over to the door opening. Having to hold on to the lid made it impossible to get my hand all the way out, so I would have to feed myself like a baby bird through the gap. This left an oily forensic trail as damning as teeth prints on butter. My entire arm would be coated. I learned the hard way to bring a roll of paper towels with me before beginning Operation PB.

To clean up, I would have to put my left arm in to take the lid and hold the place for my right arm so I could wipe the oil off my right hand and switch back to replace the lid. I'd wipe the seal, the door, the chain, and the floor; hide the paper towels at the bottom of the trash can; and shower to remove the oil and smell of peanuts from my skin. The energy used in this process made it so I was hungry again right away. Sometimes I'd have to go back in for another round.

The scarcity I felt at home made Bubbe's house feel like the Promised Land. In between all the meals and snacks, Bubbe would sneak up behind me and shove even more food in my mouth, a skill she has perfected. To this day, I can be on the phone chatting away, and before I even see her beautiful, long piano fingers in my peripheral vision, a piece of chocolate will be halfway down my throat. She is a true master.

After one of these stays, my parents chastised Bubbe for enabling me to gain weight. On my next visit, she decided to be more careful. The once-accessible candy dish that sat on her counter was now in a cabinet out of reach. I was resourceful, though, and I quickly came up with a plan that involved a chair, some large pots, and a pair of tongs. I stuffed as much candy as I could into my mouth and then covered my tracks. When Bubbe confronted me, I denied, denied, denied, but my siblings weren't here this time and there was no convincing Bubs that she had done it herself in her sleep or that her handywoman must've misplaced it. When she insisted that it was me, I called her a "bitch" to her face.

She was shocked. She decided to try out a new disciplinary tool called "time-out" that her friend Dorothy, a therapist, had mentioned after hearing some stories about our feral-wolf-pup behavior. She sat me on a tiny stool in her kitchen, facing a wall, and told me I had to sit there until I was ready to be honest. She told me she didn't care about the candy, but she did care that I didn't lie to her. Six hours later, at two in the morning, I realized I couldn't manipulate my way out and finally confessed. And, for extra measure, I apologized genuinely. I had no interest in hurting this woman who had taught me to crochet and who kept everything I had ever made her, hung all my art on her fridge, and had my two little handprints preserved in the cement of her driveway. She loved me. We talked about what had transpired and we ended up feeling closer than ever. Until now, no one had really confronted me about my behavior. It was easier not to. My parents had to conserve what little energy they had in order to handle all the massive changes coming their way, and there just wasn't time to spend six hours waiting for me to confess to sneaking candy.

When my dad came at the end of the week to pick us up and take us home, he saw how well behaved and calm we were, and he begged Bubbe to keep us for another two weeks. Bubbe knew we'd had a break-through of some sort, and she wanted more of whatever wisdom this child-rearing genius Dorothy could channel. Although she was running a day care out of her home, she agreed to keep the three of us for two more weeks and, in that time, paid Dorothy to make a house call.

Dorothy was a "self-esteem counselor," which was the eighties ver-sion of today's life coach. She dressed in a way that I can only describe as violently plain: short "church lady" hair, padded-shoulder jackets, Sears slacks. She sported that very particular Therapist Aesthetic that I would come across frequently over the next decade, with very few variations. There was always a neckerchief involved.

By way of introduction, Dorothy quietly let herself into the upstairs bedroom where I was hiding after being told she was coming. Right away I could tell she was afraid of me the way adults are afraid of kids who see through them. I questioned her intentions to myself. Did she want to help me, or did she want to tell everyone that she'd helped Roseanne's daughter? I would give Dorothy the Silent Treatment until I figured it out. If she pushed me too hard, I'd pull out the Belligerent Maniac, but for now, we could just carefully size each other up like am-ateur battle rappers.

Then she asked me if I'd like to go for a walk around the block.

Hmm. This threw me. I *did like* the outside. And walking around the block. Utah in the summer is beautiful. I liked looking at all the people in their yards and the cars going by and the cats in the windows and the dads moving things back and forth like dung beetles and the endlessly pregnant moms with lawns full of identical blond kids who were either all nine months apart or multiples, you could never tell. So we walked. She asked me questions, loaded but sincere ones. Maybe she really wanted to help me? I started answering them, feeling a little on guard, but also welcoming someone's undivided attention.

When we got back to the house, she and Bubbe went off and whis-pered about yet another "breakthrough." Bubbe called my parents and told them how well I was responding to her methods and how I even seemed happier because of them. My parents thought maybe the whole family could benefit from Dorothy's wisdom and invited her to come on an all-expenses-paid trip to stay in the back house behind our newly rented place in LA. That way she could teach us all how to communicate with one another and better handle all the new changes. She agreed to come and showed up like a New Age Mary Poppins with a suitcase full of worksheets and a big, cocky smile.

Poor Dorothy. She had no fucking idea.

Live-in therapy began with daily family meetings where we all sat around in a circle to talk about our feelings. The first thing Dorothy taught us was something called making "I" statements, a productive way to discuss your own feelings without hurting other people.

"Each one of us needs to take responsibility for our own feelings," Dorothy explained, as if she herself had invented the idea. "So we're going to learn how to say '*I feel*' not '*You make me* feel.' Why don't you go first, Jessica? Tell us all how you feel."

"Well, I *feel* . . . like you're a bitch," said my then-nine-year-old sister.

For a second Dorothy looked like a priest who had gone out on a routine house blessing only to have his own crucifix shoved up his ass by a poltergeist. She concealed her shock as therapists are trained to do and turned to me.

She flopped her head to the side, another thing all therapists do. Maybe, like the way corsets ruin spines, the kerchiefs atrophy neck muscles.

"Okay, Jenny. Can *you* tell us how *you* feel?"

"I feel . . . like you should go back to Utah." Jessica and I exchanged satisfied glances. We'd given her the ol' one-two punch, something all members of my family do. We will be mid-murdering one another and an outsider will chime in and we will stop everything to combine forces and take them down.

After this session, I could see Dorothy had been defeated, though I could also see that she didn't know it yet. I felt a little guilty. Dorothy and I had had a previous relationship. But now she was trying to make me do things I hated, like communicate with my family.

We tried a few more sessions, and they all ended in some version of this dialogue. Anything she said to me now felt loaded, as if she wasn't trying to help me anymore so much as trying to get "Fixed Roseanne Barr and Family" on her résumé. Years later, she included us without permission in a book she wrote. Her entire story was misleading and skewed toward making her a hero. My bubbe stopped talking to her after that. Bitch, don't fuck with my bubbe, or I'll write about *you* in *my* book.

She was the first of what would be a litany of specialists, each tasked with the (always expensive and usually impossible) job of trying to cure whatever was wrong with our family. In the coming tumultuous years, my parents would consult dozens of these "experts" to help deal with the issues my mom's growing fame would cause. This was the early eighties, the era of radical self-help: "est" and tough love, Wayne Dyer, and Phil Donahue. My parents were so busy making money now that solutions to any of our problems had to be fast and easy, something we could either buy, swallow, or pay someone else to do. We didn't have time to fuck around and do the actual work needed to get better.

Dorothy realized that her attempts at rescuing us were futile, and she took her padded shoulders back to Utah, but not before laying the groundwork for our next self-help adventure.

As a parting gift to us, Dorothy suggested Weight Watchers Camp as the perfect answer to my parents' ongoing childcare problem. We'd be cared for around the clock while my mother was on the road and Dad was back in Denver selling our childhood home, and, as a bonus, we'd lose weight.

The only problem with this solution was Jake. First of all, he was only seven; the cut-off age for Fat Camp was eight. And though Jake had been a fat baby—the deep folds of his thighs had made it look like he had several butts—Jake was *not* a fat boy. He was totally skinny. Still, my mother managed to convince Fat Camp to let us bring him, their rule bending an increasingly common occurrence and a harbinger of future institutions that would happily take a big check (or even a small one with her autograph on it) from my mother, even if her children didn't need whatever treatment they provided.

I did not want to go to Fat Camp. This would be the longest we'd ever been away from our parents, and I already hated being away from home. A whole summer felt impossible. Also, having just turned ten, I was not as self-conscious about my weight as Jessica was. For her, Fat

Camp was a chance at total transformation. But since I was still riding the coattails of her coolness, hoping to accidentally gain a personality by osmosis, I decided that if I at least had Jessica there, it would be okay.

Today, sending your anxious, chubby kids away to a place you refer to as Fat Camp for two whole months might constitute some kind of bad parenting. But this was Hollywood, where, if you weren't actively cultivating an eating disorder disguised as a healthy lifestyle choice, you might as well just pack up and move back to Iowa.

The first thing my dad did when my mom started earning money was to buy gadgets, starting with an elaborate VHS video camera and tripod setup that came with extra batteries, an external mic, and its own lighting package. It was overkill for home videos; he could have done a professional newscast with it. The morning before we left for Fat Camp, we awoke to a VHS tape with a sticky note in his handwriting instructing us to "watch this" before leaving. Beanie was going to drive us to camp because my mom and dad had a meeting to go to that day and wouldn't be there to see us off.

Awww! My dad had made us a sentimental video about how much he was going to miss us and how much he loved us! Let's watch! We popped the tape into the VCR. At first there was nothing but a locked-off shot of my parents' bed. Suddenly my dad appeared from behind the camera, smiling into the lens like the host of a kids' TV show. He was holding something under his chin, but it was just out of frame. He began to talk.

"Hi, kids, Dad here, just to say I'm going to miss you so much while you're all away at Fat Camp. But I'll be thinking about you—*God, this is so good!*" At this point he lifted his hand higher to reveal a plate full of Sara Lee Cherry Cheesecake, which he began to fork into his mouth while talking. My dad was thin, save for a small belly that never went away, and he didn't join us on most of our diets.

"But Fat Camp is going to be so much fun. You're gonna feel so great about yourselves when you get home—*Can I just say how delicious this is? God, I wish you were up to enjoy it with me*—anyway I want you guys to be good . . . [chew, chew, chew—moan] and to remember we love you and can't wait for your return . . . *Mmmm, this is just so good . . .*"

My mom jumped on the bed beside him and joined in. She ate several ecstatic bites while my dad finished his monologue and then she wished us well as my dad ate the final bite and got up to turn the camera off.

It was a hilarious and perfect send-off, the humor of it melting away some of the anxiety I was feeling about going, as was intended by my parents. This was our love language.

I had been vacillating between the excitement of this new experience and total terror about being away from home. My dad was in charge of getting us ready for camp, which included helping us iron all our names into clothes he'd purchased in a hurry at the local Kmart. My haul included my first real bra, a thin, white cotton thingy with no distinguishable back or front; no sweet "coming-of-age" shopping trip for me. Sweatpants and oversized T-shirts were my thing, giant sweaters and clothes that could double as duvets if desired.

Jessica was mortified by my dad's clothing selections for her, pinching every giant shirt or pair of baggy sweatpants between her fingers while packing, examining each item like it was dosed with smallpox, muttering, "Ugh. What the fuck?"

This would be the first of four summers of Fat Camp, and it took place on a college campus just north of Los Angeles. I arrived anxious and not knowing what to expect, looked around, and . . . exhaled. I instantly felt comfortable. Everyone here was fat. And there were a lot of Jewish kids, too. Also, I didn't have to share a room with my sister, but she was in the same dorm building, a perfect mix of independence and codependence. I could make my own friends and maybe even get a boyfriend that Jessica could judge and make fun of for his disproportionate head or lack of musical taste, while simultaneously telling him humiliating stories about me.

This was a branded Weight Watchers camp, and we followed the program with its "points" system and regular weigh-ins, made less humiliating because we were all subjected to them. Every morning we gathered in the center of the campus to do morning aerobics, or the more masculine "calisthenics," as it appeared on the boys' calendar, though the exercises were identical. That was followed by breakfast in the main hall, where the walls were decorated with pastel- or neon-colored posters telling us to "Think Thin!" and "Get Fit Don't Quit!" After breakfast, we'd play sports and swim. The hot afternoons were spent in the arts-and-crafts studio imitating famous artists or in the theater, where we'd practice a shortened version of *Grease* or plan a talent show. It was like any other summer camp, except fat. Once a week there was a dance or a social event. Parents visited once or twice, though only my dad came, as my mom's career was already all-consuming.

The food wasn't terrible. A square of baked egg, a palmful of sausage, one veggie portion, each worth a certain number of "points." Over the course of the summer we learned how to keep a tally of those points. If we stayed within our individual limits (which were determined by an algorithm that considered our current weight and our goal weight), we could reward ourselves with a dessert. My choice was always a slice of Weight Watchers brand German Chocolate Cake. I still crave it even though it has been discontinued, as all good things are.

For the most part, everyone was supportive of one another. If you managed to move the needle only a pound or two, we'd all still cheer one another on, especially those kids who would frustratingly stay the same weight all summer; looking back now, they probably had undiagnosed thyroid issues.

Only once in the history of Weight Watchers Camp did a person gain weight during their stay and that person was Jake. He had showed up with a baby six-pack, and though they were touted as healthy options at the time, the low-fat, sugar-free foods took a toll on his metabolism and he left with a layer of pudge over his former abs.

After the end of that first Fat Camp experience, my parents tried to adhere to the Weight Watchers system at home. They'd buy the right foods, mostly frozen TV dinners, and we'd go back to posting schedules on the fridge, counting points, and taking family walks around the block. Though my parents played along, they were never invested in the diet themselves. My mom had always struggled with her weight, but now it was part of the persona that was making her money. It wasn't in her best interest to slim down right then. My dad was only a few pounds overweight, and it was all in that small fanny pack of flesh around his belly. He loved food, but he was not a foodie. These can be mutually exclusive. My dad loves burgers and fries, meat and potatoes, steak and steak. But he is also frugal, so: McDonald's. It would take only a few weeks for all of us kids to go back to eating whatever we could get our hands on, preferably with extra cheese on it, and we would gain back whatever we'd lost, plus some.

When the next summer came around, I was excited to find out we were going to camp again. Not just because I might lose the weight I'd gained back, but because by now I liked being away from the increasing tension and frenzy at home around my mom's career. I was able to focus on myself in the way that preteens need to. I liked the anonymity of being somewhere new, even if someone would eventually spill the beans. I liked the fact that I would see friends from the year before. I liked the structure. But mostly I just liked feeling average.

That year, Jessica made immediate friends with a ten-year-old girl named Muffy, who had the most incredible wardrobe Jessica had ever known anyone to possess: Contempo Casuals chunky sweaters, lace-trimmed socks, neon scrunchies, hoop earrings, and leggings in every color imaginable. Beyond weight loss, Jessica's only other goal was to have unfettered access to Muffy's closet. And Muffy's only goal was to make my cute, skinny nine-year-old brother, Jake, her boyfriend for the summer.

By the time we had unpacked our Kmart wardrobes, my sister had quietly and successfully pimped Jake out to Muffy in exchange for access to her closet. He was oblivious to his own human trafficking. So while Jessica walked triumphantly around Fat Camp wearing Muffy's Benetton sweater, Muffy trailed after a confused Jake, trying to convince him to hold her hand for just one second. Jake was ecstatic when the summer was over and he could reclaim his bachelorhood. I, however, would be counting the days until next year, when I could once again walk among my people.

3B.

Diets I Was On

Rice Diet (rice for three meals and chicken breast at dinner)

» The idea was to eat like the rest of the world who were skinny, but for their swollen bellies. This was definitely not supposed to be Minute Rice, but no one really specified that.

Grapefruit Diet (one grapefruit with every meal)

» The idea was that grapefruit had fat-burning properties. Not true. You lose weight because grapefruit makes everything taste like earwax and you lose your appetite.

SlimFast

» The idea was Soylent Green–inspired and made it so you didn't have to think. The whole point of dieting is so you have something within your control to obsess about and you needed to think to obsess.

Jenny Craig

» All your meals were planned out and already prepared and came in a shelf-stable box. All your meals tasted like . . . a shelf-stable box.

Nutrisystem

» Another all-inclusive boxed meal situation. Just as bad if not worse than Jenny Craig, but it had some novel appetite-suppressing snacks that were worth going on the diet just to experience, like the flavored mouth sprays. Their peanut-butter-and-jelly flavor tasted like burned hair on teriyaki pork, and the chocolate mint tasted like a chemical spill.

Weight Watchers

» This one was the same as the two above, but also accounted for the possibility that you might eat real food, too. It was a good mix of thoughtless planned frozen meals and free will. The diet included some really delicious desserts, even if they were the size of a saltine.

The Fat-Free Diet

» This diet was 100 percent sugar and 0 percent fat so it destroyed your metabolism and made your brain malfunction, but SnackWell's Devil's Food Cookie Cakes with a marshmallow layer were involved, so who cares?

Private Chef

» This was another one where all your meals are planned, but they are made fresh every couple of days by a professional. Maybe if you got lucky with your chef, this would have been good, but my parents always hired one who was actually a nurse about to get caught for murdering her patients and was now hiding out under a fake identity.

Hermione

» This was an old lady whose apartment I had to visit twice a week. She would feed me frozen strawberries and give me one triangle of

Laughing Cow cheese. She was an old frail British woman. I can't remember why I had to go to her house and sit there. I don't remember her discussing diet with me or anything. Maybe she was a witch.

Hypnotherapist

» Once a week, I would go to a hypnotist. She would put me under and tell me I wasn't hungry and I craved healthy foods. My mom would come pick me up after the session and take me to KFC.

When I was nineteen, I got a gastric bypass and quit dieting altogether. I still go up and down, but the obsessive thoughts were gone pretty quickly, and I hardly think about my weight at all, probably because I'm too anemic and vitamin-deficient to spend energy obsessing over anything.

4.
The Pilot

In October 1986, when I was ten, my mom was offered a special on HBO. Everyone has one on Netflix these days, but back then it was a huge deal. Only the best of the best, like George Carlin and Eddie Murphy, would be offered that opportunity. She was still touring, either with Julio Iglesias or with the comic Louie Anderson, who was represented by the same talent agency as her. They planned to go into production on the HBO special immediately after her last tour date, so she was writing the script for the special while simultaneously touring and performing in Vegas. Her final show was August 1987, and the HBO special aired in September. It was a year of sheer chaos.

During this time, twelve-year-old Jessica focused all her attention on curating her musical tastes and wardrobe and becoming popular. She had started a club called I Hate Diana, which I wasn't allowed to join because I "didn't even know Diana" so I couldn't properly hate her. She was in Jessica's class, and I believe that was her only offense. Jessica and two other people made up the entire club and wore homemade buttons to school with the letters IHD on them. I'm not sure if Diana knew what was going on, but Jessica probably did her best to make sure she did. Jessica was extremely smart, born knowing that you didn't rise to top dog by being nice. Not only was she smarter than all the other kids, she was also smarter than her teachers. She made one cry and quit because she corrected the way the teacher was pronouncing "Penelope" (like "pen" "elope").

I didn't know anyone in the whole school except my siblings, and since Jessica was too busy being cool to acknowledge me, I followed Jake around like a stray dog. The problem was, our classes were separated by a chain-link fence, so I had to find ways to play with him through it. This was apparently illegal, and when the teacher told me to stop talking to Jake, I flipped her off. Which was also apparently illegal. I was sent to the principal's office, where they called my mom, thinking she'd be appalled. She wasn't. She wanted to know why I had flipped the teacher off, and when they told her, she asked why I wasn't allowed to talk to my own sibling. They had no answer. I felt very supported at that moment and was shocked to find out that, even though I was right to question authority, I would still be suspended and grounded. Fine. Whatever. Not being allowed to go to school didn't seem like much of a punishment, honestly, and being grounded back before handheld electronics just meant you had to stay in your room. Someone punish me like this now, please.

Jake was spending all his time playing G.I. Joes or dressing up like a soldier and filming himself taking cover behind houseplants with his water gun aimed at our dad's precious camcorder. I would do his special effects at times, making black eyes and bloody lips with my mom's extra stage makeup, and set dressing by moving furniture around and hanging sheets behind him. Despite having begged for a BB gun for the last four years, Jake got a G.I. Joe aircraft carrier for his ninth birthday, and we all spent a year walking around it, as it took up the entire floor in his room. Weekends Jessica would go to the mall with her friends, and Jake and I would go to another mall together (Jessica wouldn't allow us at *her* mall) and buy more G.I. Joes. We'd each get a twenty-dollar bill, a small price for my parents to pay for five hours of peace. It was enough for one Mrs. Field's white chocolate macadamia nut cookie, one action figure, and a personalized gold-dipped rose (or the like) from one of the hundred engraving/gift shops that were in every mall in the 1980s.

When we got home, we would present our parents with the cheesy gift they'd begrudgingly accept, and then Jake and I would have a GI

Joe war in the backyard. We'd bury the dead under the avocado tree, not our new Joes but the older ones whose rubber-banded joints had deteriorated, leaving leprous limbs all over the ground.

The pressures inside our house were rising from all angles. There wasn't one aspect of any of our individual lives or our collective life as a family that wasn't in complete upheaval. My mom was overwhelmed trying to manage her work/life balance; my dad was struggling with his new role as the supportive stay-at-home husband. Jessica was becoming a textbook Mean Girl. I was being slowly swallowed alive by my anxiety, and Jake was silently watching it all happen, which was maybe the most disconcerting of all our reactions. Our family was falling apart, and the stress of falling apart was making us fall apart even faster.

We all kept trying to maintain, though, and when my twelfth birthday came around and my parents said I could have anything I wanted, I wanted to go to RJ's in Beverly Hills. With just them. No siblings. Just me, the center of attention, RJ's sloppy barbecue ribs, and bottomless Diet Cokes. No mention of diets. My parents were to tell me all the reasons I was their favorite while I chiseled away at RJ's World Famous Mile High Chocolate Cake. My mom would absolutely *not* dump the rest of my Diet (not) Coke onto my chocolate cake when she'd decided I was done. I'd eat as much as I could and then the staff would wrap the remainder up in a golden foil swan and I would take it home and eat it for days. I had an agenda. I could tell there was reluctance on their part, and I tried not to take it personally. The tension at home followed us into the car and across town. There was an uncomfortable silence the entire way. I kept trying to break it with incessant chattering, as I was convinced I could change the mood if I just told the right story. Plus, this was the first time in a long time I had been able to get a word in, and it was intoxicating. I couldn't stop.

I was elated when we pulled into a parking spot just steps away from RJ's heavy carved wooden doors. As I prepared myself by putting my Keds back on (I still take my shoes off at any opportunity), my mom mumbled something under her breath at my dad. I didn't hear what it was over the sounds of my struggling to reach my feet in the tiny space behind my dad's seat, but I could tell by tone that it wasn't pleasant. It took a full ten seconds of passive-aggressive banter for them each to be scream-spitting inches from the other's face. That's when my mom reached across the center console and slapped my dad in the back of the head, shocking us all back into silence.

In a loud, shaky, adrenaline-poisoned voice, my dad apologized: *"I'm sorry, we are going to have to postpone your birthday dinner. We will try again another night,"* and pulled out of the parking space and drove home. I cried the whole way back. At least 20 percent of my sorrow came from mourning the loss of my golden swan cake leftovers.

My parents had separated before, but I was never aware of it. I knew they fought and yelled, but then they'd always be snuggled up on the couch soon after, the calm blue glow of the TV washing over them. I knew they were both stubborn as hell and stressed beyond belief. I knew all their dynamics and roles had been in constant upheaval for years. But it never occurred to me that that wasn't just part of marriage. We were still in an era where divorce was a shameful failure. Only the weak, the selfish, and the godless would choose splitting up over a lifetime of pious suffering together. If your parents were divorced, your class-mates would either pity you or taunt you for it, and any bad decision you would ever make would be blamed on your broken family. I never thought divorce was a possibility for my parents, yet now it seemed im-minent and I was scared.

I ran away sobbing the second our car pulled back into the drive-way, and my dad spent an hour or so following me and calling to me from the new-used Mercedes he'd bought from our landlord with his post office severance check. I eventually got in the car when I heard the squealing of several sirens down the next block. I wasn't ready to live alone on the mean Hollywood streets. We went home and my parents continued as if nothing had happened, but things were never really the same again. A distance was growing.

In May 1988, just as we were starting to settle into our lives in Hollywood, Jessica graduated from elementary school. We knew we would be looking for a house in the Valley if things kept going the way they were, so it was decided we would find a junior high for her there. I would switch schools now, too, to make my transition the following year easier. Jake would stay at his school another year. Jake's elementary school campus was in the opposite direction from our new schools in the Valley. The double commute turned my dad from a stay-at-home parent to a stay-in-car parent. He spent four to six hours a day navigating the multiple stops and the traffic, not to mention every "goddamned fucking moron" who had no business having a license.

A thing about my dad is that he absolutely loves to drive. He's amazing at it. He will premeditate things even professional truck drivers who live on the road don't think about. He knows which way to turn the wheel depending on which tire blows out and exactly what to do if your brakes fail. He turns driving into an exercise of imagining worst-case scenarios and then mitigating their disastrous effects. He also does this with life. He loves long drives and road trips. He's been emotionally attached to every car he's ever owned, compartmentalizing his years into chapters according to which make and model he drove at the time.

Another thing about my dad is: he has road rage. It seems ironic that he loves driving so much until you understand the psychology behind it. For someone who feels out of control in his daily life, nothing beats a wheel in the hand. We have video games for this now, but back in the day, barreling down a highway at seventy MPH while screaming obscenities to yourself was all the rage. My dad's dad was the same.

Being in a car with my dad is an adventure. Every swear word I ever learned came from sitting in his passenger seat. All the basics, but also an entire new made-up language of curses he invented, grouping old swears in new combos like a lyricist, usually rhyming "cocksucking" and "motherfucking" somewhere in there.

His anxiety and road rage, coupled with the constant bumper-to-bumper traffic and Jessica's commandeering of the radio to play whining New Wave alternative music, was almost too much to bear. My shrill insistence that Jake was breathing too hard and Jake loudly countering that he was, in fact, *not* and I was *insane*, was usually the final straw. My dad would violently wave his hairy nonsteering hand as far behind him as he could while craning his neck sideways to aim a scream at us. *"You're going to make me crash and we will all die. Is that what you want?"*

I didn't know until thirty years later, but apparently feeling like an electrified ice pick is piercing your pineal gland while every nerve ending in your body is being bitten by fire ants just because someone is breathing or chewing gum has a name. It's called misophonia, and it's *real*, Jake. It's a real disorder. Yeah, I'm sorry for the way I treated you, but also you were kinda being an ableist asshole.

When the HBO special finally aired almost a year after she had been given the green light to make it, my mom became recognizable in public, mostly among white, privileged older people who could afford HBO. The special got really good reviews, and my mom was offered a commercial for a major grocery chain. She was becoming the face of white American mothers, an underrepresented group at the time. TV really represented only white men. I mean, not much has changed, but at least we're aware of it now. If you were to say anything about it back then, you'd be condescendingly laughed out of whatever conversation you were temporarily allowed to witness (if not participate) in.

My mom felt compelled to represent all women and was wholly aware of the sexism on TV and in the world in general. It was understood at some point that, though men were making the majority of the income, women were the ones deciding where that money went. She was talking directly to these women and they were listening, and so she became a commodity. The revenue from the commercial was enough that we could finally buy a house.

Now that she was making money in the entertainment industry, she was exempted from the rule that women were just nagging sidepieces or submissive arm candy. She could be the real, complex feminist she was. She could talk about sex and periods and equal pay. Well, so long as she did it playfully from the kitchen. Her feminism was the thing that made her so marketable to her fan base, who were awakening to pervasive sexism more and more each day, but what the executives failed to account for was the depth of my mom's convictions. It wasn't just about noticing she was oppressed and accepting it with a few surrendered jokes; it was planning and executing an escape that left a path behind her for everyone else.

After the commercial aired, we couldn't go anywhere without someone recognizing her. People would do a double take and snap their fingers and stare and point and say "Hey! You're that *lady*!" It was so surreal that I began to feel outside of my own body and life, like someone just about to realize they're on a hidden camera show. This gave me a strange, objective view from which I could see behavior patterns I'd never noticed before. It was another language I was learning, one of subtext and intent. I could tell the second she was being recognized and could guess what the person's reaction was going to be before they themselves even knew it.

Would they come over and talk to her? Would they talk *about* her as if she couldn't hear them? Were they jealous and confrontational? Resentful? Did they want to put her back in her place for having the audacity to go public with her fatness and general unfuckability? Did they want to fuck her? Did they have a joke to "give" her? Did they have endless "constructive criticism" for her, both professional and personal? Did she inspire them? Had she saved their life in some way? Did they want to be her best friend? Did they think she was their mom? Would they attempt to befriend one of us kids as a way to get to her? Did they want to be her? Most important, were they dangerous? We needed a buffer, a safer home with less accessibility.

My parents found a perfect house up in the hills in the San Fernando Valley. It had a long enough driveway to simulate privacy. It was big, but not unmanageable. It had a bedroom for each of us and a pool. If America had its dream of puritanical apple pie and capitalism, California's dream included fertile land and gold, and Los Angeles's dream included Moving to the Valley. You'd come from a small dead town and discovered you were Special. One day you'd be a waitress and the next you'd wake up as an It Girl, or your screenplay would be bought and optioned by some studio executive for whom you made cappuccinos. You'd pack up the small Hollywood apartment you shared with several struggling roommates, and you'd move to the Valley in the Hills. It was like playing slots. You were surely going to win any minute if you just keep putting coins in.

We were in escrow with our Valley home when the 5.9 Whittier Narrows earthquake happened. The house was three days away from closing and had been tented for termites, making it impossible to check for damage. We had to finalize the sale not knowing if the house was destroyed inside or not. We call these strange coincidences that always seem to occur around us the Pentland Curse. It's like Murphy's Law, but specific and personal and usually much more humiliating.

We were getting better at taking these leaps of faith, which were more like deciding just to enjoy the fall halfway down after being shoved off a cliff. They seemed to be working in our favor for the most part, but not without their taking a toll on my dad and his mental health. He was more and more overwhelmed with every new change taking place. From an outsider's perspective, you'd have no idea that he was so stressed because he came across as jovial and lighthearted, steadfast and calm. He was extremely likable. Only those of us closest to him knew about his road rage and his rage in general. It was never directed at anyone in particular, but it was loud and could be scary. My dad started losing his hair when he was just nineteen, and by the time he was twenty-three he was bald, save for a strip from ear to ear around the bottom of his skull. This left a very vulnerable head in the care of a very clumsy man.

As kids, one of our favorite stories about our dad was the time he taught us about knife safety. He did so by taking an empty gallon milk jug and holding it in his left hand while taking our sharpest knife in his right, and stabbing the jug to show how easily a sharp blade could cut. Unfortunately, his demonstration was too good, and he sliced right through the plastic and into his left hand. He had to drive himself to the ER for stitches. I can guarantee he was screaming obscenities the whole way.

Most of the time, he would just hit his head. He'd hit it on car hoods, cabinets, doors, trunks, bed frames . . . anywhere, really. In all of my early memories, he had a perpetual scab above where his hairline had been. You knew before you'd see blood that he'd hurt himself, though, because you would hear the screaming and swearing. The more tense he was, the more distracted he'd be. The more distracted he was, the more he'd hit his head, and the more stressed he was, the louder the yelling and cursing when he did.

He was preoccupied with all the new responsibilities and dynamics of our move and our new lifestyle, and I wondered constantly when he was going to hit his limit. The good news was that his daily commutes took only an hour now, so there was significantly less time spent reinforcing those road-rage synapses. The bad news was that being preoccupied meant being distracted and . . . see above.

We moved into our new, seemingly intact home and did our best to settle in quickly. While unpacking boxes, my mom got a call from an executive at ABC who told her that she'd been trying to reach her for a year. The network had an idea they had taken to her manager Herbie Nanas several times, but he kept saying no. That idea was a sitcom based on her act and her life, and they wanted to make an offer. Herbie had plans for my mom's stand-up career, and they didn't involve television. My parents liked the idea so they fired him and hired Bernie Brillstein and Brad Grey, who helped make the deal with ABC for the sitcom and got the green light for the pilot. Not long after that, they hired a woman named Arlyne Rothberg instead. She was extremely talented and great at managing my mom's career, but also at managing life in general. She also suggested we hire an accountant, a cook, and a nanny.

Arlyne adamantly insisted we be transferred to private schools, but my parents wanted the least amount of change and disruption as possible, and, because they didn't know if the show would be a success before committing to private school tuition, they decided to wait until the pilot aired to see what the reaction was. Arlyne rolled her eyes. The accountant suggested my parents lease new cars, but my dad wanted to pay cash and own something outright. The accountant rolled his eyes. The cook wanted to make us chicken Florentine, but we wanted pizza. The cook rolled her eyes. We were getting this reaction a lot. In everyone's perception, we were basically the Beverly Hillbillies. It's true, we didn't know how to have money or status or fame or any of the things coming our way, and the people who did know about those things resented our greenness.

Now that the pilot had gotten the green light, a script was outlined and written and ready to be filmed. Once that was done, the production crew was staffed, the cast selected, and the stage crew hired. The writer's room was filled, and future storylines were laid out just in case the pilot was a success. The script was rewritten and rewritten until it was ready to be filmed. Once it was finished and edited, it would sit on a shelf until the executives strategically decided the right time to air it.

We were at a bit of a standstill, just continuing on with our lives hoping that at some point the pilot would be a success and a whole season would be ordered and make us enough money to keep our new house. We had to be careful with money now that we had a mortgage again, but we had a little room in our budget. I got a perm to tame my frizzy hair. I wanted Amir, a boy at school, with his dark olive skin and black eyes, to notice me. I bought a couple of skirts to wear with my oversized sweaters and invested in some makeup. Jessica began to veer from her Popular Girl path into a more goth one, spending her disposable cash on black clothing, black Manic Panic hair dye, and white pancake makeup to wear under her black eyeshadow. Jake continued buying G.I. Joes and playing war games alone and begging for a BB gun at every opportunity.

The show was being developed as a sort of mid-year replacement during the 1988–89 season, but the Writers Guild of America strike had just begun in March, and this created a shortage of content. All four networks were desperate for new material. The pilot had done especially well in test markets, so the production company Carsey-Werner (who had *Cosby*, the number one show on NBC) called in a favor to ABC and asked for the coveted Tuesday night slot after *Who's the Boss* and before *Moonlighting*, and they miraculously got it. This was like winning the lottery! It would still be months before the pilot would air, but everyone seemed certain it would be a hit.

In the meantime, I met a girl named Christina in homeroom, and we made each other laugh in class so much that we started hanging out outside of class and then outside of school. We became best friends. We were both rebellious but not yet ready to commit to any of the compulsions we were feeling. When Christina came over, we'd both follow Jessica's lead on music and clothing. She was our unwitting goth mentor, and she hated it. She started smoking around this time, and Christina and I would sneak one of her cigs every once in a while.

We were starting to get in trouble for fucking around in class and being called out for being disruptive, which made us want to be more disruptive. We would make little noises and jokes at the teacher's expense.

The thing is, I didn't like being told what to do. I still don't. If someone says, "Don't put your hand in that fire," I probably will. If they say, "If you put your hand in that fire, you'll get burned and it'll be extremely painful. Your skin will swell and blister and peel and be so sensitive that you will feel the clouds moving. Your nerves will be damaged permanently," then I most likely will not. I'm not oppositional. I don't mind direction, especially if it comes from experience, but I hate control for the sake of control, and it was everywhere. Every teacher, every adult, my mom's manager Arlyne, nannies, cooks, Weight Watchers counselors—*everyone* had an idea of how we were supposed to live, and the more attention my mom got, the more the suggestions flew in. Everyone wanted to be at least the ringleader, if they themselves could not be the main circus act.

One day in school I drew a really well-done (I must say) cartoon of Jim Davis's slobbering idiot Odie humping Garfield from behind with his notorious I Hate Mondays face. Everyone laughed and passed it around the classroom. My teacher saw it and took it and was irrationally pissed about it. She called the principal to come speak to our whole class. I was mortified. Even though I didn't like following pointless rules, I *hated* getting caught and scolded.

When he showed up, the teacher handed him the page and I turned beet red and started sweating. I didn't know what kind of trouble I was going to get into, but I imagined it was going to be embarrassing regardless. The principal grabbed the paper, looked down, and coughed through his nose. He was trying not to laugh, but he couldn't stop himself. He tried to regain his composure and couldn't, so he held the paper out, shook it, shook his head no, and left the room, choking. I wasn't disciplined further, and every time I saw the principal after that, we shared a look like we just "got" each other. Good. I needed at least one ally here.

The teachers had been acting more and more strangely as the rumor spread that the nasal-voiced lady in the Ralphs commercial was my mom. They were calling on me more in class, drawing more attention to me. They were asking increasingly personal questions. Some of the teachers spoke in curious and excited tones, and some, like the art and creative-writing teachers, sounded cynical and resentful. I started to hate going to school again.

Toward the end of the academic year, Papa Woody had a heart attack and was hospitalized. My dad flew home to see him. When he came back, he seemed defeated. Apparently my grandpa didn't recognize him and yelled at him to leave the hospital room. My dad was devastated, and even more so when Woody died a couple of weeks later.

We all went back to Colorado for my grandpa's funeral, where there was an open-casket wake beforehand. Papa Woody's body was in a small room, so no one who didn't want to see him would have to. I wanted to. I loved him so much, and I just wanted to see him one last time. I walked into the room behind my dad and peeked around him.

My eyes landed on what appeared to be a mannequin lying in a fancy coffin. *Who the fuck was that?* I was in shock. I said out loud, "That's not Papa Woody," as I continued to stare. He wasn't there. I couldn't *feel* him in the room. There was no warm mist of grandfatherly love in the air. I tried to come to terms with the absence of him in his presence. I realized that the feeling of another person did not come from their body, and my mind was blown. I wanted to get closer.

I approached him curiously and first noticed his makeup. I remembered my uncle and aunt's wedding in Colorado Springs a few years earlier. Everyone's look was similar. It was that eighties aesthetic: A thick layer of skin-colored powder spackled over their pores, a thick streak of bright pink on top of various cheekbones, light blue shadow on all the eyelids. Eyeliner, mascara, bright-colored lipstick. Colorado Springs was small enough that there might have been only one makeup artist in town, and it's likely that she would have had to hustle a bit to make a living. Weddings were only on weekends, and you could probably pull off only one to two max. That leaves five other days in the week. I was doing the math in my head as I admired Papa Woody's hip, neon-pink cheeks. As I looked closer, I could see that what I thought were mascaraed eyelashes, were actually tiny stitches holding his eyelids shut. *This* was supposed to bring closure and peace? I was ready to go home now.

We returned to California and finished the last few weeks of school, and then packed up for another summer at Fat Camp, our third. This time was different. The playfulness of the past two years was gone, and Jessica and I were serious about following our own paths. While I would spend the majority of my summer staring at the boys and trying to get felt up, Jessica was desecrating holy altars and masterminding a snack-food cartel.

I'm not kidding. One night, Jessica had broken into the campus church in search of alcohol and taken a half bottle of holy wine right off the altar to bring outside for her waiting friends. I was tagging along as usual, pretending I was cool, but my real mission was making sure

Jessica didn't do anything too dangerous. Everyone took a swig and passed it around until it was empty. When the bottle came to me, I pretended to throw back a gulp, but kept my lips mostly closed, just parted enough to scent my breath so my squareness wouldn't be discovered. It tasted sweet, cheap, and perfume-y—not holy, at all. I imagined Jesus in our circle, taking a slug and then spitting it out, offended that this was supposed to be his blood as we bonded over being misrepresented and misunderstood. Jessica had also scavenged a half-smoked cigarette from the staff area, and she lit it with a book of matches she had also taken. We passed it around, taking a puff each before it was gone. The filter was wet with wine and spit, none of us knowing you weren't supposed to suck it like a straw, until it collapsed under the intense heat of too many hits in a row. It tasted like shit and gave me a headache.

When we finished, we hid the empty bottle and cigarette butt in the bottom of the trash can outside the church and went back to the dorm. I was sure I was going to get busted. The dorm head would just look at me and know right away that I had been drinking and smoking and lock me in a room and force me to confess and name names. I struggled to stay calm as I watched Jessica float back into the building, carried by a breeze, completely guiltless and sure of herself. I hid in her literal shadow, hunched over and avoiding eye contact until we got back to our rooms. I climbed into my top bunk and waited an hour to see if we were busted before letting my guard down enough to sleep.

This was the same summer Jessica sneaked off campus and found a twenty-four-hour grocery store a few miles away. After loading a cart full of junk food (mostly manufactured by the same company that owned Weight Watchers), she returned and promptly started a sugar black market; she'd charge double for the product plus tack on a "risk fee." It didn't take her too long to figure out that frosting was the drug of choice here. It was so loaded with preservatives that it could be safely kept in a footlocker or under a bed. It was ready to go at all times. It was the sweets equivalent to the savory Easy Cheese that we all secretly love. All you had to do was choose: chocolate, vanilla, or Funfetti.

She took me on one of these product runs once when nobody else would go with her. I was so nervous and sketchy that you'd think I was crossing the border with a balloon of heroin up my ass. As we walked back to campus with our backpacks full of frosting, a cop car drove by. I felt like I was going to pass out. I considered flagging it down just to confess preemptively, knowing that cops respected honesty. My punishment would be less harsh that way. My heart was pounding in my chest and my vision was blurry with anxiety. Every muscle in my body was tense and my breathing was tight and shallow. Under her breath Jessica whispered, "Act natural." Unfortunately this *was* natural for me.

The cop car rolled by without even registering two preteens out walking alone at midnight. We returned with the goods and doled them out discreetly as, one by one, kids came in the room to pick up. Jessica was in her element and had found her calling. I, however, wanted out. This career in organized crime was not for me. I just needed a simple life, a house full of kids, some animals, a garden. I was anxious to get started on this dream, but I had to get a man first.

The boys here were nicer than the ones at home, who would make jokes about my body and clothing or, worse yet, ignore me. They were quietly sympathetic, too, since they also struggled with beauty standards. I don't know which comes first, sensitivity or weight gain, but those two things are locked in an eternal chicken-and-egg cycle. It doesn't matter. Knowing the answer won't make it less painful.

There was one boy in particular I liked, Zach. He looked like a chubby River Phoenix from *Stand by Me*. He had dimples and a sandy-blond crew cut. He smiled a lot and had perfect teeth.

One night, there was a dance and I got all dressed up in my finest Kmart leggings and oversized Sade sweatshirt and sat against the wall with a few of my girlfriends. We watched the older kids pair up with the ones they'd been flirting with all week, wondering if maybe *next* summer, we would have that kind of luck. I saw Zach and a group of boys saunter up to the entrance, and I sighed at his handsomeness. The group stopped, scanning the room. Then they started doing this breathtakingly sexist eighties movie thing where they each singled out the girl they liked by pointing and saying, "I want that one." One of Zach's friends pointed out a girl next to me. "I want *that* one." The next boy did the same thing, and the next boy. When it was Zach's turn to pick out a girl, he quickly scanned the room to look as if he'd considered everyone, his eyes landing on me.

"And I want . . . *that* one," he said.

I was vibrating from the thrill of finally being properly objectified! Like all the girls on TV and in movies and songs! No Bat Mitzvah or menstrual event could even compare to this true rite of passage into womanhood.

Zach asked me to dance. We stood face-to-face, our hands on each other's shoulders, stiffly stepping side to side, middle school–style. After a few songs, Zach asked if I wanted to take a walk. We weren't supposed to wander around the preparatory school campus that Weight Watchers rented every summer, but I was a woman now and could make my own decisions. We walked outside and ended up behind a dorm in an area that was meant for smoking and snack breaks during the regular school year. There was a Pepsi vending machine that had been emptied by the staff in preparation for the arrival of the fatties. We sat on a bench, bathed in the glow of the Pepsi logo, and talked and giggled. He asked me if I'd ever kissed anyone. I said yes, though I meant Keith, my across-the-street neighbor back in Denver, and the peck at our pre-K childhood "wedding" before his sister punched me in the mouth.

Zach leaned over and stiffly put his hands on what was probably going to be my waist in a few weeks, and kissed me. With tongue. I still remember the celery taste of his kid breath and the weird same-temperature feel of having a chunk of another person's body inside of yours.

After that, Zach reached around and let the full weight of his arm rest on my shoulders. We stayed like that for a long time.

So *this* was a summer fling. I had checked all the boxes. Summer. Check. Objectification. Check. Body part in my mouth. Check. There was no going back to the Jenny who had arrived here weeks ago. I sighed, looking upward into space.

"Holy shit, did you see that?" I said to Zach.

"See what?"

"That was a UFO! It did a straight line then a weird circle around that star."

"No, it didn't."

"Yes, it did! Then it stopped for a second, then *shot across the sky!*"

"It was probably an airplane."

"No. I know how airplanes move. It wasn't a satellite either." My blissful state was shattered, though I tried to act like nothing was wrong. Sitting on this bench at Fat Camp, backlit by a corporate logo, arguing with some guy who didn't believe a word I was saying, I was *even more* a woman now than I had been minutes ago. I realized that, in order to let Zach's arm rest on me, I had contorted my body in such a way that my ass, arms, and legs were now asleep. This was so overrated.

I shifted a bit to move my blood around, then zoned out, thinking about the chances that the mostly teen staff might have accidentally left behind a single can of soda in that machine. I thought of all the ways I could get it out. I could tip the machine, but it would fall on me and I'd die. I could shove my arm up inside, but I'd get stuck and the fire department would have to come saw me out of it. I'd be kicked out of Fat Camp. I could think of nothing my family would love more than to make jokes about that for the rest of my life. I wasn't going to give them that satisfaction.

Instead, I was going to sit here tucked uncomfortably into Zach's pubescent armpit and fantasize about those aliens coming back around to beam me up. Maybe they could impregnate me and I could skip this whole boy thing.

School started again in August, and now I was in seventh grade, a budding tween who had seen a dead body, smoked cigarettes, been kissed, seen a UFO, drunk stolen holy wine, and assisted with a black-market cartel. I had big plans for my coming teenhood.

However, a month into the school year, the show that had been sitting on the shelf for the last ten months during the writer's strike *finally* aired in that special Tuesday evening time slot.

It was an instant hit, and we were wholly unprepared.

5.

Are You Becky or Darlene?

One question I could never get used to was: "Are you Becky or Darlene?"

These characters were amalgams pieced together by Matt Williams, the head writer, who had come to our home to study our family before attempting to write the script for the pilot episode. I vaguely remember him showing up at our old rental house to learn our dynamics. I knew why he was there, which made it all the more awkward.

I usually loved having people over. It was like the kid version of traveling to Europe or something. A whole new energy and culture would wash over the house. It'd smell different because someone usually frantically cleaned and put something delicious in the oven. Also, your parents were on their best behavior. Instead of yelling at you like Joan Crawford, they would coyly apologize for your precociousness, and sigh-laugh while squeezing you a little too hard, and then they'd bargain with you to leave the room by giving you something you usually weren't allowed to have.

I preferred their comic friends to anyone else. They were rough and crude, inappropriate and warm, nonjudgmental and hilarious. I mostly loved the gruff old men, as I've said, and that was the majority of them. I had a particularly obnoxious crush on Allan Stephan, who was one of the Outlaws of Comedy with Sam Kinison. Any time I caught wind of a visit from him, I would put on my cutest outfit and do my hair and put on my Bonne Bell Lip Smacker and sit and stare at him until my mom would yell at me for making him uncomfortable.

I figured this was going to be another situation I might eke a distracting crush out of, but, upon meeting Matt Williams, I quickly lost interest. I was shocked at this other breed of creative. He was a writer, not a comic. He was geeky and pale and had clearly never been outdoors, let alone sped a motorcycle through the desert while drunk on whiskey and trying to get to Vegas to pay his bookie with coke money. Not interested.

Something about Matt's presence felt invasive. You could see the wheels in his head turning at all times. He was watching us, but without seeing us. We weren't people, but characters, and going through his childless intellectual male filter, those characters became caricatures. He couldn't help but offer an impersonation of our family in lieu of representing it. He took whatever it was that he learned back to the writers' room and started scripting it.

From the very beginning, my mom and Matt were a bad match. He wanted to call the show *Life and Stuff* and my mom, whose life and personality the show was based on, wanted to call it *Roseanne*. This wasn't an ego trip. It was a calculated move to reduce the risk of losing her intellectual property by being fired. They couldn't very well make a show called *Roseanne* without Roseanne.

In the two years prior, several women, including Cybill Shepherd and Valerie Harper, had fought their removal from their shows because of differences with their mostly male coworkers. And because they were demanding treatment equal to the men they worked with, they were being called difficult and bitches. If my mom was going to be called a bitch, at least she'd make it so she couldn't get fired for it.

The taping schedule was grueling. Mondays the writers would meet early in the morning to start developing the storyline for the week. Once the basics were decided, they'd begin working on structure and dialogue. A writer's assistant would compile all the notes and info into an actual script, which would then be sent to a few select people for approval: My mom, my dad, Matt, and a couple others. My mom would bring the script home and spend the rest of the night making notes with Aunt Beanie and my dad, who was also a writer and consultant for the show. Then she'd take the script back on Tuesday. The writers would use her notes and build another layer of story, and then the same process would happen again. Wednesdays the script would get final approval, be "punched up" (essentially meaning dick jokes were added), and then a hundred copies in different-colored paper were printed and sent to the right departments. Set design, art department, wardrobe, camera crew, lighting, etc., would all receive a copy and make their own notes, each doing their part so that on Thursday, while the actors were doing a table read and making final notes on the script, the whole stage would transform into life-size dioramas in which to tell the week's story, the living room set always staying the same, with its trademark crocheted throw slung over the sunken couch.

Gaffer tape would line the floors to show where the cameras should roll. Lights were pointed at all the right places. The wardrobe department would be pulling several outfits for each actor and for each scene, taking Polaroid pictures of everything for reference later. Legal teams would be combing the script to make sure there were no trademark infringements or inappropriate subject matter that might cause the advertisers to pull their ads. A table full of a million kinds of processed packaged snacks and drinks would be restocked all day. Meals were delivered to the set on days the actors weren't there. On days they were there, huge, catered feasts would be ready in a nearby tent, rows of stainless troughs full of whatever food fads were popular, warmed by little Sterno cans. One of about fifty production assistants would bring in a steady supply of frappés from Coffee Bean all day long.

There were so many things to manage and so many different employees and departments, it was amazing that it ran so smoothly most of the time. It was more than a well-oiled machine. Each show was a miracle. A very expensive miracle.

At home, things were not going so smoothly. With our teachers' and fellow students' growing interest in our lives, and the paparazzi exploiting our accessibility by showing up in school parking lots or calling the office to get personal information under the guise of being a family member, it was becoming obvious that we needed more protection than the public school could provide. Since we were already a couple months into the school year, we decided to finish it out and then transfer next year with the help of Harriet, the woman Arlyne had brought in to help us find better placements. In What If hindsight, it may have been better just to switch schools then, but in Real True hindsight, nothing was going to make anything any easier. Except surrender, extreme and ultimate surrender. And maybe time.

Portola Middle School was overcrowded and had been easy to get lost in, with the huge classes, my one friend, my mediocre grades, my mediocre looks, my learned submissiveness, and my chameleon-like ability to get along with most people. I had enjoyed that anonymity as a natural-born wallflower. But now, with every episode aired and with every interview published, that freedom was diminishing.

Although I had started the year ready to be noticed and make a space for myself in the world, I wanted it to be on my own merit. The space that was in fact opening up, and the role that had been assigned to me, were not ones I related to at all. Instead of being a sexy, curvy young woman with Amir as my boyfriend, I was just the fat daughter of a fat celebrity, with terrible grades and a bad attitude.

There was a boy named Ben who made it his mission to make me cry every day. He called me fat and disgusting and made grossed-out noises near me every time I ate. He looked at every girl as if she was made out of pig shit. I tried to stand up to him once, but he physically intimidated me by standing over me and yelling. I would have to find another way to take him. I dug through our mail pile until I found one of the witchcraft zines we periodically received. I thumbed to the back looking for just the right spell kit. I found one. Bind Your Enemies, it said. Yes. Perfect. I scrounged up change from all the junk drawers until I had the right amount of money to send in, included a self-addressed stamped envelope for my order, and put it in the mailbox. Because it weighed forty pounds from the change, the mail carrier didn't take it and my mom found the envelope before it had the chance to bind my enemy.

She confronted me about it, truly worried that I was moving outside of the white witch realm into the dark arts. She asked me what my intention was. "I don't want to kill him," I said. "I just want him to suffer a little." Not being able to purchase the spell, I made do and put together my own kit using leftover Hanukkah candles, a sock doll, and rubber bands, of which I layered as many as I could over the doll's mouth.

And miraculously, he all of a sudden left me alone. Maybe it was the dark arts, maybe it was the calm and knowing smirk I had given him the last time he'd called me fat when I thought my kit was on the way. Now to deal with the other two thousand students.

As the year continued, the questions began. They started slowly with "Is Roseanne Barr really your mom?"

You'd think that question would be easy to answer, but there was a small electrical shock and disconnect each time because, as I said before, she was still Mrs. Roseanne Pentland to me. Also the word *really* gave the whole topic an infamous, unbelievable quality.

FAQ:
» Is Roseanne Barr *really* your mom?
» Is she really that funny at home?
» Are you Darlene or Becky?
» How much money do you have?
» How much does your mom weigh? How much do you weigh?
» I heard Roseanne is a Jew. Is that true?

Along with the too-personal questions were the surreal ones.

» How come your dad is on the show and you're not?
» How come your siblings are on the show and you're not?

And my personal fave: Why isn't your last name Goodman? Think about this one for a few hours.

At first, when the questions were new, they were fun to think about and answer, but eventually the answers became automatic and exhausting. Coupled with these questions were their deep underlying subtexts. I would have to learn to read the intent of the person first in order to know the actual tone of the questions they were asking.

For instance, the question "Is Roseanne Barr really your mom?" can be read with emphasis on every single word, each giving it new meaning, but also, along with audible emphasis, there is an underlying energy emphasis. "Is your mom *really* Roseanne Barr?" can mean (1) You're a liar (the more famous she got, the harder it was for people to believe that she had actually given birth to me). (2) You don't look rich. (3) You don't look like a Jew. (4) Why do you get to have a famous connection? (This one was entertainment industry–specific.) (5) I'm about to tell you why I don't like your mom though I know nothing about her. (6) I'm going to rope you into a conversation and then milk you for personal info I can use for personal gain. (7) I want to be in your family.

I got pretty good at knowing what I was dealing with earlier and earlier in the interactions, and eventually I was so good, it bored me. People thinking they were the first person to come up with a joke or an idea and presenting it as if it were genius was tiring. Everyone deals with this to some extent. Especially people in retail who hear things like "It doesn't have a price tag! Must be free!" all day.

There was a special set of questions for us Roseanne-Adjacents, and then similar versions that were directed at her.

I'm a polite person, but I'm also easily bored, and I came to hate being asked these questions, and even more when they were directed at my mom, because she was sick of them, too, and not as nice about answering as I was, and that was embarrassing to me and my Midwestern people-pleasing gene.

How do you read intent? You read it with your solar plexus, and you don't let your eyes or ego get in the way at all. When determining intent, you have to pay attention to the exact words used. You have to go drag the micro-perceivable movements you usually pick up subconsciously into your conscious brain. It's a rescue mission, and only sometimes do you come out unscathed. It's hard to trust your intuition at first, but eventually you get so good at this, you can name archetypes and then come up with an effective course of action to handle each.

My mom was starting to be interviewed a lot. Everyone wanted to know the story of how a regular fat housewife got a big break in Hollywood. People were really shocked to learn that the *Roseanne* show was based on our actual lives. We were a working-class family of five: three spunky kids, and two loving, if unconventional, parents who hustled to get by. We ate Cheetos instead of meals sometimes and played Beat the Bank. Our furniture looked like Grandma died and left it all to us. Until we moved to the Valley, we had a small, lived-in house in the suburbs, which we were growing out of. We fit in but also didn't.

As to the pressing question "Are you Becky or Darlene?," everyone at school wanted an answer. It was strange enough to have a TV character based on me without the added strangeness of being asked who "I" was based on. My answers were always a friendlier version of what I was thinking (They're prime-time, idiot; any real version of us kids would have to air on cable), but I'd answer, "Both." Jessica and I were both sarcastic and sardonic like Darlene, but we were both basic and typical in some ways like Becky.

My mom absolutely could not relate to Matt's one-dimensional version of us and she tried and tried and tried to explain to him in a thousand ways what he wasn't getting, but he wasn't getting that either. He was confident he was doing it right. He was following the sitcom formula, imitating what was already out there. This was *our life*, though. Matt couldn't understand and my mom couldn't compromise about her life's work. It was a match made in hell. Rumors started spreading that my mom was a bitch, impossible to work for, difficult, a shrew.

My dad fell into some kind of mediator role between my mom and Matt, and was doing his best to keep tensions at bay so my mom wouldn't be seen as difficult. It was backfiring on him, though, as my mom wanted him to convey the intense righteousness of what she was saying, as opposed to keeping the peace.

While my mom was busy fighting for her voice, we were busy taking advantage of her distractedness. Jessica's behavior was becoming increasingly brazen, and my parents were spending more and more nights in her room with the door closed trying to talk her through it, but she was dead set on being the Baddest Girl Alive.

The previous summer, when Jessica's reign as the Godfather of Fat Camp had ended, she was jonesing for more adrenaline and continued acting out. She started smoking and drinking and sneaking out regularly. The parental chats in her room were becoming more frequent by the day, their tone escalating in fear and worry. There was less talking and more bargaining and pleading now.

First it was simple: Jessica wanted a coffin for a bed *and* her room painted black. My dad was actually arguing on Jessica's side this time. His logic was that allowing freedom of self-expression would remove the need for rebellion or dishonesty. My mom did not want to see her baby in a coffin, so everyone compromised and one day my dad came home with a gallon of black paint and did her entire room, hoping that this would be enough.

Next was the talk about not stealing the rum offering from the voo-doo altar in my mom's dressing room. My mom was still close friends with Chai, a woman she had met at the bookstore. She was a voodoo priestess and had taught my mom some things back in Denver. The al-tar in the dressing room was for the support of female energy against oppressive forces, and so the rum was constantly being restocked as the gods needed massive amounts to take on *that* task in Hollywood. Jessica seemed to have a thing for sacramental spirits.

Then there was the talk about why you cannot take that aforemen-tioned stolen voodoo rum to school and drink it in the bathroom with twelve-year-old strangers because not only is it wrong but you will get caught and suspended.

Then the one about how you cannot hide said twelve-year-old strangers in your closet for two weeks because they don't want to go home. That is an illegal act called "harboring a runaway."

Also, you cannot steal a car and drive it, especially when you . . . can't drive . . . and are thirteen. Jessica had sneaked out at night with two friends, slipped my dad's jeep into neutral, pushed it down the driveway until it was safely out of the parental vicinity, and then started the en-gine and gone for a joyride. My dad noticed the odometer by chance the night before was on a particular number like 33,333k, and so the next morning, when it read 33,450k, he knew. She was busted. After being pressed for a while she admitted it, saying, "Okay, fine, I stole the car. Who are you? Sherlock Fucking Holmes?" making my dad chortle.

Our parents decided to let her know where the path she was on led. They closed the door to her room again. Jake and I jumped right into our places outside to eavesdrop, but this time the tone was calm and too quiet for us to hear, the most terrifying kind of conversation in a Jewish family. When Jessica came out of her room, her usual teen angst aesthetic seemed less performative and more serious. I *had* to know what was said.

I pushed and pushed and asked Jessica a thousand times. She told me to ask Mom. I did. Over and over and over. She said she would tell me later, but I wouldn't let it go. The next morning, Mom finally cracked and told me the cautionary tale she had told Jessica to warn her off of misbehaving. She explained to me and Jake that we had a sister somewhere out in the world that we didn't know, who didn't know of us. My mom had given birth to her in Colorado when she was just seventeen years old at a home for unwed mothers. She was given the name Elishia at birth, but no one knew what name had ended up on her adoption papers. My mom had left her information with the agency back in the day in case Elishia decided to find Mom when she turned eighteen, which was in just a few more months. It was a secret we weren't allowed to share with anyone else. Even people we loved and trusted could turn on us and sell the story for a lot of money, and my mom didn't want the paparazzi going after her.

My siblings seemed to be just a bit surprised by the news. I, however, felt like my whole world was flipped upside down. Not in a bad way, it was just that family meant everything to me, and my siblings were my reason for living. I remember being about five and crying myself to sleep at night thinking about having to grow up and move out and have a family of my own. It was a devastating thought. I couldn't imagine ever loving anyone as much as I loved them. I figured we'd be the exception to the rule and always live together, just us five.

AND NOW THERE WERE SIX! THERE WAS ANOTHER ONE OF US! AND A SISTER, NO LESS!

MAYBE THIS ONE WOULD PLAY DOLLS WITH ME.

5B.

The Fifteen Archetypes (and Three Subsets) Experienced by the Fame-Adjacent

1. **The Shocked:**
    Genuine inability to assimilate info, as if you've been told aliens exist. Lots of openmouthed staring, intermittent blinking, a tight grab or slap to your upper arm to test the Matrix. They say, "Are you serious?!" over and over. Protocol: Stop answering "yep" and pull your arm away. Thank them for their interest as you walk away quickly.

2. **The Networker:**
    Acts calm but their voice sounds like it's being squeezed through a tube. They buy time with small talk while figuring out how to use you to their advantage. Protocol: Talk about God.

3. **The Fan:**

Impressed by the actual work. Breathy and faint, like a Beatles groupie. Runs through entire body of work, repeating lines back to my mom that she doesn't remember saying. They are sweet and unpretentious, which means they don't realize that you're eating dinner or that one of the teens dressed in all black at your table is cutting herself with a steak knife. Protocol: Wait them out.

4. **The Fanatic:**

Impressed by celebrity itself and not the body of work. They have no idea what it is that you do and they don't care. They ask generalized questions and answer their own questions out loud before you can. Protocol: Stare back at them.

5. **The Conner:**

These people think Roseanne Conner raised them. They tell me that my mom is their mom, or call my mom "Mom" with a little laugh. They either had no parental supervision so always sat in front of the TV after school watching *Roseanne* or else their entire family watched together over dinner. Protocol: Say "Roseanne Conner might've raised you, but Roseanne Barr raised me."

6. **The Man:**

Men wanting to put my mom back in her place. They usually start with "You aren't as fat as you look on TV," "You're actually kinda hot," or "How does your husband feel about you working?" and "Who takes care of your kids?" Booooooooring. Protocol: Wait for the patriarchy to eat its own tail.

7. **The Cuck:**
   Men wanting my mom to put them in their place. They usually laugh overzealously at her jokes and say self-deprecating things, trying to get her to jump on board. Protocol: *Do not* say mean things to these men. They will never leave you alone again.

8. **The Damsel:**
   Women wanting my mom to rescue them from or teach them how to manage Mans and Cucks. Protocol: Tell 'em.

9. **The Hater:**
   People just wanting to let her know they hate her and her work and everything she stands for and everything she does or ever did. These people are self-important as fuck, which is why they get so mad when other people are "important." Also, why do they think you care what they think? Protocol: Smile big and say, "Thank you!," which will confuse them deeply.

10. **The Conspiracy Theorist:**
    People who have received signs from the universe that Roseanne is part of a universal plan that also relies on them and a few select others like Richard Simmons and Chuck Woolery. There is usually an Elvis reference in there. They all have leaky pens and write their manifestos in illegible cursive. Protocol: Enjoy the fuck out of those manifestos, but also keep them in case there's ever a police investigation.

11. **The Bulldozer:**
    A person who sees anyone around my mom as a roadblock on the path to her, or else a fill station on their way to her. Condescending, singsongy, and overly touchy. They grab you

by the shoulders and physically move you to the side and hold you there while excitedly chirping in her face. Protocol: Lean backward as hard as you can until they're unable to maintain their stance.

12. The Punisher:

Someone who makes anyone around my mom pay for their disdain for her. It is always unjustified and seems to be a reaction to some character they have built in her place and then hold her accountable to. I got this one a lot. Protocol: Try to explain they are mischaracterizing her until you hit peak frustration and start crying and don't go outside for a week. I guess I haven't mastered this one yet.

13. The Interrogator:

This person asks questions so fast you can't think and are caught off guard, accidentally revealing personal information. Protocol: Count to ten before answering anything.

There are a thousand more archetypes, but none matter as much as the Unimpressed. This group is the biggest mindfuck. There are three major branches to this group and they are all dangerously similar. Much like confusing a garter snake with a black mamba, you *do not* want to err here.

14. The Unimpressed:

The Nonchalant: This person is more like a regular stranger meeting a new person. It is usually someone from another country or a completely different walk of life. They're curious and kind without disdain or contempt. Genuine questions are asked. Respect is obvious and felt. Protocol: Fall in love.

The Undetectable: Any of the above archetypes, but disguised. I hate this one. It's hard to know what lies underneath and how to proceed. Protocol: Deal with the consequences of your misjudgment later.

The next and final one, though, is the most terrifying of all. Run-ins with these people have large and devastating effects on everyone's lives. They have growing roots like a cancer.

15. **The Actually and Truly Unimpressed:**
    This person is *genuinely* unimpressed because they are always unimpressed with anything that isn't them. They're narcissists and/or sociopaths. They use people like pawns and feel no empathy, which allows them to rise to powerful positions where they are extremely easy to confuse with decent, righteous people on account of their self-confidence. The main tell is how much they agree with you and insist that you are a perfect genius. They do this while also trying to change everything about you. At first, they make suggestions as to how you should conduct yourself in public or behave in private, and whom you should befriend. These suggestions turn into demands, eventually, and you lose all sense of self under their control. They always have an agenda, and they make it look like that agenda is in your best interest, but it never is. These people are dangerous. More dangerous than any conspiracy theorist who promises you're part of a divine shift in consciousness for New Earth that will begin as soon as you get them in touch with Richard Simmons. Protocol: *Do anything it takes to get away.*

6.

Sock Drawer Full of Kraut

I wanted to know everything about my new sister and tell everyone, but since she wasn't eighteen yet and couldn't consent to being found, I wasn't supposed to discuss it. Now that Season 1 of the show was so successful and my mom was a household name, we knew the tabloids would all die to break this story.

People were going through our trash regularly. (My dad had a cold once and the trash was full of snot rags, which he left on top of the bag with a note that said: "I have a cold. Enjoy.") Paparazzi were cornering our teachers in the school parking lot, and some teachers were approaching paparazzi on their own. Everyone was trying to get a piece of the action, if not the money. Everything we did or said was being watched. Rumors were constantly churned out. It didn't matter at all if there was truth to them or if they were complete fiction; once something was said publicly, it took on a truth of its own. It *was* true now, in a way.

We started hiring all kinds of people to manage every aspect of our lives, because that's what we were supposed to do. My dad fought the farming out of childcare for as long as he could, trying to do everything himself, but we just kept getting more out of control and fatter until he finally had to concede.

The education consultant Arlyne had suggested, Harriet Bay, was now finally allowed to find us private schools that could handle our new security needs. Everyone wanted to make us over and teach us which fork to eat with, not because these things are important to happiness but because they were embarrassed that white trash like us had gained entry into their club. They were only as classy as their members.

Arlyne finally talked my parents into a cook, a nanny, and a house-keeper. The first cook we hired made fresh and healthy meals that would rot in the fridge for days before she would toss them. She was disgusted by our bad taste. I remember having my best friend Christina over one day to go to the mall to make fun of Tunas (which is what we called trendy popular girls because they swam in schools and all looked the same) and being told I had to eat a meal before going so I wouldn't be tempted to visit the food court.

I politely declined the dry hunk of mahi-mahi on top of some ex-tinct grain they had found in a tomb where it belonged and planted back into existence. I was told I couldn't go to the mall until I ate it, and so I lost my shit.

It probably appeared as though my guttural screaming was because I was fat and spoiled and wanted pizza instead, but it was actually be-cause I felt humiliated in front of my only friend. Christina was terrified and went home, and I was embarrassed. I didn't get to go to the mall that day and sat in my room instead, full of building rage. As a fat per-son, people tend to treat you like a jolly mythical kitchen marm, or a universal mother, or some other representation of a loving, nurturing pillow person, but that is only the Taurus ones (astrology joke for the Pisces reader). The rest of us are bubbling over with anger. Our fat is ectoplasm, not beanbag. I still hate mahi-mahi.

Part of the reason we were able to get fatter under the watchful eyes of our help was that all three of us would get an allowance of ten dollars a week, and as soon as we were home alone, we would call Domino's Pizza. We would scarf the pie down, leaving not a crumb of evidence, and then discard the box behind the wooden toolshed in our backyard. We couldn't put the boxes in the trash because we feared the paparazzi writing a headline with a collage of hundreds of pictures of pizza boxes stuffed all different ways in our trash can. "Roseanne Barr binges on pizza every day!"

The toolshed butted up to a steep wooded hillside, so you couldn't see the pile of boxes behind it. It wasn't until two years later, when the house was put up for sale, that a real estate agent giving buyers a tour discovered the cardboard dump. She could not imagine the backstory and so asked my dad why there was a hill of two hundred pizza boxes behind the shed. We were past the statute of limitations then, so there were no consequences aside from the deep shame felt every time that story was told. Listen, we were hungry, and hunger makes you do things.

One thing hunger made us do was blackmail a nanny. My parents had hired a woman named Imelda to pick us up from school and watch us until they could get home from the studio. She was an interesting woman with interesting advice such as "Don't do PCP . . . on weekdays! Because you're working. Only do PCP on weekends. On weekdays, when you are working," she'd say as she drove us up the winding hillside, "you should only smoke pot." I still remember the feeling of my brain trying to figure out what to do with this information. Should we jump out of the car screaming for help? Should we remain calm and decide what to do once we were safely at home? Should we ask her for a joint?

I looked at my sibs to see if they had heard the same thing I had, and their expressions said yes. We locked eyes, silently agreeing to a plan, as siblings do. "Yeah, okay. That sounds like solid advice. Thank you." We played it cool until we were home, then immediately ran into Jake's room to discuss this further.

"Should we tell Mom and Dad?" "Nah. She's not doing PCP on weekdays. She said it herself." We cackled. We were learning to trust no one but one another. We didn't want a nanny. Or a cook. Or a therapist. Or a school adviser, dietitian, or principal. We didn't want one other stranger coming in to fix us.

We decided that instead of telling our parents, we would just tell Imelda *we were going to tell* our parents. That is, unless . . . she bought us each . . . a giant jar of sauerkraut.

Why sauerkraut? Why didn't we ask for sugar and candy? Was it possible that we had some sort of starvation-induced disease, like scurvy, that we were intuitively trying to correct? Did we have pica from mal-nutrition? Maybe we were just ahead of the game on probiotics. Who knows?

We confronted her and introduced our terms. She was confused, but complied, buying each of us a half-gallon plastic tub of kraut. We kept the tubs in the bottom drawer of Jake's dresser, the same one he stored his skid-marked underwear behind so the nanny wouldn't find them. This was clearly a thing we learned somewhere, the art of hiding evidence. We tucked our tubs below his winter sweaters that weren't needed now that we lived in the Valley, and visited them often until they were gone.

Imelda hadn't had the foresight to plan for her future by bringing us a steady supply of underground foods, so after we finished the kraut, we decided the benefits no longer outweighed the risks of a nanny on PCP and told on her. She was promptly fired. Enter Angela.

Angela would talk to us about her acne while we were eating pizza. One time we went to Carl's Jr. with my dad and came home with the bags, and she said, "Jenny and Jake! You went to Carl's Jr.?" like she was pretending to be excited, but the fear was obvious behind her smile. What would happen to her if my mom came home and we were even fatter than when she left? That's all I remember of her.

Next was a woman whose name I can't even remember through the thickening fog of change. Let's call her Nice Nails Lady.

Her résumé specified that she was a hardworking woman who did dishes and laundry and would change your car oil and do some of this and a lot of that, fix your leaks, wash the dog, and give you CPR if you were to choke on any of her five-star meals. Her credentials were amaz-ing, but her nails were long and perfectly manicured, and I remember someone telling my dad that was strange for someone who was going to plumb your house then redo your roofing the same day. She never did any of those things, but instead brought in her younger cousin, Elana, who had been in the country less time than she had and spoke very little English. Nice Nails Lady made Elana do *all* the labor, while she lounged around like her pimp. One day, Nice Nails Lady said something smarmy about my sister, so I called her a bitch and she hit me. I called my mom on set screaming like I had been shot. Nice Nails Lady was fired, but Elana continued to clean for my family for years, though she'd still jump every time we came around a corner. She had seen a lot in her time with us. I try to imagine what she must have been thinking coming into the house, indentured to her cousin, not understanding what all the screaming was about.

Trustworthy childcare was proving hard to come by in the years before Google and Yelp, and it wasn't long before everyone realized we were in way over our heads. We needed more extreme solutions than others.

Harriet had found a couple of suitable private schools for Jake and me. For Jessica, they were looking for something that dealt with behavioral issues more than academic ones. One was found that boasted an emotional growth–based curriculum. It was a boarding school called CEDU in Running Springs, California.

The CEDU (pronounced see-do) motto was "SEE yourself as you are, and DO something about it," but it was impossible to get an answer as to why it wasn't just called "SeeDo." Administration was always very secretive about the name. Upon researching, you will discover that the secrecy is because C E D are actually the initials of Charles E. Dederich, the founder of Synanon, a violent cult started in the fifties. The letter "U" stands for university. There was a concerted effort never to let the link between the schools and the cult be recognized.

Dederich was a member of Alcoholics Anonymous but, after taking LSD, felt that people addicted to illegal drugs (as opposed to alcohol) needed their own program. He combined the word "syn" meaning togetherness with "anon" and started a foundation. This foundation began as a two-year residential program but, because you never stop being an addict, grew into a way of life.

In lieu of medication or psychiatric intervention, the Synanon method of therapy was called "the Game." This form of group therapy was the center of everyone's life while in rehab. The Game wasn't a game at all. You couldn't opt out. It was a condition of your residence and membership and was borderline abusive and violent. There were two sets of rules in Synanon. The rules outside of the Game, and the rules inside of the Game.

Outside of the Game, members were encouraged to be helpful and nice to one another, but inside, you were meant to examine yourself and others by exaggerating your own rage and feelings to an almost comical point. You could say anything you wanted to anyone you wanted, even the facilitators or higher-ups. Things like, "You're a fucking pervert! You make me sick!" or "I masturbate to thoughts of you."

The Game was designed to break down communication barriers, which translated to breaking boundaries. I guess it worked a little too well, since the founder and most of its members ended up fucking one another's spouses and impregnating young women and strongly encouraging abortions. It wound up being called "the most dangerous cult in America" at one point.

Although Synanon was a nonprofit with tax-exempt church status, CEDU schools were private-pay residential programs that were founded by Mel Wasserman, a former member of Synanon who used his experiences as a model for these teen schools. CEDU was a two-and-a-half-year program that was in session year-round, which meant that Jessica could start immediately. It was only a few hours' drive away, so she wouldn't be that far and could visit on weekends.

The problem was that there was no time for my parents to tour the school. The tensions between my mom and Matt, the head writer on her show, had reached a fever pitch. At the end of December 1988, my mom had threatened to walk off the show, having finished only thirteen of twenty-two promised episodes, if Matt wasn't fired. She was exhausted from struggling with him. Matt was still under the impression that he should have the final say over what went into the script, and they were locked in a daily battle over dialogue and tone. I remember hearing my mom read the script to my dad and saying over and over, "Roseanne Conner would *never* say that!" She was right. Matt's version of Roseanne Conner seemed to be some evil shrew who loved nothing more than to verbally assault her husband for being a worthless idiot.

Matt was asked to step aside and did so reluctantly. He felt that this was being asked of him because Hollywood had disdain for writers, and thought the star was more important. Though that's absolutely true, my mom was the writer first and the star second, not to mention being the actual creator of her show.

There was also a battle over the "Created by" credit. Matt tried to get his name on it, but my dad had read William Goldman's book *Adventures in the Screen Trade*, which explained how powerful a credit that was. The reason it was powerful was because it guaranteed the accredited merchandising rights, which meant you would get a cut of any money made on merchandise. This amount could easily be in the millions. George Lucas made most of his fortune off of *Star Wars* toys, not the actual movies. *Star Wars* merchandise has made around twelve billion dollars to date. He mentioned to Arlyne that my mom should have that credit. She took it to the Writers Guild and it went into arbitration. The compromise was a credit saying "Created by Matt Williams, Based on a Character Created by Roseanne Barr." So now my mom owned herself, and Matt owned Dan and the kids, which is why there was never any merchandising done. It would have been a legal nightmare.

The media was speculating that my mom was difficult to work with since she couldn't get along with Matt, although Carsey-Werner stated that my mom "is passionate about what she does and she cares very deeply about the character that she had created in her stand-up routines. And for whatever part of that she's using in the show, she cares very deeply about that. After all, she's spent years on it."

In the midst of all this, my parents tried to block off a couple days to drive to Running Springs and tour the CEDU school for Jessica, but Marcy Carsey and Tom Werner didn't want to lose her for that long. They offered to charter a helicopter to take my parents up and back in just a few short hours. They agreed.

When my parents arrived at the airport near the school, a limo took them to the campus, where they were greeted by an unpretentious (always the *most* pretentious) counselor-type and a couple of current older students whom we would later call Look Goods (kids who benefited from favoritism by helping sell the bullshit this place was churning out). The program curriculum was emotional growth–based as opposed to preparatory, which seemed okay. Neither of my parents had gone to college, and that was never a pressure in our house.

The snow-frosted campus was beautiful, and the setting was just far enough from civilization that there seemed to be no way Jessica could get in trouble. The mountains would act as a gorgeous razor-wire fence made out of coyotes, snakes, and hypothermia.

It was a wonderful pitch and it worked. They flew home and let Jessica know she would be touring this "art school" in a week. My parents drove her up and redid the tour with her, but at the end, they reluctantly told her she was staying behind, the staff standing near to support them in their moment of doubt. This had been planned weeks in advance. Jessica was shocked and betrayed and started screaming profanities. My parents were ushered away, all the while being coached not to give in or be manipulated by her protests.

Once they were separated from Jessica, my parents drove home, as was the plan. I'm sure it was emotional for them both, but they were convinced this was the best way to help her get on a better path. Jessica was escorted to her bunk, where she found her suitcase and unzipped it. Inside were several pairs of ugly Carhartt-style heavy denim jeans, a couple of ugly T-shirts, and a yellow sweater with taxi checkers on it that she had stopped wearing years ago when it became unfashionable. This was a girl who had sold her own brother for a cute wardrobe. Her vanity could not take it. Years later, other students recalled the "guttural screams of Roseanne's daughter when she first found out about the dress code" at CEDU.

When my parents came home, they sat Jake and me down to tell us that Jessica wasn't coming back for a while. They hadn't told us before because they knew we would warn her. Later that night, I sneaked from my significantly creepier doll-filled, Laura Ashley–like room into Jessica's black cave with the Cure and Bauhaus posters everywhere and went through the drawers that she'd never allowed me to look in. I played some of her cassette tapes to decide which ones I should borrow indefinitely. I couldn't sleep knowing that I'd be walking into my wretched school alone every day for the rest of the year. I was scared for Jessica. I was scared I was next. I was scared at Jake's lack of being scared.

Two days later, my dad got a call from the police department in Running Springs. Jessica was in custody. She hadn't eaten in days, a common practice among girls who ended up in these places. She had left campus in two feet of snow in only a pair of tennis shoes and jeans, and walked miles into town. In CEDU-speak, running away was called "splitting." The protocol was to have the police take the kids back to campus with the parents' blessing and drop them off again, Refusing to Be Manipulated. That was the plan, but the officer was a dad him-self and said to mine, "There are a lot of truckers out here, and I would not want my thirteen-year-old daughter walking around alone in the woods." This scared my dad enough that he picked her up and, after collecting her belongings from the CEDU campus and being subject to all the tongue-clicking, head-shaking, and disapproving looks from the staff, brought her home instead.

When I heard Jessica was coming home, I immediately returned her tapes to her room so she'd never know I took them. I had mourned her leaving for no reason and felt like we'd averted disaster. I thought things would just go back to normal. I thought she'd been sent there to scare her and now that she'd been scared, she could come home. Kind of like when we got grounded, and then the consequences would be im-mediately forgotten.

When Jessica got home, she had a new fire in her eyes. She was now officially *bad*, having been to a reform school, become a runaway, and been to a police station. Like when someone gets a face tattoo, she was now fully committed to this identity. She immediately found pot in my parents' closet, stole and smoked it, got busted and spanked, and called the cops to report my parents for child abuse. When the cops came to our house, Jessica told them there was a trash bag full of weed in their room. She was hoping they'd bust my parents, but instead they fawned over my mom, rolled their eyes at Jessica, and talked about how much they loved the sitcom. Jessica's flames were fanned by this experience, and obviously something else had to be done. Harriet was back on the job.

Another placement called Community Psychiatric Center (CPC) was decided on. They had a teen unit on the second floor. It was a locked facility with 24/7 supervision, and there was no way out of this place without consent. That was enough of a selling point. The only problem now was getting Jessica there. They had already tricked her into touring CEDU, and that ploy wouldn't work a second time. There was no rea-soning with her. There was nothing to manipulate her with. She could get whatever she wanted on her own.

Enter the bounty hunters. Well, that's what we called them. I'm not sure what it said on their business cards—assholes for hire, professional bullies, troubled teen troopers. They were just adult civilians with athletic builds, the reform school equivalent of mall cops. May they all get inguinal hernias from wrestling noncompliant teens.

About two weeks after my dad brought Jessica back to her black room, she woke up with two large adults standing over her bed. They told her she was going to CPC whether or not she wanted to and that the only choice she had now was how difficult she wanted to make it on herself. I was on the couch outside her bedroom, listening and watching in horror. I had no idea what was happening, but I had just gotten Jessica back and did not want her to go again.

She knew she had no choice, so she surrendered. She just wanted to brush her hair first. Since she was calm, the bounty hunters let her go to the bathroom, but on her way, she took a quick sharp turn past me and ended up at the serving utensil drawer in the kitchen. I was silently cheering for her as she pulled out a small serrated steak knife and held it out in front of the two. There was about a five-second standoff before the lady laughed at her, said, "What are you gonna do with *that*?" and quickly jumped on her and restrained her. The other person jumped in, too, and they dragged her, screaming, past Elana and myself and stuffed her into the back of a door-handle-less car.

I wouldn't see her again for a while.

I missed having her to argue with in the car. I got the front seat and control of the radio now, but I had no idea what music was good without her input. I hated the pressure of being in charge, as I had a short attention span and would zone out while changing the stations. I'd always end on a Spanish-language one where I didn't recognize the words enough to be distracted from my angst. I missed having someone else around at school who knew what I was going through and could field half the questions about Darlene's behavior.

Weeks after Jessica disappeared into the privatized adolescent mental-health-care system, my mom left to film the movie *She-Devil* with Meryl Streep in New York. She would try to come home every other weekend, but it was a tight shooting schedule in order for them to finish by the time Season 2 of *Roseanne* started production. They had only a few months.

Season 1 had wrapped, but the episodes weren't finished airing yet.

In one of the last shows, Darlene got her period. She got her period before I did. Every girl I knew both feared and secretly envied an "I bled all over my white gym shorts" situation. No one *really* wanted it to happen that way, but if it was going to, might as well have a good war story that ended with camaraderie and membership in a club.

The day after that episode aired, I walked into school thinking of nothing but Amir and his deep black eyes. Maybe today was the day he would notice me. I was thinking about my outfit, my hair. I was in my own world. As I walked through the halls past acquaintances who were taking a new interest in me, I was confronted several times with "Oh my God. Darlene got her period! Is that because *you* did? Did you get *your* period?"

My dad loves horror movies, and by the time I was eleven, I had seen every single one ever made, including *Carrie*. Naturally I thought, "They're gonna dump blood on me and then I'm going to have to kill them all with telekinesis." I couldn't decide if it was more humiliating to lie and say yes, or tell the truth and say, "No. I didn't get my period. I am still a big baby and *not* a woman. I cannot bear Amir's children and am unworthy of his love." It was also humiliating to know everyone was looking at me and thinking about my crotch.

That period storyline was more loosely based on Jessica's story. One evening the previous year, both my parents had disappeared into her room to talk to her. It was a quiet and secretive talk. The door was shut, which meant it was time for Jake and me to get into position, leaning gently into the door. We couldn't hear much, but when the door opened, everyone was happy and soft and emotional, especially my dad. I couldn't imagine what it could've been about. I searched for clues and irritated everyone with questions until Jessica finally said, "I got my period, okay?!" which I believe are the exact words Darlene says.

I was starting to hate school, and although I was promised a better experience next year at a private one, I knew my hatred wasn't about location. It was about feeling scrutinized and invisible at the same time. It was about not being able to trust anyone. It was about feeling stuck in my fat body without coping mechanisms. It was about deep anxiety and loneliness. I would try every day to get out of going. At one point I became so desperate I called in an actual bomb threat. From my home number. I called the school and told them I had put a bomb in a trash can the night before, so I wouldn't have to go. There was no caller ID then, but the school called the police to trace the call, and the police called my house to tell my parents what I had done. I endured a lecture while enjoying my day off due to suspension, and plotted how to fake a fever the next day.

Days after the curiosity about my ovarian development had worn off, I was notified by Danielle, a rich-mean-cool girl who looked exactly like a tiny Steven Tyler, with huge teeth covered in silver braces, that my parents were getting divorced. Her mom had shown her the story in a tabloid.

Danielle had always tormented me, calling me fat and asking me questions about my diet and wardrobe to intentionally embarrass me, and this was just a new angle for her.

I rolled my eyes at her naivete and her inability to separate fact from fiction, so she brought the tabloid to school the next day to show me. I used the opportunity to shut her down for good.

"You brought a tabloid article to prove to me something is happening in my own house that isn't?! What an *idiot*," I said in front of everyone, finally putting her in her place.

(Somewhere this month, I turned thirteen, an important birthday for a Jewish kid. I cannot remember a single thing about it: where I was, who I was with, how I celebrated. It bothers me, but trying to piece together this year in linear time now, as an adult, howwwww would I?)

A few weeks before school ended, yearbooks were handed out. Danielle and her clan pranced over in their tiny outfits and she opened her yearbook to the back page. This is what your friends did so you could write "don't change" and "have a great summer!" inside.

"Can you . . . ?" she asked. I debated whether or not to grace her pages with my now-famous-adjacent signature. She didn't deserve it. But I'll take the high road, I thought, and took her book to sign.

". . . have your mom sign this?" She beamed.

I stared into her eyes with my pen barely touching her page while that sank in.

"Go fuck yourself," I said. Up until now, I had only ever flipped someone off behind their back or mumbled a swear word under my breath. I had never so directly stood up for myself, and it felt amazing. This was the new me.

Later that week, a random teacher stopped me in the hallway and asked for my report card like a Nazi asking for *die Papiere*. Any previous year, I would have presented it like a good little girl, but I was wiser now. I recognized immediately from her tone of voice that she was just another archetype. A punisher. I refused to give it to her, and she made a derogatory comment about my mom (there it is), then called me a "mess-up." She dragged me by the arm into her classroom and intimidated me into handing her my report card. I finally did. She looked at my pathetic grades, stared me in the eyes, and said, "That's what I thought." I let all her unwarranted contempt for me sink in for a minute and then I quietly, but not calmly, said, "You . . . are a *cunt*," and stormed out, kicking every locker I could reach on my way.

The teacher had no consequences, but I was suspended for a week. I was supposed to be grateful for this since I should have technically been expelled. Because it was the end of the year and I would be leaving for a private school (and possibly because the principal loved me for my Garfield comic), they let me finish as long as I didn't go into that teacher's building anymore. I agreed and completed seventh grade with straight Fs, ready for a final round of Fat Camp, this time in Vermont.

We chose the East Coast Weight Watchers Camp in order for me to be closer to my mom in New York. When camp was over, I'd go stay in a hotel with her while she finished filming. We'd enjoy some quiet mother-daughter bonding, and then return to LA together to start filming Season 2 of *Roseanne*.

That was the plan, anyway.

7.

She-Devil

In March 1989, the first season of *Roseanne* had wrapped taping, and a huge party was held in Las Vegas to celebrate. A bus took the whole cast and crew up, including my mom and dad. There were paparazzi everywhere, and they seemed to be taking a special interest in my parents' relationship. My dad figured it was just because the show was number one.

A month later in April, my mom went to live in New York for three months to film the movie *She-Devil*. She would continue to write for Season 2 of the show during her downtime. Her writing partner and old friend from the comedy club scene Tom Arnold would fly to New York as well and get a nearby hotel room to help her.

My dad didn't think anything of it until a reporter for the *National Enquirer* called him.

"Are you aware that Roseanne is having an affair with Tom?" the reporter asked my dad.

My dad insisted that Mom and Tom were just writing partners and worked at strange hours in their room at times.

"No, Bill. They're sleeping together in the room."

My dad thought this was an attempt to goad him into a reaction they could capture and exploit as they would often do, and he continued to blow the reporter off.

"Want to hear the tapes?" he asked my dad.

My dad hung up and called my mom to tell her how ridiculous the paps were being. "They told me you're having sex with Tom and they have audio of it! Can you believe how ridiculous that is?"

My mom was silent for too long. Long enough for my dad to finally understand that the reporter was not bluffing. The *Enquirer* must have booked the hotel room next door and put microphones against the electrical fixtures to record actual audio. (Yes, they did this.)

My dad immediately made an appointment with his therapist to try to process what was happening. During that session, Dr. Perry's phone rang and he answered it.

"Well, he's right here. Tell him yourself."

Perry handed the phone to my dad, and my mom was on the other end. "I want a divorce," she said. She had been calling Dr. Perry to ask him if he would tell my dad that news in their next therapy session when he would have support, not knowing it was happening at that moment. My dad did his best to absorb this new information and stay sane, but just two weeks later, just days after the season finale had aired, my dad received a call from a private detective. Let's just call him Dick.

"We know about *the baby*," Dick said.

It was still scandalous in Hollywood back then to have had a baby out of wedlock, and even more so to have given the baby up for adoption. There are so many Hollywood horror stories stemming from actors' public relations agents trying to hide their sexualities, or any proof of sexuality. It was a necessary component to being a sex symbol, pretending you'd never had sex. There's a famous story that Loretta Young got pregnant by Clark Gable and had the baby out of wedlock and then pretended to have adopted her own kid. Being a single mom who was adopting someone less fortunate was way more acceptable than having had sex. Their daughter didn't find out the truth until she was an adult.

"What baby?" my dad asked, having prepared for this call for one and a half decades; he was still protecting my mom.

"Elishia," Dick said, letting my dad know he had the actual birth certificate.

There were probably people who figured that my mom disappearing at seventeen to "go to school in Colorado" was hiding a pregnancy, and maybe a few who recognized her from the unwed mothers' home, but none of them knew the name on the birth certificate. My dad hung up and immediately called my mom in New York. She had received calls, too, and was "handling it." She wanted my dad to stay out of it now. They were divorcing and it wasn't his problem anymore.

Dick was a PI, but that's not the only place he made his money. Blackmail is a much more lucrative business, as my siblings and I had learned. Dick was working for a man named Petrelo, who had hired him to dig up Elishia's birth certificate after the *National Enquirer* had hired Petrelo to find Elishia.

So the *Enquirer* hired Petrelo to find proof of Roseanne's out-of-wedlock baby; Petrelo hired Dick to find the birth certificate; and Dick hired a crony to deliver a copy. The crony offered to keep the birth certificate from Dick for a fee from my parents of fifteen thousand dollars but was turned down. Dick offered to keep the birth certificate from Petrelo (even though he had no intention of doing that) if my parents paid *him* off, which they didn't. He took the certificate to Petrelo.

Petrelo was also working both sides of the street and told my mom he'd give her all of Elishia's information and keep the story from the *National Enquirer* if she paid him half a million dollars, which was a lot of money. But she did. Elishia's eighteenth birthday was just weeks away and the records would be made public. My mom could just picture this little baby whom she promised she would find opening her door on her birthday to a crowd of ethically bankrupt pigs shooting flash cameras in her face. She saw what effect things were having on us, but we had been slow-boiled in the waters of celebrity and Elishia was probably a normal girl living a normal life with no idea of the media circus that her biological parentage connected her to. It would be too much.

Despite my mother having paid obscene amounts of hush money to protect her, two weeks before Elishia's birthday, the phone at her house rang. It was Petrelo. Elishia's mom, Gail, answered the call.

"Is Brandi home?"

When Gail had adopted Elishia, she named her Brandi, which Petrelo had discovered. Brandi's parents had always been open with her about the fact she was adopted, but wouldn't know anything about her birth mom until she turned eighteen and, if she chose to, asked the agency for the information. It wasn't guaranteed that Brandi would ever want to begin that process, and it was her choice whether or not she decided to find out about her birth mother. It wasn't something that would be forced on her. She had a pretty lovely life. She was born and adopted by the nicest couple ever in Denver, Colorado, where she lived with her older brother, Barry, who was also adopted, until her family moved to Texas when she was seven.

Her adopted family was also Jewish, as was both parties' wish, and Brandi was about to finish high school with a high GPA, ready to go to college. She had a large friend base from the Jewish Community Center in town. She was popular and pretty and had a jock boyfriend who was sweet and driven, ready for medical school. She had a pretty voice and loved to sing and be onstage.

Gail told Brandi to join the call.

"Your birth mother hired me to find you, and you should know, she's famous."

Knowing that her birth mom was Jewish, and now with the new information that she was also famous, Brandi started to guess who it might be. She thought about her own red hair and beautiful singing voice and guessed Bette Midler. When Petrelo told her to try again, she said Barbra Streisand. When she was out of guesses, Petrelo said, "It's Roseanne Barr," to which Brandi, in shock, replied, "I didn't know she was Jewish."

Petrelo continued working both sides of the situation. He tracked down Brandi's friends, including her ex-boyfriend, who had been her senior prom date just months before. Petrelo manipulated him into sharing photos and stories of Brandi.

He also set up a conference call with my mom and Brandi, both too elated and nervous to question why he hadn't just given them the other's number. They talked for hours and planned to meet in Los Angeles in a couple weeks. My mom would fly Brandi and her mother, Gail, out and put them up in a hotel. They could meet and hug and decide how to proceed.

What my mom didn't know was that Petrelo had recorded that conversation, and he took all his other collected information, stapled it to the transcript of that call, and sold it all to the *National Enquirer*.

The first time I ever saw my sister Brandi's face was in the prom picture her high school boyfriend shared on the front page of the *National Enquirer* while I was standing in line at the grocery store after school. I knew my mom had found Brandi and talked to her; I knew that there had been foul play and the *Enquirer* had blackmailed us and bought stories . . . but it never occurred to me that that is the way I would be introduced to her. I searched her face for signs of my own. I'm your sister, I thought while staring. You're *my sister*.

I wanted to tell everyone in the grocery store now that it wasn't a secret anymore, but looking around, I realized I'd seem nuts. I grabbed a copy and threw it on the conveyor belt to read later. I had been lost somewhere in the chain of command and hadn't received a debriefing. I guess I had to let this trash magazine do it for me.

Around this time, Tom suggested that he and my mom get married. That way, he could protect her from her agent, lawyers, coworkers, and anyone else who had selfish intentions around her. She eventually agreed and they started making wedding plans.

No one thought this was a good idea, especially Chai, the voodoo priestess my mom had befriended back in the bookstore days. Chai had been close to both my parents for a long time, but when the divorce happened, my dad got custody of that friendship and they spoke every few nights. Chai made no bones about the fact that she did not like Tom Arnold one bit. When my dad told Chai that my mom was marrying Tom, that he would live with us and my dad couldn't do anything about it, Chai said, "Don't worry. I will take care of it."

I don't think my dad asked any further questions. It was like having someone offer to pray for you. You just say "Thank you" and continue on with your life, knowing it will do nothing.

In May, Mom flew home on break from *She-Devil* to meet Brandi for the first time. Or, I guess, the second time, technically, since she'd birthed her. Brandi's adoptive mom, Gail, flew out from Texas with her for emotional support, and Beanie came as my mom's emotional support. They were scheduled to meet in a private room at the Beverly Hills Hotel. My mom was so nervous, she came early, and when she knocked on Brandi's hotel room door, there was no answer. She headed down to the lobby to get coffee and wait a little while longer, not knowing that, in their nervousness, Brandi and Gail had also come down for coffee. Beanie said, "There she is." From across the lobby, my mom and my sister locked eyes. They immediately recognized each other, ran toward each other, and embraced. Brandi introduced our mom to Gail, an awkward introduction that I incorrectly imagine went, "Mom, this is my mom. Mom, this is my other mom."

After all the introductions, Beanie and Gail left and Mom and Brandi settled in to catch up on each other's whole lives. They talked for hours, and planned to spend the next day together as well. They would have to find somewhere else to do that now that the paps had caught wind of their location. They chose the home of my mom's manager, Arlyne.

While at Arlyne's, my mom got a phone call from Tom's roommate saying that Tom had overdosed on cocaine and was hemorrhaging. My mom had to cut her time with Brandi short to rush to Tom's apartment, where she found him bleeding in bed. She had been to this apartment several times before they were dating. Tom's girlfriend at the time would call my mom and beg her to check on Tom while she was out of town because she was afraid of this exact scenario. His place was filthy and full of empty pizza boxes and liquor bottles. My mom would throw the rotten food and paraphernalia away, clean his apartment, and talk him into showering, and then come home and await another call from the fiancée in a few weeks.

This time was different, though. Tom had hit a new bottom and was basically dying in front of my mom. She somehow managed to keep calm, gather him up, take him to a hospital, sign him into rehab, and return to have dinner with Brandi. They said their farewells, made plans to see each other again soon, and then Brandi went back to Texas to graduate high school.

Mom was furious at Tom for ruining her reunion with Brandi and put their marriage plans on hold. She made him promise to stay sober and to go to AA meetings regularly. The rehab facility Tom had been admitted to was called Van Nuys Behavioral Health Hospital. They specialized in addiction, and most of the staff were actual survivors of drug addiction instead of clinical nurses or book-smart professionals.

Because of this, the friendships Tom made there were familial, and he and the staff became close. There were a lot of celebrity connections there, too, which made it all the more comfortable. It wasn't long before Tom replaced his drug addiction with a sobriety addiction. The answer to everything was AA.

I don't know how, but my dad was still holding it together. He was still living in the home he and my mom had purchased together in the Valley. He was still seeing his psychiatrist, Dr. Perry, whom he had met as Jessica's admitting doctor at CPC. Dr. Perry had quit CPC to go into private practice. Along with these three sessions a week, my dad was leaning on friends and family for support.

When Chai found out that Tom had overdosed and hemorrhaged, she nodded knowingly. She told my dad that she had, just the evening before, "pushed" Tom. She wasn't causing his abuse issues, she was just exposing them, putting a magnifying glass on them, making them come to a head faster, like putting a hot towel on an abscess. It was an exhausting process but worth it. Now my dad didn't have to spend money on PIs to prove Tom was on drugs.

With all this drama going on, I couldn't really relate to any other twelve-year-olds I knew. I held on to my comfortable friendship with Christina and swore I'd still hang out with her even though I would be going to a different school the next year, but there was no one I knew whom I could share my life with. Even with Christina trying to understand what I was going through, I was beginning to feel completely alone.

I was hoping that another round of Fat Camp, this time on the other side of the country, would cure my loneliness. No one would know me or my story. I knew that that would only last a short time, but hopefully it would be long enough for me to make some friends on my own merit. Maybe I'd get a boyfriend again and go to a further base than the lame-ass kissing of an alien-denier.

This year at camp was different. I had no siblings with me and didn't know any kids or staff from previous years. I felt strange in the East Coast climate, with its air completely different from Southern California's. There was no saltwater haze, just woodsy smells. Even the buildings felt different. Weight Watchers camps always took place on private school or college campuses in the summer, when the dormitories were mostly vacant. The buildings on this year's grounds were older and had none of the southwestern feel that the buildings in LA had. It felt ancient and European. I managed to make a few friends, but I couldn't relate like I'd hoped I would. Some had girlfriends and boyfriends at home. They wanted to talk about their Nintendo games and parents and school crushes and hopes for college. I didn't want to say too much about anything because it was hard to do without accidentally revealing that my mom was Roseanne Barr and that the family with all the drama that the tabloids seemed to have most of their focus on was mine. I lasted about a week before a staff member recognized my mom's name on my paperwork and told everyone.

I admitted and downplayed the connection and went along with things there, but I started to feel very dissociative, as though I was just watching myself play along with things. I felt like a ghost that made appearances sometimes but existed mostly in a different realm. Sometimes I would wander away from the other campers, who were all sequestered in one dormitory, and explore the rest of the campus. I found a building on the other side of the grounds that smelled like chlorine, so I went inside and explored. I walked the long hallway toward the wet cement floor. It was texturized to prevent slipping. There were locker rooms. I opened some of the lockers but they were all empty. An occasional damp towel was thrown on a bench. Through the locker room door was an indoor pool. I put my foot in. It was freezing cold. I thought about jumping in but heard a door open and ran out, scared of being caught. I sneaked out a different way, passing a vending machine full of candy bars. I stopped to stare at the snacks inside. They looked absolutely fantastical after I had eaten only prepared cafeteria foods for weeks. I felt like I had stumbled upon the City of Gold or something. I'll be back for you later, I thought. Maybe I would start my own underground sugar ring like Jessica had. No, I didn't have the balls. But I *could* buy myself a Snickers and eat it while hiding in a bush.

I wandered off farther from camp, figuring I was probably busted already so I might as well make it worthwhile. I walked a path until a branch of it led into a beautiful old two-story building. I went inside. It was stunning, a huge library empty of people but with old bound books and newer books and staircases and windows designed to let light in. I felt as if I had wandered into another dimension and was surprisingly okay with it. I lay down on a leather couch and fell asleep.

I had always had weird, memorable dreams that I could recount in greater detail than anyone could tolerate hearing. But the dream I was falling into was *not* a dream. First, I became so heavy I couldn't move. My fingernails felt as though they weighed fifty pounds each. The heaviness crept over my whole body and paralyzed me. My eyes started seeing static, like when you rub them too hard, and the static moved as if I were going through a tunnel of it. There was a thinning spot at the end of the tunnel that was becoming clearer as I moved forward. I could see shapes and people, but from a perspective I wasn't used to in real life. I panicked. Was this death?

I tried to wake myself up but didn't know how. I couldn't move. I tried to call out my own name or scream for help, but my breath felt too weak to make my vocal cords move. I was drowning in the density. I was panicking so hard, writhing around inside my own skin, that I actually made my big toe move. I felt it and knew it was a lifeline of some sort. I focused on that toe until I made it twitch again. And then again. The twitching tugged on whatever tether my spirit had to my body like a fishing line. I was able to make two toes move now, and then my whole foot and ankle, and then my leg, which I kicked so ferociously that I woke myself all the way up. I sat up, my eyes wide with fear and confusion, and breathed heavily until I could calm down. What the fuck just happened?

I walked back to the barracks hoping I wasn't caught, and when I got there, no one had noticed I had been gone. I was still scared from the weird experience I'd just had and preoccupied myself with thoughts of the vending machine.

Later that night at the big round group dinner table, I choked on an orange section. The membrane of it had pulled taut against my esophagus and breathing in had somehow suctioned it. I stood up and put my hands on my throat, the universal sign for choking. The entire group sitting at my table thought this was another one of my jokes. I stared into each camper's eyes, trying to get one to notice I was serious, but no one got it. I remember thinking, This is how I die? At Fat Camp? Choking? On a fucking orange? Because everyone thought I was trying to be funny? I refused this fate, reached down my own throat with my thumb and pointer finger, and pulled the membrane out right before I was about to pass out. I inhaled air so loudly that all the kids turned around to look at me.

"Oh my God! We thought you were kidding!" They all got quiet and we sat for a while. I thought about my experience earlier in the day and decided that the two events must be related: the universe was trying to kill me. I had opened some portal. I could feel the darkness from my library dream clinging to my sternum. We dispersed and went to our dorm rooms to get ready to sleep, which would not be easy for me from now on.

While my roommate played "Toy Soldiers" on repeat on her tiny boom box, I lay in bed, terrified to go under. I felt a heaviness on my skin I couldn't explain or understand. For the next ten years, I would have to deal with this. Falling asleep on my back made me instantly go into paralysis. It never got less terrifying. I got better at getting my toe to wiggle sooner, but I couldn't master getting it to stop altogether. Sleeping on my stomach helped sometimes, but sometimes, it didn't. I was afraid to go to sleep, and not all that excited about being awake in the mess that was my life.

A few weeks later, camp ended. I think a driver came to pick me up and drive me from Vermont to the Plaza Hotel in New York, where my mom was staying. I vaguely remember all the counselors being disappointed that they didn't get a glimpse of Roseanne.

When I arrived at the Plaza Hotel, I knew right away I wasn't going to fit in there. Have you ever read the Eloise books? Imagine if she was a feral wolf-child with PTSD, possessed a sixth sense manifesting itself in terrifying out-of-body experiences, endured a powerful food addiction, and had a roving band of salacious assholes snapping pictures of her every move.

With Jessica in California, Jake had come to New York a week before camp ended to spend alone time with our mom, and we were the only kids in the place. Everyone was clean and thin and well dressed. They were well behaved and walked like they were trying not to wake someone. I was always ultra-polite to everyone, even when I was being a little shit. I wasn't ungrateful, just untrained. Jake and I would try to keep ourselves entertained by pushing all the buttons in the elevator, ordering massive amounts of room service, running up and down hallways, eavesdropping on any room from which we heard voices coming, and hanging out in the lobby, people watching.

After several of the hotel staff complained, my mom had the wherewithal to fly Beanie out to watch us while she was on set. Beanie was my favorite babysitter and possibly my favorite person on Earth. She was endlessly present for us and found ways to support us that no one else thought of or had time to do. She was also scary intuitive, like the rest of the women in my family, and her gift was bypassing all your bullshit and seeing right into your soul. She would reach into your subconscious like a psychic chiropractor and adjust your spiritual spine without your even noticing. She loved us kids, so this was always done with kindness and love, but if you pissed her off, well, then . . .

Beanie had a hard time holding down a regular job because of her inability to eat shit from people. She had been fired twice for telling her bosses off. When we first moved to LA, Beanie had to sit next to a woman in the medical billing office who made openly anti-Semitic comments constantly. Beanie went to HR several times to address the issue, but they kept telling her the woman just had an unusual sense of humor, or "didn't mean it."

One day while in the bathroom, the anti-Semitic woman came in and was washing her hands at the sink. Beanie sidled up next to her to wash her own hands. The woman took out a bottle of perfume and nervously sprayed herself a bunch of times while Beanie stared at her in the mirror. After an uncomfortable silence, Beanie turned to look her in the eyes and said, "Your pussy can't *possibly* smell *that* bad."

It was apparent to everyone that Beanie couldn't have a regular job, and Beanie was constantly working on ideas that would set her free from the demands of wage labor. At one point, she had a prototype for a weeble-wobble man-doll that, when knocked over, would say sexist things, making you want to knock it over harder the next time. Though the character Jackie was based on Beanie, there was no way that 90 percent of Beanie's persona would have made it past the censors.

On Mom's days off, we all did the touristy stuff you're supposed to do in New York City. One of those things was seeing a Broadway show.

We decided on *Cats*. Despite my cynicism and inability to take adults in leotards seriously, I did my best to enjoy the performance. It lasted for hours, maybe even days. When it finally ended, I was exhausted and my head was pounding. I had been getting migraine headaches since I was eight, and they were crippling. I wanted to curl up in the luxurious bedding at the hotel and pass out.

It was a warm and beautiful night, so we decided to walk back to the hotel. Beanie and Mom walked right behind Jake and me, keeping us rounded up like sheepdogs. I loved this sensation of walking city streets at night. It was beautiful and mysterious and, although I felt exposed and nervous, it was exhilarating. People watching at night was a whole different game, and I was hyperaware of everyone around me. I noticed a man in a long jacket acting strangely ahead of us. He was turned sideways and watching us peripherally around the hood of his coat. I wondered if he was going to rob us, but then I heard Jessica's irritated voice from tagging along on her escapades in my head. "Ugh! You're so paranoid and dramatic! Chill out!" I was being ridiculous, I decided. I straightened my back to send a message that I was not an easy target, just in case, and looked to make sure the robber had lost interest in us.

That's when I saw him start to approach us. He reached his right hand inside his trench coat and started to pull out something shiny and metallic from his breast. I couldn't see what it was in the dark, but I was certain he was going to shoot us. My mom grabbed Jake's arm and mine and started running, dragging us with her. I couldn't see what was happening anymore, so I just started running, too. I checked to make sure Jake was keeping up as the three of us sprinted through groups of people on the street. I was completely disoriented and running blind. My mom finally pulled us down some stairs to an underground lobby of some sort and we stood inside, panting. I was too scared to try to understand what had happened; I just wanted to make sure we were all okay. Mom's eyes were darting around, Jake's eyes were sunken and scared and he was quiet, and Beanie . . . where was Beanie?! A few seconds later she came down the same staircase and into the lobby. She was fired up, her eyes full of flames, her body shaking, but her almost sociopathic smirk calmed me. I knew she had handled the mugger, and I knew he would never be the same. Beanie had powers.

"That guy had a gun!" I said.

"Nah. He's paparazzi. It was a camera. It *was* a camera," Beanie said.

When Beanie had seen the look of fear on our faces, she had turned and run toward the guy chasing us. She saw the camera around his neck and ripped it off of him. She threw it on the ground, smashing it to pieces, and she stomped on it, then turned back and came to find us.

On a walk to Central Park the next day I tried to figure out why anyone would chase us with a camera. We would have gladly posed for a scheduled shoot had we been asked. Why was this happening? My mom confessed to us that it was because she was dating Tom. The paparazzi were stalking her to get info about their relationship. I hated this idea. My parents' divorce wasn't finalized, and I worried about my dad alone in Los Angeles, all of his kids away, seeing the stories on the covers of the tabloids while buying bachelor groceries. It was all too ridiculous. I laughed a big hearty maniacal laugh and stepped off the curb to cross the street. My mom grabbed me and pulled me back seconds before a bicyclist would have hit me.

I wasn't sleeping well. When I was awake, I was worrying about Jessica, my dad, the divorce, paparazzi, starting a new school, losing weight, Jake's increasing quietness, my sister whom I had yet to meet, the feeling that I had no one to talk to who could possibly understand what I was going through. When I lay down at night, all these things would swirl around me until I'd drift off into sleep paralysis. After I'd conquer it with my big toe, I'd have nightmares for the rest of the night. I'd wake up hungry, an immediate reminder that I was fat and hated my body. Then I'd eat and feel terrible about the food choices I'd made. I'd get dressed in clothes that didn't feel like mine because my clothing options were limited to whatever was available in my increasing size. This was before Lane Bryant and I had two options: stretchy pants and oversized shirts, or large billowing waistless muumuus with giant floral prints. You could look like a slob or a couch. Pick one. One thing I didn't worry about was my mom. She was clearly right where she was meant to be. She seemed completely in control and impervious, like some sort of superhero. She was so quick and sharp, any talk show she did made the interviewer seem completely out of their league.

The days my mom was filming, we would go on set with her, hovering around the craft service table sneaking junk food as we had learned to do back in Los Angeles. We would sit on the set and watch them film the same scene a few times, and then we'd get bored and go hang out in her trailer and watch TV. We were invited to be in the scene where Ruth is shopping at Neiman Marcus, but quickly got kicked out for taking all the clothes off one of the mannequins on the live set. We ruined a whole scene before anyone noticed. Our part was cut, and so were we.

On a day off, we went to the famous deli E.A.T. to try a real Reuben sandwich on rye. When they brought me my sandwich, I couldn't believe it. It was *huge*. I ate as much as I could, but there was so much left we had to ask for a to-go box. This seemed like it was already expected of anyone eating there, and the waiter brought us a kit to pack it up. That's when I noticed a homeless man leaning against the window of the deli. He was cross-legged on the ground and huddled somewhere inside of several layers of coats and clothes. He was dirty and his hair was matted outside the rim of his beanie. I'll give the rest of my sandwich to him, I figured. I carefully packed it up so I could hand it off with minimal humiliation for either of us. We paid our bill, I grabbed the bag, and we walked outside. I approached the man on the ground and held out the container with the sandwich in it. He jumped to his feet. I stumbled back a bit at seeing his height but continued to hold the leftovers out. He threw his coat open and I saw inside of it a Nikon camera swinging from his neck. That's odd, I thought. He could probably trade that for food.

By now, you know the drill. He put the camera up to his eye and took shot after shot of my mom trying to hail a taxi while simultaneously trying to shield our faces from the lens. You can still find these pictures online. Please admire my Sun-In bleached hair, my oversized shirt, and my stretchy pants. Also please notice that I am a terrified thirteen-year-old and my brother is only eleven, and that this photographer is a pig.

We couldn't go anywhere without being followed. We went to Tom's hotel room for lunch one day and five or six paps lurked outside the lobby for hours waiting for our next move. When my mom and Tom were together, they were like mischievous teens, which I enjoyed as a budding troublemaker myself. We could see the paps from the fifth-floor window of Tom's room, so we decided to go to the local drugstore and buy some balloons. The paps followed us there, and then they followed us back to the hotel and took their places right under the window. We filled the balloons with water, opened the window, and dropped one at a time onto the pile of photographers. They screamed and dispersed, looking up to see who had done such a thing, but we had all retreated from view. A part of me felt ashamed for being petty, but that goody-two-shoes inner voice of mine was quickly being drowned out by a new voice. This new voice was adamant that the paps deserved it. She was right.

On the set of *She-Devil*, my mom had a fancy trailer because she was the star of the movie, alongside Meryl and Ed Begley Jr., both of whom also had deluxe trailers. While all the minor trailer-less actors had their makeup done on set, the stars had their own stations. This meant that the huge hairy mole that my mom's character, Ruth Patchett, had on her face, along with several backup moles, lived on a pumice stone in the trailer, too. Jake and I would do everything possible not to look at them but, after every makeup touch-up, it would be in a different place and would sneak up on us. One time, it was sitting on the coffee table in the living room. Jake panicked and couldn't take it anymore. He left to sit outside the trailer, away from the mole. I stayed inside to snoop.

After playing with her stage makeup and going through all her cabinets, I set my sights on my mom's purse. I rummaged through it, reading labels and trying on perfumes. I fished inside a little pocket, and found a tiny vial. I held it up to the light. It was brown glass with a powdery substance inside.

Cocaine.

I don't know how I knew what it was. Maybe it was all the After-School Specials I had watched. Maybe it was from spending too much time in a comedy club greenroom. I was livid. I threw open the door to the trailer, finding my mom standing outside with some wardrobe stylists. I held the vial out and self-righteously and said, "What is *this*?"

My mom's face dropped and she excused herself to come into the trailer. She shut the door. She was obviously pissed that I'd gone through her purse and had come at her like that in front of her coworkers. I knew I'd crossed a line, but I felt justified. My sister had been taken away and locked up for less than this, and I was angry at the hypocrisy.

She told me it was Tom's. She had taken it from him earlier that day and had nowhere to put it. She was trying to help him get clean. He had a problem, and she loved him and wanted to help. I felt horrible for my reaction. She was just trying to help someone, and here I was thinking she was some kind of secret addict. As a child of the eighties, I grew up with Nancy Reagan in charge of at least some of my thinking.

My mom sent Jake and me home the next day. Taking care of us while also trying to star in a movie, get a divorce, start a new romantic relationship with an addict, help said addict get clean, connect with her long-lost daughter, write a second season of a number one show, handle the pressures of escalating fame, and flee paparazzi all at once was too much for her for some reason.

When I got home, Jessica was there. She had manipulated her way out of the mental hospital in June to go to Fat Camp in central California. She told her doctor that her behavioral issues stemmed from the low self-esteem caused by being overweight, and that if she were allowed to go to camp and lose twenty pounds, her issues would be cured. It was a ruse to gain more freedom, of course, but they fell for it. She's masterful.

It had taken two weeks before she was kicked out of camp for being a bad influence, smoking, and tagging her new handle, "Orbit," on the walls of an outbuilding where she hid to ditch the scheduled exercise activities.

A new plan had to be formulated for Jessica. Again. Harriet, the consultant, who was becoming more of a family member these days, found an alternative school called Concord that promised to be the perfect environment for her. Now my parents just had to figure out how to get Jessica to Concord in Century City, me to Newbridge in Santa Monica, and Jake to Landmark in the Valley.

They also had to figure out how to figure anything out, since they could barely talk without things escalating to a fight. The solution was hiring an emotionally uninvested auxiliary parent, a nanny for everyone, including the adults. Sharon was a fifty-year-old grandma who was calm and quiet and under the impression she was just providing basic childcare to a few preteens. God bless her, the poor thing.

7B.

Crumb-Brushers

I don't remember who coined the term, whether it was my mom or Tom, but all of us new-money, rags-to-riches types noticed the phenomenon of Crumb-Brushers Syndrome.

It started with your first fancy meal in a five-star restaurant, where, in between the appetizer and the salad, a waiter would come clear the previous course's designated plate and silverware. This was like any midrange restaurant experience, but at these really fancy ones, a butler would come by after the waiter and use a metal scraper to pull all of your crumbs into a receptacle, returning your place setting to its original and immaculate condition.

The first time this happens, you don't know where to put your hands. You watch and you're aware of the decadence and you're insistent that you don't require such things and the butler ignores you so instead you apologize for the burden you've become.

The second time, you're still shocked and embarrassed. You still try to make eye contact with the butler to let him know this is not your idea. You're on his side.

The third time, you move your arms and continue whatever

conversation you were in the middle of before you were rudely inter-rupted. You say "Thank you" without making eye contact.

The fourth time, you don't bother saying thank you.

The fifth time, you demand to know where that slow idiot of a crumb-brusher is.

The irritated and angry entitlement sets in quick. You can see it wash over people's eyes like the dark filter of Sauron whenever some-one gets ahold of the Ring of Power in Middle-earth in Tolkien's *Lord of the Rings*. There are few Frodos in Los Angeles. They all escape to the Shire, aka ranches in Montana.

8.

Wedding Singer

Divorce always sucks but not everyone gets to walk into a 7-Eleven and see their ex-wife mud wrestling her new man in a five-page full-color spread in *Vanity Fair* shot by Annie Leibovitz. Not only was my dad getting a divorce, but he was also losing his job writing for a number one TV show and losing custody of his kids for half the time. He was a mess, and he decided to go back to Colorado for a couple weeks to see friends and family and attend his twenty-year high school reunion. While there, he met a woman and they started dating, which was at least a step in the direction of a new future.

My parents had surrendered to the situation and were co-parenting well. They worked it out so that when the movie wrapped and my mom returned to LA, they could live separately and continue to be on friendly terms. My mom would rent somewhere near the studio, and my dad would stay in the house they had bought together until their assets could be divided. It was a progressive divorce for progressive people. The custody arrangement would remain as flexible as possible to minimize the stress on us kids, who were starting new schools and dealing with an immense amount of change.

As for their own stress, to minimize that my parents entered into a contract that granted them a legal divorce before all the terms were set, called a bifurcation. A major part of that preliminary agreement was that Tom was not allowed to live with us. My dad had resigned himself to the fact that my mom was dating him, but he didn't want him around us if he was on drugs, drunk, or unpredictable, and as far as everyone knew, that's exactly what he was.

Tom still had his small apartment in town.

The movie wrapped in July, and production for Season 2 of *Roseanne* began in August. Mom rented a château in Benedict Canyon and had Sharon help with getting us to our three schools as well as mediating between my parents to coordinate our schedules.

We also had to coordinate the two sets of rules we now had. During my parents' marriage, they were always careful to be a unified front when making decisions, but now they could vote separately. There were cracks in this arrangement that allowed us kids to get almost anything we wanted if we finagled it right. Like many children of divorce, we learned how to manipulate the system pretty quickly.

For instance, Jake finally got a BB gun after years of begging and my mom saying no. He just had to keep it at my dad's. He immediately took it into the backyard, aimed it at a bird, and pulled the trigger, never considering he might hit the target. The bird spun to the ground and died in front of Jake, who turned white and mute and cried for days. It was ages before he touched the gun again.

While Jake was recovering from PTSD after killing a living creature, I was getting in trouble with Christina. Her parents were divorced also and therefore distracted, and we had four houses between us to pull our antics in. Jackpot. One weekend at her dad's bachelor pad, we went for a walk. We bought eggs and shaving cream and went on the hunt for an expensive car to destroy as a commentary on capitalism. We found a Mercedes-Benz parked in an alley and threw the eggs at it one by one. I took out the shaving cream and started writing swears on it. All of a sudden, the gate right next to the car opened and a man popped his head out and yelled, "What the *hell* are you doing?!" We froze.

He was the owner of the car and was angry, but also clearly had children because he was not as pissed as he should have been. He was that brand of dad-disappointed that destroys people. He coerced us both into his backyard by threatening to call the cops and shut the gate behind us. He went to rinse his car before the shaving cream ate the paint off. I noticed Christina walking the perimeter of the yard, and I watched her as she found a gate to slip out from. She left my ass there. I was angry but impressed. I was too scared to try anything like that. That kind of ballsiness is exactly why she went on to become a reality show star on *Road Rules*, a stand-up comic, and an extremely talented podcaster. She hosts the popular *Your Mom's House* podcast with her husband now.

When he came back out and saw Christina was gone, he forced a confession from me and made me tell him my parents' phone number as a trade for not calling the police. He tried to get Christina's information from me, but I wouldn't snitch. I gave him my parents' number and sat there formulating a story to tell them while he called them. In the half hour I had to sit in this man's yard, he brought me water and seemed genuinely perplexed as to why I hadn't also had the wherewithal to escape like my friend.

I denied guilt for years, saying I had seen someone else egging the car and tried to stop them. I had a journal that I kept, knowing full well that my mom was reading it. Everything in it was a lie. I left it in "hidden" spots, like under my pillow or in the top drawer of my dresser, to make it look like I didn't know. I wrote the false account of how I had seen some kids egging an old man's car in an alley and intervened, but no one believed me. Such was the life of a martyr.

Finally I got fed up and filled that journal with debauched, slutty stories about all the motels I was sneaking off to in order to suck old businessmen's dicks for drug money, and then at the end I wrote: Hope you enjoyed, Mom! It was so funny that she had to admit that she was reading my journal so she could laugh with me about it. Even in the midst of all the shit, being funny was the most important skill you could develop in my family. You could defuse any situation and tell the most brutal truths without consequence if you could just make everyone laugh. It was a risk, though. If you didn't absolutely nail the joke, you were *fucked*.

After a story broke in the *Enquirer* about Tom paying thugs to beat up paparazzi in front of the famous restaurant Spago, my dad did what any concerned Hollywood dad would do. He hired a PI to do some recon on Tom to see if he was dangerous to have around his kids. "How do I know you're any good?" he asked the PI. "Well, I know about the pink Chrysler in your driveway." My dad indeed had a pink Chrysler in his driveway. He was hired.

My dad's only glimpse into our lives away from him was what he read in tabloid articles or what gossip was passed to him from insiders. He never asked us kids probing questions because he didn't want to put us in a bad position, so he had to imagine worst-case scenarios and act accordingly. Sometimes that meant hiring spies.

What had actually happened at Spago was that the paparazzi were stalking my mom and she jumped in her car to escape. They stood in front of her car so she couldn't exit the parking lot and set off dozens of flashes in her face. She was gracious at first and let them take a few shots, and then she asked them to move. They wouldn't. Instead, they started baiting her with their antagonistic questions. A couple of ruffians were walking by and yelled, "Hey! Do you want us to get rid of these guys for you?" My mom and Tom accepted the offer, and the ruffians laid into the paps while my mom and Tom escaped. Of course the paps' employers wrote an article about the confrontation and made it sound like my insane mom and her violent boyfriend had assaulted these poor guys who were just trying to do their job. That's a job the way being the school bully is a job.

A couple of months and twenty thousand dollars into my dad's surveillance of Tom, he had nothing concrete. Mostly because my dad refused to do anything illegal or immoral to get information (although he received several offers), which made it difficult, but it didn't matter anyway. Tom himself would answer the question "Is Tom on drugs?" soon enough.

This was the time when "entertainment news" segments started showing up on the regular news, which before had been devoted to covering things more important than a TV star's messy divorce. Soon, shows that were exclusively gossip started popping up on network TV, like A Current Affair and Hard Copy, and then whole cable channels devoted to it were launched, like Movietime Network (later known as E!). There was a lot of new airtime to fill, and our family was an easy target. The success of the Roseanne show, all the drama surrounding us, and the rebellious and playful ways we handled it provided endless content. We weren't a conventional celebrity family; we were a regular-looking, overweight, middle-American, rowdy bunch. We were loud, inappropriate, and slobbish. We didn't fit into the Hollywood scene at all.

I always tried to do what was expected of me, but my mom would set me straight and remind me I didn't have to. We didn't have to be grateful for being stalked. These people were making money from humiliating us. We had to play the game a bit, but we absolutely did not have to believe our own bullshit. I can't imagine what kind of "I'm over the moon" horseshit I'd be tagging my Instagram photos with today had she not taught me to walk that line.

There was another reason we were an easy target: Tom was doing a lot of the reporters' work for them. He would call the paps and tell them where he and my mom were going so they could show up and get photos. On the night that the paparazzi had been roughed up outside Spago, Tom had both taken money from the reporters whom he told about the plans he and my mom had *and* paid thugs to beat up those reporters for invading his and my mom's space. We found this out from the paps themselves. They told us that Tom had been the one who had leaked the story about Brandi to the *Enquirer.* He was using the extra money for drugs and alcohol.

We all started our new schools at the beginning of August. Jake went to a place in the Valley that specialized in teaching children with learning disabilities, even though he was never actually diagnosed with anything other than being disorganized, and I went to a little hippie school in the heart of the Jewish area of Los Angeles. Jessica went to Concord, a precocious rich-kids' school.

At the beginning of the summer, I had interviewed with the prestigious art school Crossroads but was turned down. I blame the black clothes and white pancake makeup I wore under my black eyeshadow and eyeliner to tour the school. And also my straight Fs from the year before. And possibly my very obvious disdain for being awake and alive. And maybe my transcripts that said I had a problem with authority and also never showed up.

My new school was called NewBridge. Every place we ended up at had a name like this one, something that sounded academic but also emotionally promising. I'm sure most parents who paid that much money for a private school were at their wits' end, and a name like NewBridge felt like a guarantee of some kind.

All of our new principals had been debriefed about not talking to paparazzi or mentioning my mom's celebrity to any students or teachers, and I was hoping to take advantage and start fresh. NewBridge was small, with only one hundred students from kindergarten through twelve. There were fewer than ten kids in each class, which was supposed to mean I would get more of the teachers' attention, but I did everything in my power to keep them, and everyone else, at a distance. I wasn't starved for attention, as some of my behavior apparently suggested. I was starved for autonomy.

A few months into the school year, Season 2 started taping and airing, and we were back to our previous crazy schedule, only now we were moving from house to house and dealing with the divorce and even more paparazzi because of it. There was always one pap staked outside of each of our schools, and several outside our houses. This was before Rupert Murdoch owned everything, so there were still four different media outlets in serious competition with one another. Sometimes all four tabloids would have a reporter stalking us, and they would be fighting to get the good stuff. They'd yell over one another, trying to be loudest so we would look at their camera. They'd trip over one another as they walked backward in front of us.

Any time we left a driveway, a car would get behind us. It was scary to be followed all the time, but we made light of it by holding our middle fingers up to the back window, or sometimes exposing our naked asses. Making a joke of it all took some of the sting out of feeling like we couldn't let our guard down or trust anyone. The downside was that the paps loved drama and games, and every time we did something like this, it was an invitation for them to incite us further to see how crazy they could make us. They were like annoying puppies—you throw a ball once and then get locked into an eternal game of fetch.

I was experiencing physical symptoms of the stress I was under. My stomach hurt all the time and my migraine headaches increased in strength and frequency. I could barely get through a day without being in pain. I went to doctors, but nothing they suggested helped. It was just puberty, they said; I was thirteen and was probably going to get my period soon. I hoped so. I was ready to catch up to my peers and become a fertile woman who could escape Los Angeles and bear ten children in the wilderness.

I started refusing to go to school on account of the headaches and stomachaches, and there was no talking me into it if I had decided not to go. At first, my parents would spend hours trying to get me up and ready, alternately threatening and coaxing me, but I just couldn't. I couldn't be away from my family. They were my only allies. I couldn't be out in the world. I couldn't be among strangers. I didn't want to leave my bed. I didn't want to answer any more questions about my mom or have it pointed out that I was fat. I just couldn't do it anymore.

I was losing interest in everything academic. History was first, then Spanish. All I retained from that class was *"Los dos muchachos son muy aficionados de los deportes"* (The two boys are very affectionate of sports) and *"No tengo mi tarea"* (I don't have my homework), which was really all I needed to know.

Art was the last class I lost interest in. I remember working on carving a lithograph of a nearby apartment porch I had scouted and sketched during a class walk. This class taught actual skills. Art was just math without all the confusing numbers. I was learning how to see things differently, from different angles; how to draw what was really there, instead of just what you were expecting to see. I loved the exercises of drawing upside down or with your eyes closed or with your nondominant hand, the difference between subjective and objective views, and learning about negative space. There seemed to be deep universal truths hidden in each approach that you'd accidentally process while your monkey brain was out of the way, busy doodling.

I started going to school only on days when I had art class, which was twice a week, and because of all the school I was missing (or so I thought), someone called CPS to do a wellness check on us. We didn't know who made the call at the time but found out later that it was a reporter from one of the tabloids. They weren't concerned about us at all; they just wanted to write a story about CPS coming to Roseanne's house.

The papers did things like this: they would hire people to pretend to be lovers or doctors or whatever and send them to our house. They'd ring our doorbell, we'd answer, and they would take pictures of us talking to these entities. Then they would write a story about it. That's all they needed to do. A lawyer once told my dad that this tactic was called "the dog fucker." If you accused someone publicly of fucking dogs, thus associating their name with the idea of fucking dogs, it didn't matter at all if it was true or not. They would be known forever as the dog fucker. Say it enough times and loud enough, and it was as good as true. Facts were totally irrelevant. For example, it made a much better headline to say "Crazy Female Actress Terrorizes Intelligent Professional Males Just Trying to Do Their Job" than to say "Artist Has a Vision and All the People Riding Her Coattails Are Working Against It, Thinking They Know Better."

I was intensely lonely at NewBridge, even though I had made a couple of good friends. My favorite was Darwin, a tall redhead with a great sense of humor. We'd walk to the tiny park across the street after school with a couple of other kids, stopping at a 7-Eleven on the way to load up on nachos and pump cheese. There were no limits to how many pumps you could have: as many as would fit. Sometimes I'd skimp on the chips so I could load more cheese into the container. I lived in fear that a pap would snap a photo of me, wide-eyed and licking the paper boat, and print it with the headline "Four-Time Attendee of Weight Watchers Camp and Roseanne Barr's Daughter Jenny Drowns Her Sorrows in Queso." That wasn't far off from the actual stuff they would print about us, so we were always on guard.

Aside from my small group of friends, there weren't many teachers or kids I connected with. I had managed to keep my secret for a few weeks at the beginning of the year, but it wasn't long before everyone knew who my mom was. I didn't even bother to speculate how they found out. It was pointless. There was definitely a Fucked-Up Teen Circuit in Los Angeles, since there were limited places to put troubled kids, and two of Jessica's goth friends from her last teen placement were here now, Spidra and Widow. (Not their birth names, I'm guessing.) They knew and may have told someone, but they seemed less than impressed by it. I just figured it was one of the adults because it was *always* one of the adults.

One of the perks of private school was the school having the money for amazing extracurricular activities, like the weeklong field trip we took to Yosemite National Park. At first, I didn't want to go. I didn't want to be the fat kid struggling up the trail, lagging behind everyone else and waiting to be singled out by a predator. I didn't want to have to shower in view of classmates or drool in my sleep. I still was anxious being away from home and would have horrible stomachaches when I was separated from my family. I had to go as part of the school curriculum, and because I had missed so much school already, I would be held back a year if I missed a whole week.

The bus ride we took to the park was awful. I wanted to cry the whole way. I distracted myself the best I could by drawing scenery in my sketchbook. When we got to our cabins, it was already bedtime. I lay in my bunk, feeling the deep pangs of homesickness that went with me everywhere. But something changed in me when I woke up in the morning and went outside to walk to the cafeteria. I wasn't prepared for the beauty that surrounded me when I stepped out of the cabin. It overwhelmed me and I was speechless. Like even inside my head. I don't remember ever being inner-speechless until then. It was life-changing in a way I couldn't interpret. I felt small and insignificant, and that, strangely, was so comforting. None of my problems mattered. In fact, they were so ridiculous that it was *hilarious*.

I took stock of the last few years and decided that I was the subject of a joke God was telling itself, and I wouldn't know the punch line until my dying breath. I just had to accept my role as jester, and I'd be okay. Maybe one day I'd write a book about all these strange things that seemed to happen, and that would be motivation enough to survive it all. I could just compartmentalize everything into chapters and put them away to process later. The more ridiculous and scary something that happened was, the funnier I could make it by compressing it into a single run-on sentence. "I saw my sister for the first time on the cover of the *National Enquirer*." "My parents padlocked the fridge so I couldn't cheat on the Rice Diet." "Blackmailing PCP-smoking nannies for sauerkraut." Where is the tragedy? Nowhere. It's gone immediately as soon as you say the magic words: "That's one for the book."

Going back to the regular classroom after that trip was extra-painful. I just wanted to be back out in the woods and objectively looking at my weird-ass life, as opposed to subjectively living in it. Yosemite reminded me of camping weekends with my dad, when life was simple. It always made me happy to see him relax out in the woods, making black coffee on the camp stove and lounging in his hammock. I missed seeing him carefree. Now that I spent half my week away at my mom's house, per the custody arrangement, the toll life was taking on him was incredibly obvious each time I saw him.

Season 2 was well underway and now included a newly sober Tom, who kept busy by weaving his way into every aspect of the show. There was little he wasn't involved in, which pissed everyone off for different reasons. An air of contempt began to form around everyone and everything on that set, and the once family-like environment started to feel like a war zone. Eventually it split into two groups, Us and Them. Us were the people who understood my mom's vision and actively worked to support it, and Them was everyone else.

Tom's role became protector against the "Thems." He would say anything my mom was afraid to say. He was six feet tall and large and intimidating, so the men who had intimidated my mom up until then were rendered powerless, and that really pissed them off. Where once they'd had unfettered access to her, now they couldn't control her. Their next power move was to destroy her in the press.

The new head writer they'd hired to replace Matt, Jeff Harris, took out an ad in *Daily Variety* saying, "To my friends at Carsey-Werner Company, ABC, to the cast, crew and staff of *Roseanne*: My sincere and heartfelt thanks to all of you. I have chosen not to return to the show next season. Instead, my wife and I have decided to share a vacation in the relative peace and quiet of Beirut."

Not surprisingly, he was also fired, which they spun back on her as well. Whoever had the most friends at the newspaper was the winner. You had to walk a very fine line by not completely dismissing the reporters but giving them something in exchange for their leaving something out. You had to work with these scumbags, and my mom was willing to do that only so much.

Most of the responsibility and blame for any difficulty fell on my mom, but at the same time, all her creative control was being wrestled away from her. The tabloids put stories out left and right about how difficult she was, and every time she tried to stand up for herself, they'd spin that, too. It felt very much to me like everyone was trying to put her in her place, but she wasn't having it anymore. She had backup now.

Tom was very different from my dad. My dad is a peacekeeper, and his decisions are carefully calculated and rooted in fear. He was afraid that my mom would get fired and lose this opportunity she had worked so hard for, so he fell into a position of mediating between her and the studio execs and tried to tame her. He became her minder when she needed an ally. Meanwhile, Tom was my mom's biggest fan. He stuck up for her and took her side, no matter what. It was his personal mission to protect her from all the things everyone else had failed to protect her from because their own interests got in the way. This was a weight lifted from my mom, and she became a playful teen in love. They couldn't keep their hands off each other or be apart for even a minute.

Tom was also very entertaining and charming, and his jokes, if inappropriate, were really funny. He had a way of teasing people that made it okay for them to laugh at themselves, but sometimes he couldn't sense when to stop and it bordered on cruelty. By the time you processed his last dig at you, he was already on to another. He left a lot of people speechless. Once, Jessica called a teacher a *cunt* and my mom was called to the principal's office. Tom went with her, and the principal concernedly recounted what had happened: "Jessica called Mrs. Brown a *cunt*," and Tom replied with, "Well . . . *is* she a cunt?"

This boundarylessness was easy to confuse for closeness, which we overlooked in our desperation for tribesmen. We would take whatever we could get in the way of allies.

On December 12, 1989, Tom relapsed. My mom was devastated. Tom was breaking all the promises he'd made her and she was beginning to doubt his commitment to her. She called off the wedding just one month before it was scheduled to take place.

Tom spent the next weeks apologizing and promising to stay sober if my mom would give him one more chance, and she eventually agreed. The wedding was back on. When my dad heard this, he crumbled. He didn't want Tom around us even when he was six months sober, and now it would only have been a month at the time of the wedding, if he could even manage to stay clean that long. He called around, looking for lawyers that could help him. None of them wanted to go up against a star. They didn't want to get blacklisted in Hollywood. He kept calling until he found one that agreed to take the case because, and I quote, it was "sexy."

What was sexy about it, you ask? When I think about sexy, I think of ten empowered women reading to one another around a table at the bookstore they own and run. I'm sorry to point out that Hollywood's version of sexy is simply "exploitable."

Just one day after the divorce from my dad was finalized on paper, my mom and Tom had their wedding at the rented mansion in Benedict Canyon. I wore army boots and a red velvet dress I had purchased from Goodwill the day before and sloppily stitched with lace around the neck, cuffs, and hem. Even though it was meant to be private and no invitations had been sent, the press found out about the event and the paparazzi swarmed the gate at the bottom of our long driveway. There were about twenty reporters camped there trying to get a clear shot of the guests as they pulled up.

These are the worst people on Earth, I thought. Subhuman. Parasitic. Gossips. Witch-hunters. You can't go much lower than that. Can you imagine following people around and taking photos of them and their kids, baiting and goading them into a reaction so you could make money from it? When I'd complain about their behavior, I'd hear, "That's just part of being famous," "You shouldn't have become famous if you don't like it," and other such "She was wearing a short skirt in public and drinking alcohol" victim-blaming nonsense as justification. These comments usually came from the same people who put actors on a high pedestal and then get angry when they act human.

Inside the house, the small wedding was a simple get-together, but outside it was world news.

I heard a helicopter crossing back and forth overhead and craned my neck out of the window near which Jessica and I were smoking cigarettes. The helicopter had a three-letter news station name on its side and was flying so low that I could see a photographer leaning out and taking pictures. These people are relentless! I took the speaker that was hooked to the stereo in my room and set it in the window frame. I aimed it at the crowd outside our gate. I found one of my sister's punk tapes and put it into the player and blasted it out the window. The paps turned toward us and started shooting video and photos. Some had those now-obsolete giant news cameras that sat on their shoulders like a bazooka.

I heard panicked footsteps running up our stairs and my mom's brother, Ben, swung into our room, sternly saying, "*Turn that off right now! This is your mother's wedding! Have some respect!*" I didn't feel like having respect for anyone. I didn't want my mom to marry some other guy, especially one who ate goldfish for a living like Tom did in his act. I felt sorry for my dad, and I was scared of what our family would be like with this new dynamic.

Jessica and I missed the actual ceremony and vows because we were smoking with our friends. The small room it took place in was too crowded and we didn't really feel like we should be there. We both felt like we were auxiliary guests at best, and burdens at worst. The whole day was tense, and not just because of our karaoke, which had mostly gone unnoticed by anyone but Ben and the paps.

The Barr family contingent consisted of my bubbe, my grandpa, and their four kids. They all loved my dad despite his being goyim, and many exceptions were made for him because they loved him so much. My dad was grateful for their acceptance, and he didn't bat an eye at their eccentricities and strange ways of doing things.

This new guy, however, they were wary of. He was flighty and messy, immature and tactless. He made jokes that made everyone uncomfortable, and he lacked boundaries. He had no experience with children and was unpredictable. They were suspicious of the way he micromanaged my mom, and his growing involvement in all aspects of her career and life. Although they were going along with things, they were vocal about their concerns.

Tom had admitted to selling stories about us for drug money in the last month as part of working his program. Like any convert, in his excitement to become this free, better person, he was eager to share his testimony with everyone else. In the last month, Tom's new sobriety had become a family issue. Now that he was in a twelve-step program, that's all he saw. We were all dysfunctional. We were all addicted to something, or codependent on someone who was. Everything Jessica and I did was scrutinized and dissected. I was now a codependent compulsive overeater, and Jessica was an alcoholic and addict (cigarettes). Tom's focus started shifting from his working his own program to fixing us kids. My resentment was growing with each label attached to me and with each attempt to solve me.

When I'm pretending to be spiritual and take the high road, I think about how poorly I would have handled being in Tom's shoes. He had a tumultuous past of his own in small-town Ottumwa, Iowa, that had stunted him. With an emotionally distant family and a job on the kill floor at the local Hormel slaughterhouse, he was very different from us. Not to mention that he was only twenty-nine, ten years younger than my mom, when he married a celebrity, inherited four teens, and got sober.

I'd like to give Tom the benefit of the doubt and say he was really trying to be a good partner, that he was just out of his wheelhouse and in way over his head, but I'd also like to not be that moron who gives everyone the benefit of the doubt when they don't really deserve it, so . . .

9.

Million-Dollar Cab Ride

Immediately after the wedding, Tom moved in with us and started to micromanage our home the same way he did the studio. He was trying to help my mom make parenting decisions that weren't his to make, and so my dad got lawyers and then Tom and Mom got lawyers back.

The original point of hiring lawyers was to work out a viable plan for custody and co-parenting, but with all the dynamics of a stepparent, fame, money, and troubled kids mixed in, it became a sort of gladiator duel, our family being the swordsmen who had to fight each other to the death for our freedoms, and the ruling class of lawyers cheering for their team from the stands.

Hollywood lawyers are different from other lawyers. Everything is a game, and there is strategy involved in being the winner. Often, the clients just want to find a compromise and get out, but the lawyers talk them into fighting for something extra. A publicly covered case was free advertising, so they had to "win" at any cost. If they could get a high-profile celebrity anything she wanted, then every celebrity would come to them and they'd be set for life. Consider their hourly pay and this was a genius-level scam.

My parents and Tom were locked in an endless cycle of this tug-of-war, and we kids were right in the middle. We were the little pawns. At the lawyers' advice, any action we took was recorded and used to further the narrative of whichever parent was suing the other at the time. If I came home to my mom's house from my dad's with dirt under my nails, they would write that down. If I gained weight, the lawyers would note that, too. If I wore an all-black outfit, if my hair was dyed, if I had missed a day of school, if I seemed extra tired or grumpy, they would record it as proof of some kind of neglect. Things that my parents had previously considered acts of self-expression became red flags that the other parent was failing to address.

I would see stories in the news and tabloids about court dates and fights, but I didn't know what was real anymore. I was in a dream state of some kind. I remember writing in my journal, "I feel above and to the right of my body. Like I've been knocked a few seconds into the past and can't catch up." It was as though my soul was doing a merciful thing, being slightly misaligned from physical reality. If I had been all the way in my body and all the way in my feelings, I would not have made it. I would zombie home from school, and then zombie to school, and zombie through school, and then fall asleep and fight paralysis and nightmares all night, get up, and do it again.

I was tethered to this fat little anchor of a body for some reason, and I wanted out. I didn't necessarily want out of being alive, I just wanted out of being in a reality I didn't co-sign for.

One day I sat on the school blacktop during lunch, pulled my sleeve up, and raked the back of my forearm with a wood carving tool I'd taken from art class. Maybe I could prove I was alive if I felt pain and bled. Maybe the pain would sew me back into my body. Maybe if I localized my feelings into a small space and gave myself a *reason* for the pain I was feeling, I could contain and manage it. Maybe I wanted someone to see and ask me why I was cutting my own skin. There were times when people noticed I wasn't doing well and checked in on me, but as soon as I'd start to open up, they'd suggest I had low self-esteem from being fat or ask me something personal about my mom, which would shut me down immediately.

It didn't help that I was overweight, but even I knew that was a symptom and not a cause. I didn't really see it as my problem so much as a problem of society, or of other people holding me accountable to their own ideals. I thought it was strange how fixated other people were on my weight and wondered why it bothered everyone so much. People seemed to need something tangible to blame for the way I was feeling in order to want to help. No one is strong enough to delve into the abyss of someone else's darkness without a belay.

When the day of my eighth-grade exams came around, I knew I was going to fail. I had been absent a lot of the year, and on the days I did go to school, I couldn't pay any attention. I couldn't care, even though I wanted to. The teachers pleaded with me, as if they could change my mind, but it wasn't *my* mind at the moment.

I couldn't take any more disappointment, so I went to the nurse's office with a fake migraine and asked her to call my parents. She rolled her eyes and asked if my headache had anything to do with the tests. "What tests?" I asked. "Oh! Yeah! Today is finals! I forgot. Well, I guess I can just take some Tylenol and push through." I figured that would be enough to convince her that I actually was sick.

"Okay," she said. Hmmm. I needed a new plan. That's when I started to "see halos that made it impossible for me to read fine print." I had gotten very good at this game. No one could beat me.

"I can't see. Please, just call my parents. They'll be upset to hear you had me take an important test while I was blind."

"Go see the principal. I don't know what to do with you."

I talked the principal into calling my parents, but they didn't answer. My mom must have been at work. It was Friday, which was a taping day. She'd be there late and so couldn't come to get me. The principal rifled through my file to find an emergency contact number. It took a while to be passed and transferred around until I could reach my mom. I begged her to come get me and she said she couldn't. They were shooting. I asked if I could take a cab to the studio and she could pay him when I got there, and she reluctantly agreed. She had to get back to the set.

The principal called a cab for me and told me I could go sit out front and wait, so I did. About ten minutes later, a man pulled up. He seemed disoriented and confused and very young. I got into his cab and immediately felt a huge knot in my gut. Something was telling me not to go with him. I looked at his license, which was posted over his radio, to see what his name was in case I had to file a police report. I noticed that he'd had an active license for only twelve days. *Nope.* I apologized and jumped out of the cab. I was absolutely not going to assist the universe with reactivating my Pentland Curse. He got irritated and swore at me and drove off, and I went to have the principal call another cab.

"Why didn't you take that one?!" she asked me, completely irritated.

"I had a bad feeling." She blinked at me as if to say I was ridiculous and tried to reason with me, but halfway through her sentence, she just gave up and called for another cab instead.

I went outside and waited again, this time for thirty minutes. When that cab arrived, I climbed and looked at his license for reassurance. His posted license was from *four days ago.*

I didn't want to go back inside and drag this out any further. It had already been an hour since I'd gone to the nurse's station and I wanted this day to be over. I wanted to crawl into the king bed inside my mom's air-conditioned dressing room trailer and listen to the show being taped over the monitor while I ate plentiful craft service snacks. I decided to just literally ride this one out.

The driver asked me where he was taking me and I said, "Studio City Studios." And he nodded as if that were not a problem and pulled away from the curb. He seemed a little curious as to why a thirteen-year-old would be headed to the studios in the middle of the day, but he was too busy struggling to make sense of the street signs to ask me anything, for which I was grateful.

I stared out the window and started to fall asleep with my head against the glass, dropping into that slow humming daytime sun nap in a too-hot car. It was quiet and I hadn't heard silence in what felt like forever. Occasionally the driver's radio would make some boo-bop sounds and a staticky, barely audible voice would mumble something. All this added to the hypnotic effect. Sleeping while sitting up and sleeping during the day seemed to be the only things that would bypass the sleep paralysis I had been suffering with since my summer at Fat Camp in Vermont, and so I slipped into a deep rest.

I woke up refreshed for the first time in ages and yawned and stretched. I noticed that the cab had pulled over and the driver's door was open. I tried to make sense of my surroundings. There were green grassy hillsides and tall phone towers. The air was cooler than Studio City's would have been. I sensed by the trees that I was at a higher elevation than I should have been. The meter was at some ridiculous number, and the clock was two hours past the time I'd last looked at it.

I started to panic. I had been kidnapped and was finally going to be murdered like us latchkey kids had been promised daily. I sat up and started planning my escape when I noticed the driver yelling into a pay phone in a language I couldn't understand. I looked around me for anything usable as a weapon.

When the driver saw that I was awake and staring at him wide-eyed and scared, he panicked and yelled louder into the phone while staring at me. He started waving his arms around and yelling to me, "It's okay! It's okay!" His body language was submissive and apologetic. His shoulders were down, and he took a step backward. He seemed on the verge of tears. He was freaking out worse than I was. I knew now that I wasn't the victim here. Only a few days into his new job, he had abducted a child. I could tell how much he had riding on this by his trepidation, and I felt compelled to calm him.

"Yes! It's okay!" I smiled to let him know I understood.

The driver took notes over the phone until he finally seemed to have a sense of where to go from here. He got back into the car and said "sorry" about twenty times, then made some turns. It took us about thirty minutes to come down from Encino Hills, where we were, and get on the 101 to Studio City. I was so happy to see the freeway and recognize street names. The dehydration from the hot car and the daytime nap had started to give me an actual headache, and I figured I deserved it.

We finally pulled up to the CBS Studios' Radford lot. The security guard looked in the window at me and said, "They're looking for you." I was so caught up in just getting back that I hadn't thought about what my mom must be thinking. The guard let us through and I pointed out to the driver where the set was.

When we drew up, the lot was vacant. There was none of the activity of a regular Friday, just a few cars in the assigned spaces, but no wandering people with headsets or arms full of scripts or coffee. None of the child actors were sitting on the stairs chatting. The makeup room's door was closed and there were no flashing lights. It was eerie. I told the cabdriver to hold on and I would go find someone to pay him, and he reassured me he would charge for only half an hour, per his boss. I got out and started looking around for *anyone*, but no one was there.

I was about to hyperventilate when I saw John Goodman walking from his dressing room to his car. I ran up to him.

"Do you know where my mom is?" When he realized it was me, he seemed irritated. "Yeah! She went home and so did everyone else. They shut down production and canceled the taping because you were missing. That cost about a million dollars," he said, like a disappointed dad trying to convey the severity of the situation. I stood there letting that weight sit on me a minute while he got into his car and left.

Fuck.

I went back to the cab. "Can you take me to my house? No one here can pay you." The driver was petrified. "Wh . . . what is your address?" he asked.

"Um. I don't know," I said. Back in Denver, I knew my address and phone number by heart as part of the latchkey kid protocol, but we had moved so many times since then, no one could expect that of me anymore. The driver went white.

I suggested we go back to the guard gate, and the guard was able to track down my mom's assistant through Carsey-Werner's office, call my mom to say I'd been found, and provide the cabdriver with the address to take me home.

I stayed awake this time and shouted to the driver when I recognized milestones, and we made it back to the house only four hours after I had gotten permission to leave school. We pulled up and I went inside with the intention of sleeping for a week. The nightmare was over.

OR. SO. I. THOUGHT.

I got out of the cab, my backpack and shoes in my hands, opened the door, and dropped my things inside the house. Our nanny Sharon was standing right inside, staring me down. "I'm okay!" I said, about to explain. She dead-eyed me and brushed past to go out and pay the fare. I followed her out to say goodbye to the driver. He looked absolutely wrecked as he took the cash, pulled away, and sped off. Goodbye, comrade. I'll never forget you. We were both POW/MIA together for a day. I felt a kinship.

"Get in the car," Sharon ordered.

But . . . I wanna go to bed.

"Your mom is waiting for you at the bottom of the hill." We had coffee dates at the bottom of the hill sometimes, so I was happy to go meet my mom and explain what I'd just been through.

I tried to tell Sharon what had happened, but she was absolutely silent and seemed uninterested. It was as if she was refusing to hear my bullshit or something, and I felt confused. It was only a ten-minute drive down the hill, and we pulled into a parking lot and parked next to my mom's car. I got out of Sharon's and went to get into my mom's car but the passenger door was locked. She got out of the driver's side and walked around to me.

She was sociopathically cold as I just kept trying and trying to tell her what had happened. She started walking somewhere, and I followed her, still trying to get a connection, but there was none. She was walking faster and I tried to keep up on the hot asphalt.

"Ow!" I said, and she looked back at me.

"Where are your shoes?!"

I had left them at home in the rush. I was trying to explain all of it, including how we got to where I left my shoes, and somewhere in trying to find all the right words, I realized I had followed my mom into an elevator.

"Where are we going?"

She didn't answer me but instead pretended to take interest in the story I'd been telling. *Finally.*

"Yes! We were at the end of Mulholland!"

"Wow! That's far!" she said, obviously feigning interest while distracted. I followed her out of the elevator and into what looked like a waiting room. I stopped telling my story. I knew what this meant.

"Mom. What's going on?!"

"I want you to just talk to this really cool lady. She can help you deal with some of the things you're going through." Was she gonna help me with my sense of direction and bad luck? Maybe the Pentland Curse was reversible?

I was in the waiting room less than a minute. The second we walked in, the secretary recognized my mother, jumped up, ran into the closed office, and came out a second later, avoiding eye contact with me. Now, the door seemingly opened on its own and a woman in her thirties appeared from around the corner. She wore an ankle-length skirt with a blouse tucked into it, with one-inch sensible heels, and her long blond hair was tied halfway up in a clip. She looked like an eighties version of a seventies version of a Victorian schoolteacher. She "invited" me into her office and closed the door behind me. My mom stayed in the waiting room.

I shut down immediately. I felt tricked and trapped. Misunderstood. Disregarded. I worried that I would end up in a psych ward like my sister, who had disappeared for months and still wouldn't really talk about what had happened.

"I'm Dr. Jolie," she introduced herself. "And you are?" Bitch, you know who I am. I refused to answer any of the questions she aimed at me, and I folded my arms across my chest. I was so tired and now I was also angry. After several attempts to engage me, she stood up from her desk, put her hands on top of it, leaned over, and said to me, "How . . . would you like . . ."

I already hated her for this dramatic pause. She reminded me of an actor who just kept going with a monologue, unaware that the audience had lost interest.

". . . to get away from it all?"

Oh, fuck. I knew what that meant. Jessica had recently gotten "away from it all."

"If by 'it all,' you mean *you*, then yes. I would like to get away from it all."

I think she thought I'd be grateful and excited by her proposition, but I was no fool.

"No, I'm talking about a facility where you can go get help."

"Nope, but thanks a lot for the offer!" I got up and started to leave.

"I'm afraid you don't have a choice. You can go willingly or you can go with assistance." I recalled watching Jessica being dragged out of our house by bounty hunters and weighed my options, settling on running away that night.

"Intake is at noon tomorrow. And if you run away, you'll just make things worse."

When I came out of her office, my mom was gone and only Sharon was in the waiting room, ready to take me home. Though I wanted to run for my life, I went with her, fully aware that if I did not have a travel buddy to guide me, I'd be lost and dead in San Diego within a couple of hours.

When we got home, I immediately went up to my room to smoke my last cigarettes before I turned myself in the next morning. I stayed up all night, lying on the roof under the stars and swimming in the dark in our pool.

I didn't really know what to expect on the other side of those walls that separated me from Jessica when I'd go visit her. They'd bring her downstairs into a conference room that was clean and clinical. The walls were a baby-blue color and the floor was beige linoleum. I never did see the actual unit she was living on. Was it full of drooling psychopaths in hospital gowns? All the Weird Kids from across the state? Gang members and drug addicts? The only gauge I had was how tough Jessica's exterior was when she'd walk into a family therapy session, and it was pretty tough.

There was no reason to waste my last bit of free time speculating when I'd have those answers tomorrow.

10.

Too Fat for Shoes

When I woke up the next morning, I was slow to get out of bed, though I was wide awake. I stared at the ceiling, trying to get myself to jump up and run. Just run. I could figure out where I was going later. I thought about places I might go, but every imagined scenario ended in disaster. If I ran to my dad's, he'd get in trouble. If I ran to any of my friends' houses, they'd be charged with harboring a runaway. I knew that from when Jessica had the kid in the closet.

The intake procedure was humiliating. I don't remember who took me, but I was dropped off on the first floor and waited until two escorts (one male, one female) came down to get me. They used a key to call the elevator and took me up to the second floor. They took me into an office that looked like a medical exam room and had me stand behind a curtain and strip. I had to hand them each article of clothing as I took it off so they could thumb through the seams and pockets looking for contraband. When I was naked, the female told me she had to make sure I'd given them everything and then came around the curtain to see me standing nude. I was freezing cold and totally humiliated and scared, which came off as anger. They were both unfazed by my bitchy commentary and continued to talk to me softly and calmly while they went through their process. They gave me scrubs to wear and a pair of hospital socks with zigzagged rubber paint on the bottom to replace my army boots, and took the rest of my clothes.

They introduced themselves as Peter and Kelly. They were nurses. This wasn't some boarding school or therapy-based community center. There were *nurses*. This was a *hospital*. A mental hospital. A *One Flew Over the Cuckoo's Nest* kind. I tried to hide my fear as they led me out of the exam room onto the unit.

To my right was a giant heavy door and, through the reinforced glass pane, I could see a long hallway. The unit was L-shaped, and in the crook of the L was a diamond-shaped nurses' station encased in bulletproof glass. It had two windows that faced out: one to our unit and one to the unit on the left. I didn't know what the separation was for, and didn't want to. The nurses' station window slid open and closed manually from inside, and next to the handle was a box with a giant red button on it. A nurse sat at a desk behind the window and watched the units through the glass. Behind her was a room. It also had a heavy door with a reinforced glass window at eye level. Above the glass was a placard that said "Observation Room 2" and one single bed in the middle of the room on a metal frame that appeared to be bolted to the floor. The mattress was bare and made of plastic. Behind it was a giant window looking out at the street below. The glass was tinted and seemed to be thicker than a regular window.

Peter and Kelly walked me up to the nurses' window and signed me in, then told me they would "give me a tour." We walked about three feet. On my left was a room about ten by ten with couches and chairs lining the walls, a TV set, one table with four chairs around it, and two thick tinted windows.

"This is the Family Room." I looked at the four or five miserable teens rolled up on the couches with their sleeves pulled over their hands and their rubberized sock-covered feet tucked up by their butts while they watched Paula Abdul prance around with a cartoon cat on MTV. In the corner was another fat girl, and we made eye contact. "That's your roommate, Phoebe," Peter said.

Why would they put both of us fat girls in one room? That drew even more attention to our fatness! Phoebe and I broke eye contact, both clearly having the same fat-girl thoughts and not wanting to shame each other by feeling ashamed.

They continued to walk me down the long hallway. We passed a laundry room and a few rooms with doors open where I could see there were two beds in each. There were about ten rooms like this, then at the end of the hall were two much larger rooms. One had chair desks and was clearly a classroom. Fuck. They have *school* here? The other room across the hall was full of long tables, and I could see basket after basket full of arts and crafts supplies. Hell to my left, heaven to my right.

Peter and Kelly took me back down the hall and stopped at one of the rooms. They took me inside and showed me which of the two beds was mine. I looked around the room at Phoebe's things, trying to determine if she was a Goth or a Tuna, and that's when I noticed the cassette tape on the nightstand.

New Kids on the Block.

It turns out Phoebe was not only a Tuna, but also a Top-40 pop fan. I could not do this. This was the last straw.

"I thought we couldn't have radios and music?" I said to Kelly, hoping I'd just busted Phoebe and they would take this cursed cassette away.

"You can earn use of a cordless battery-powered radio, and your roommate has done that. Stay out of trouble and you can move up to level three and earn the same."

"What level am I on now? One?"

"Zero," Peter said.

Peter and Kelly left me in my room and told me they would see me in an hour for "rounds." Rounds were when a staff member would come to your door and peer in to make sure you were present and alive every hour around the clock.

When dinnertime came, we were all called to the Family Room. We sat on the couches and waited for a kitchen staff member to come up in the elevator with a cart stacked with insulated plastic trays full of cafeteria slop. They would hand us each a tray complete with a dull plastic spork and leave us be for thirty minutes. The TV would blast music while we all sat and stared. Eating was not a joyous event. The too-thin girl would move her food around and even hide it in a napkin or give it to one of the thick teen boys, which was illegal. Phoebe and I would look down and eat slowly and carefully so as to not seem like wild hogs, and the boys would scarf their food without chewing. Occasionally someone would throw a piece of food at the wall or TV or glass that surrounded the nurses' station. We'd all laugh and get riled up and start throwing food, too, and the nurses would run in and tell us to calm down and threaten to call a Code Red.

A Code Red was when that red button came into play. If they pushed it, an alarm would sound with a voice saying, "Code Red, Unit Two!" a couple times. Alarm lights would light up the hallways, and any available staff from all five units would come in the elevator and grab whoever was being violent or out of control. They would restrain them on the floor until they were calm, or they would inject them with Thorazine and wait for it to kick in. Then they would move the kid to the Observation Room and shut the door. They would lie on the bed until the drug wore off, or they'd be restrained in "five-points," which meant all four limbs and forehead were strapped to the metal frame of the bed.

In bed that night, I found out that Phoebe was here because she had tried to kill herself when her attempt at self-liposuction with a vacuum cleaner failed. She had cut a slit in her thigh and stuffed the nozzle into her leg and turned the machine on, but all she got was a terrible infection. I felt so deeply sorry for her. I knew this level of desperation.

She was there for only a couple weeks, and just as I was beginning to get close to her, she reached level four and got to go home. I got the sense that she didn't want to go home, back to where her dad called her names daily and her mom said nothing in her defense, but she had "earned" it, as the staff said.

The next day Dr. Jolie came to visit and told me she worked here and would see me three to five times a week, depending. I didn't want to see her. I already hated her for putting me here. I made sure I didn't make it easy for her. I sat silently through some appointments. I said mean stuff through others. I challenged every single thing she said to me.

For the next eight months, this was my life. School three mornings a week, occupational therapy (crafts) the other two mornings. I made a lot of moccasins and wooden clocks and bookends in the time I was there. I made friends, but most left after a few weeks. Some would return occasionally when they'd relapsed.

I was getting fatter, and my doctor was being held responsible. It was suggested that I was running an underground food railroad here. I hadn't thought of that! Good idea. I was doing nothing other than eating three cafeteria meals a day and sitting on my ass inside a mental institution where the only exercise we got was the two hours a week we were dragged upstairs to the third-floor rooftop volleyball court.

The third floor was the adult unit. We'd take the keyed elevator up and walk the long corridor to the end of the hall. I'd glance in all the rooms at the people rocking or picking their arms or staring blankly into space. These were truly mentally ill people, not bratty kids on drugs. We'd be led to a patio, which had a small bulletproof reinforced window right at face level, and let outside. I am using the term *outside* loosely.

There were four stucco walls surrounding us, and ten feet up, where a roof should be, was a thick layer of chicken wire laid across the top, so no one could jump off the building. A volleyball net was hung low enough that the lightweight foam ball could pass through. Occasionally, a patient would take a bite out of the foam ball. It was a different patient each time, and no one had suggested they do this. Biting a chunk out of foam must be some sort of universal impulse that most of us ignore. We'd stay up there an hour tossing the ball back and forth, the game being more about getting the ball through the gap than hitting the ball to each other. It didn't bounce. For the twenty-eight weeks I was there, all fifty-six times we played this game, a man would stand at the door and hold up a Polaroid of a younger man. Maybe his son. And stare at us. I would go to the window and look at the picture like it was the first time I'd seen it and give him a thumbs-up, which he always seemed to appreciate. Not one of us ever broke a sweat before heading back to watch more MTV.

I did not have an underground food ring, but I did have a cigarette one. I had a roommate named Clarissa, who was skinny and blond and therefore hot. Our room faced an apartment complex. We would watch the guy in the window opposite ours come and go. He was a hesher, as we called it, which meant he dressed in skintight black, with chains and metal band T-shirts, and most likely drank and smoked a lot while flipping his long hair around. One day Clarissa and I decided he was our ticket to cigarettes. We waited to see him exiting his apartment and banged against the thick bulletproof glass until he heard something. He looked around, trying to place where the noise was coming from, and looked up to barely see us through the tinted window. We had to get his attention. We lifted our shirts and waited for him to understand. He ran back inside and came out with binoculars. We flashed him again and put our shirts down and then he pointed at Clarissa, gave her a thumbs-up, asking her to flash again. I wasn't attractive enough for this degenerate's attention, unfortunately. Clarissa scrambled to write down the number of the pay phone on our unit quickly and held it against the window while I stood by, dejected. He jotted it down and went inside.

Clarissa and I waited by the pay phone. He called pretty quickly. She told him she would show him whatever he wanted if he would just tie a box of cigarettes and matches to the string we would lower through the window vent the next day at seven p.m. This vent was the only contact with the outdoors we had besides our caged-in volleyball games. I would sometimes stand on a chair and shove my fingers down the vent and have the tip of my longest digit be technically outside, or press my nose up and huff the LA air, remembering the smell-taste of gasoline and smog.

We had an hour in our rooms at this time, but most important, the administration staff that worked in the offices directly below us would be gone then. We had occupational therapy that day and would steal a roll of twine and lower it. He agreed, obviously seeing how hilarious the whole situation was. He asked our ages and we said eighteen. There is no way he believed us, but he pretended he did.

Mission Tits for Cigs went down perfectly, and we enjoyed our reward later that night, but Clarissa left a few weeks later, and my currency was gone. I'd have to find another way to get smokes.

My next roommate was Hilary, a girl who was doing time for being violent. Turns out she was violent against an abusive stepdad. He was white and hated her for being black and said horrible shit to her, so she beat his ass. She was chubby, too. One night we stayed up late plotting how to escape. I had been here for four months and never got past level two. I was done trying to work for my release. I was just going to have to take matters into my own hands. We decided that we were going to pretend we were exercising, running up and down the corridor, and when we got to the end, we would throw both of our huge bodies against the giant secured emergency exit door, take the stairs down, and be outside before they could catch us.

The first few laps, we were just scoping the situation. One of the staff actually complimented us on our initiative to lose weight. We said thank you, then ran to the end again, gave each other a sign, and rammed the door as hard as we could.

It didn't even shake. The magnet that held it closed, I found out later, could lift a car. We knocked the wind out of ourselves and fell to the ground exasperated and in pain. We both cried and lay there until we caught our breath, and then went to bed.

The next morning we sat together, bruised and defeated, in the Family Room awaiting our breakfasts. We knew we needed another plan, and before we could even formulate one, a miracle occurred. A new nurse came into the room and introduced herself. "I'm Nancy and I'll be taking all level threes downstairs for breakfast today, so line up if that applies to you."

I was on two and she was on one, but we made eye contact and knew what we had to do. We both got in line and waited to be caught. The elevator doors opened and we shuffled in with the level threes. The elevator door closed! We grabbed each other's hands, not wanting to make eye contact, and felt the elevator drop underneath us. It stopped and the doors opened, and we two fat bitches ran like hell through the front doors and out onto the street. The last thing I heard was, "Wait, girls! The cafeteria is *this* way!" As if.

The thing with running away from a private institution is that, once you're off the property, the staff can't touch you. They have to call the police, and that would take a while. I tried to get my bearings to see where the nearest 7-Eleven was. I knew one was around from my visits to Jessica, but since I have the worst sense of direction, I started walking the wrong way. A couple blocks down and I was feeling great. The sun was shining, the air was clean and moving around me in ways I'd forgotten that it did. I had beat the system! Or so I thought, until I saw Dr. Jolie's car pull up next to me.

Fuck it! She couldn't do anything! She wasn't a cop. At this point my roommate flipped and ran off and left me there alone. I never saw her again, but I heard she went to the top of a nearby building and tried to jump before the cops got her.

Now that I had no ally, I had no idea what to do. Dr. Jolie asked me what it was that I wanted and I said cigarettes. She offered to buy me a pack if I went back, reminding me I had nowhere else to go. Although my dad technically had joint custody of us kids, he was in a powerless position. Since we were "out of control," *something* had to be done. If my dad protested the measures taken, he was essentially keeping us from getting help, and that didn't look good for future custody battles. He had to walk a very fine line. Since the hospital's main interest was filling the beds, they did and said whatever they needed to in order to make my mom feel like she was doing the right thing by keeping me in their program. If she took me out, she was sabotaging my therapeutic recovery.

I agreed to meet Dr. Jolie near the hospital while she went and got me cigs. When she came back, I grabbed the cigs and chain-smoked for the next hour. A staff member from upstairs had come down to be ready to escort me back up when I gave in. I taunted him by repeatedly putting my foot on their private property while standing in the street. When he'd advance toward me, I'd pull my foot back and laugh. He only fell for it once, but I continued anyway. At some point, I got sick from smoking and went back upstairs. I was put in the Obs Room for twenty-four hours and I spent the whole time looking at the street below, wishing I were braver.

An emergency family therapy session was called to chastise me for running away, and that was punishment enough. The family therapy sessions were horrible. Tom talked about nothing other than my weight and insisted there must be a reason for it that needed to be exposed. My anger issues and defiance and trust issues must come from somewhere. Tom was in therapy at the time for being sexually abused as a child, and so it just made sense to consider that I was a victim of sexual abuse, too. I felt like that was something I might remember clearly, since I remembered every thought I'd ever had and every word I'd ever said.

Tom's paternal interest in me always felt to me like a fuck-you to my dad, as opposed to actual concern for my well-being. Around this time,

Tom went on a talk show like *Charlie Rose* or *Larry King* or something and talked about how he had spent the evening before helping us kids with our homework. He said it in an accusatory way, though, like he was the only one who had ever tried to help us. He looked into the camera and said he was "the best dad those kids had ever had." The funny part was that Jessica and I were both locked up in separate hospitals, leaving only my brother Jake at home. The special school he went to didn't give homework.

I got in trouble with the head nurse once for refusing to wear sneakers because they hurt my feet too much. Tom told me it was because I was a compulsive overeater and was "too fat for shoes." This kind of indictment was in line with the tough-love school of thought that shockingly brutal honesty was the best way to show you cared. Thanks, whoever came up with that idea. I felt like his involvement in these sessions was just to distract from the relationship problems he and my mom were having. Humiliating me was a bonus. Later that year, a podiatrist would confirm that I had a birth defect in my feet that made wearing shoes painful and would require surgery when I was an adult. I wanted to gloat about the fact that it wasn't weight-related, but then gloating about a birth defect that requires surgery for any reason seemed kind of dumb.

During one of these family therapy sessions, I met Brandi for the first time. She was on summer break from her first year of college, and our mom had decided it was time to introduce her to the rest of us. I cannot imagine what it must have been like for her coming to Los Angeles to meet us, but I imagine it would be a lot like Dorothy being swept up in the tornado and dropped in some weird land full of mentally ill people. I had seen her face on the cover of the *Enquirer*, and I'd seen some photos that my mom had showed me, but it was entirely different to see her in person. She had big green eyes. Up until now I was the only green-eyed child. Jessica and Jake both had deep dark brown eyes and darker complexions. Brandi's skin was fair like mine, and she had reddish tones in her fine, wavy hair. I saw both the similarities and differences simultaneously and watched in awe as she displayed the same mannerisms as the rest of us, like the way she would turn her head to the side when she was saying something cheeky. It was a powerful meeting. We bonded right away, as I had hoped we would, and I'll never forget her asking, "Why are you here? You're the most normal one I've met so far." I loved her immediately, but we would have to wait four more years to spend any chunk of time together.

The eight-month mark rolled around, and the only kid who had been there longer than me had held a loaded gun to his parents' sleeping heads and the gun jammed. If it hadn't jammed, he'd be in prison. I started to wonder if I might actually be insane, because the mark of insanity is thinking you are sane and I believed I was sane, which meant I wasn't.

Dr. Jolie was trying to figure out what to do with me next. I couldn't stay here forever, but she didn't want to send me home. She looked into having me emancipated instead of returning to the same situation that had landed me here. I didn't even have my period yet! I couldn't possibly have my own apartment and a job without at least menstruating. I had turned fourteen on the unit, though I don't remember it at all. All I remember was Beanie sending me a birthday package full of arts and crafts supplies, the last I'd hear from her for ten years.

Eventually Dr. Jolie moved me downstairs to the residential unit. I was the youngest of the other kids there. There were only, like, seven of us, so I got my own room. I could smoke and have shoelaces and candles, and the doors were locked only at night and for our protection. We could walk to the nearby 7-Eleven if we had an adult with us. I could breathe actual air. I had school every morning instead of just three times a week, but I got kicked out almost every day for messing around with my friend Jarod. We'd draw pictures of the grim reaper doing normal daily activities, like playing golf or fishing, but with a scythe and people's heads. We would get sent out to the hall, where we would scream-sing metal and punk songs and then wrestle and beat each other up. I knew the first time he put me in a headlock that I loved him like my own kin.

I spent the next three months burning treasure candles in my room with Bauhaus playing on my boom box, and painting a village of tiny ceramic houses in my alone time.

I got to go on a couple of home visits from here, and they were disappointing. The house that my mom and Tom had been renting in Benedict Canyon was infested with rats. The attic and walls were full of them. They could be heard scurrying through the drywall all day and all night, and every vent or closet smelled faintly of rodent piss. When my mom discovered this, she moved out and rented a house in Malibu overlooking the ocean. All of this had taken place while I was away, so on my first home visit, Tom picked me up and drove me out to the Malibu mansion.

He stopped at KFC on the way to pick up lunch. I stayed in the car, but when he came out he had a cardboard box full of food and a young employee carrying another box. He was also holding a paper bag in one hand, which was also full of food and plates.

I asked if we were having a party, and he said no. I asked who was at the house and he said, "Your mom and Jake." Hmmm, I thought. This is a lot of fried food for four people, one who is on leave from a mental institution she's in for, as far as she can tell, being fat. When we got back to the house, Tom finished off the majority of the food while I looked around in a daze. This was my family's house. All their stuff was in it. Jessica had been here when they moved in and left a room full of her goth stuff behind before getting locked up again. Jake had a whole life in the house; toys and cameras and tripods and props for reenacting his favorite film *Die Hard* were everywhere. There were shoes by the front door and plenty of food in the fridge, and I didn't recognize any of it. I felt completely left behind and lost. When I got back to the hospital from my two-day visit, I felt like I was home again, and that scared me.

After a particularly bad family therapy session, I asked Dr. Jolie if I was ever going to be able to go home for real, and she hesitated. I didn't understand. I needed to know why. What was wrong with me? I demanded access to the very thick chart they kept about me behind the nurses' station. Dr. Jolie wouldn't let me see it, saying it was confidential. "IT'S MINE! IT'S ABOUT ME! LET ME SEE IT!" I tried to break into the locked nurses' station to steal it. She told me to go outside and calm down before they had to call someone (meaning restraints). I kicked at the door and went outside to smoke and just started bawling. What was wrong with me? What were they hiding? I knew I was a brat, but I must actually be a monster. I started spiraling.

One of the staff members named Cal came outside and saw me crying. He lit up a cigarette and stood by me. He was gruff and a recovering addict, as opposed to a nurse or trained professional. He had been through some shit; you could see it on the deep wrinkles on his face. He wore a leather jacket and jeans so he could ride his motorcycle home after work.

"What's going on?" he asked me calmly.

"Am I crazy?! I must be crazy! Only crazy people think they're not crazy! If I *am* crazy and I *know* it, I can work with that! Dr. Bronner escaped from a mental institution before starting his soap empire. He just incorporated his crazy right into the business model. I could do something like that when I get out. If I get out. I just need to know if that's the route I need to take. I have been here longer than anyone! Am I crazy? I wanna see my chart! IT'S MINE! WHAT THE FUCK IS EVEN IN THERE?!"

He waited for me to get winded and take a breath. He took a long drag on his cigarette, held it while looking me in the eye, blew it out for what seemed like hours, then said, "You have the best mental health insurance policy I've ever seen. You're worth a million a year, babe."

I went cold. My blood drained and my brain did that montage thing of calculating information. It took a minute for the answer to come to me. Could that be true? Could it be that simple? Oh my God. I'm not *crazy*, I'm *profitable*. I gotta get out of here.

I went to my room and packed a pair of underwear, an awl I had stolen from Occupational Therapy in case I had to defend myself, and whatever change I could find, which was about four dollars, and put everything in my metal lunch-box purse, which also could double as a weapon if needed. I went door to door asking the other patients if they had any money I could have. We always supported one another and loved helping someone else escape. I had once distracted a nurse so my friend Ymir could push an emergency fire button in the nurses' station to open all the magnetic doors so he could walk out. He made it to the sidewalk downstairs before he was wrestled to the ground and drugged, while I cheered him on from the second-story window. We were all in this together.

Someone gave me a five, and now I had nine. A girl named Jill offered to come with me. Sure! I had failed at my last attempt to run away and thought this could be just the thing I needed to succeed. Jill had street smarts and I had nine dollars and an awl. We were a good team. We planned to meet at the back door at six p.m., right after rounds.

Jill took charge immediately. She suggested we go to the Westside Pavilion, a huge crowded mall a mile and a half away. We could panhandle for money and find some food and a place to sleep. I was relieved to have a partner in crime with her head on straight, and I followed her.

When we got to the mall, Jill started immediately approaching people to ask for food or money. Watching the posh mall-goers with arms full of bags look at her and turn away like she was trash was a wake-up call. We must have looked frightening. No one wanted to get involved. No one was going to help us. Someone would call the police and we'd be taken back or put in jail for soliciting. I suggested we leave and go find somewhere warm to sleep. She had other plans, though, and as we left the mall and walked through the parking lot to go somewhere else, she went rogue and started approaching men who were alone.

"If you give me and my friend a place to stay tonight, I'll suck your dick," I heard her say. "Um, I won't be sucking any dicks. Sorry. I'll sleep in an alley first!" I told Jill. She assured me I did not have to suck a dick. She would do it. She didn't mind. I was both horrified and appreciative, but started wondering if Jill was as together as I'd thought she was. But I had no other choice than sticking with her.

We ended up at a gas station across from the mall and Jill told me to wait outside. She went in without me, came out three minutes later with a six-pack of beer, and told me to get in the small sports car that sat in the employee parking space. I got in the car and she did, too, and we each drank a beer. I drank only a few sips to seem like I was on board while I tried to understand what was going on. Jill had "worked out a deal" with the guy who was working inside. He would give us a place to stay the night when he got off work in thirty minutes.

I looked around his car and saw nothing but warning signs. It was immaculate, as if he'd recently cleaned it with bleach. The rear windows were tinted. His air freshener was a sexy lady. After fifteen minutes, I panicked. "Jill, I can't do this. I have a horrible feeling. Let's go! Let's get out of here!" She was reluctant to miss out on a place to stay, but I started getting out of the car and she had to follow me.

I walked toward the busiest-looking place I could see. It was a small café, but it was packed, which seemed strange for so late at night. A few feet from the entrance, I heard a man screaming from behind us. It was the gas station attendant and he was *pissed*. He was screaming that we owed him and started chasing us. He jumped in his car and drove after us screaming, "Fucking bitches! Whores!" I ran into the café and Jill followed. I bought us each a soda and found a corner to wait in, expecting him to bust in the door at any minute and drag us out. A half hour passed. I was sure he was outside waiting to accost us when there were no witnesses, but the café was closing and we had to take the chance.

We sneaked outside slowly and he wasn't there. I was scared to walk down the street, though, so I suggested we go up the stairs to the second floor and make a plan. There was a watch store up there, and we huddled together in front of the door as it got colder out. We stayed up there a couple hours. We started to talk about our situations, and that's when Jill told me her story.

She had been severely abused her whole life both physically and sexually. She had an imaginary adult male friend as a kid who protected her, but when she was about eight, her stepdad threw her into a burning hot shower and shut the door on her. Her imaginary friend tried to help, but he received third-degree burns all over his face and body and now he looked like Freddy Krueger and he wasn't there to help her anymore. He had turned that day in the shower and he tormented her now, telling her to kill herself constantly. She was on medication that helped her keep him away.

My guts hurt for her. I could see the eight-year-old in her face. It hadn't been that long ago. I told her some of my story, and we both started shivering. The temperature was still dropping and now we had adrenaline coursing through our veins after recounting our traumas. I told her I was cold and we should find a warm twenty-four-hour place to stay until the sun came up. We walked down Pico toward the beach, hoping we'd find a place before hitting the ocean, and an hour later, we were at Dunkin' Donuts.

We went inside and I counted the change I had left. It was about four dollars. I figured if I bought one thing per hour they'd let us stay, so we split a glazed and talked more about our lives. Occasionally I would notice Jill looking over my shoulder in an almost hypnotized way, and then she'd look back at me and her eyes would focus again. It started happening more and more in the next hour, so I asked if she was getting tired. She told me that her friend was back. In my ignorance I told her she had better take her medication, and that's when she reminded me we didn't have access to our meds. They were kept in the nurses' station. She had missed her evening dose and was about to miss her morning one, too.

The cashier started looking at us funny, like we were teen runaways or something, probably because we were. Jill was acting more and more agitated and I was down to my last couple dollars after buying another doughnut and a large hot coffee. It was about two a.m. now, and I was falling asleep sitting up. I figured the coffee would jolt me enough that I would be able to think clearly about our next move. I drank it all and bought a refill.

Jill was starting to tremble occasionally, and it was getting worse. She explained that it was a side effect of coming off her medication, and then she bumped the table and the coffee spilled in my lap. It wasn't that hot anymore, but now we had to leave. I had no more money for coffee or doughnuts. The staff had run out of patience with us, and Jill had no more meds in her blood. I sighed and realized it was time to go back.

Jill didn't want to go back, but I talked her into it. I told her I had to go back and I needed her to help me, so she did. The unit was locked when we got there, and I had to bang on the giant steel door for us to be let in, and when the doors opened, the nurse on duty rolled her eyes at us. I told her Jill needed her medication and that I was going to bed. She said okay, and I figured I would have to deal with the consequences tomorrow. I went and lay down.

About fifteen minutes later, I heard banging on the big steel doors, and it dawned on me that I wasn't going to get to wait until tomorrow to deal with the consequences. I knew those were the thuds of an angry parent, and I went out into the hallway to accept my fate. My mom and Tom were standing there, and their expressions scared me. I ran into the nurses' station to escape them but they followed, backing me into a corner. They both grabbed me and dragged me out of the building and into their car. We sped off, and I had no idea where we were going.

10B.

How to Smoke an Illegal Cigarette in a Lock-Up Facility

Smoking the cigarettes we cunningly procured while under the watchful eyes and numerous alarm systems at CPC required an elaborate drill.

First, you had to go in the bathroom, turn the shower to the hottest setting, put rolled-up towels at the bottom of the door, stand on the toilet, and hold your hand up to the fan vent in the ceiling.

You had to inhale hard and quick, put your hand back up before smoke could vacuum back out the end, then hold the smoke as long as possible and blow the remainder up into the fan. When you were done, you had to take a last drag while jumping down off the toilet, throw the cig into the water to extinguish it, and jump back up to exhale into the vent one last time, jump down again, flush the toilet, and then shower and brush your teeth. After that, you took a washcloth and rubbed toothpaste all over the walls from top to bottom, waited, then washed it off. You could only handle this big routine once in a while.

11.

Too Fat for Cake

I would soon find out we were going to Van Nuys Behavioral Health Hospital in the San Fernando Valley. I knew about this place not only because this was the rehab Tom had been admitted to when he had overdosed and hemorrhaged, but also because Jessica was currently a patient here. About a month before this, Jessica thought she was going to a routine therapy session with my mom and Tom and ended up being brought there. This technique had become the method of choice for putting us places.

Now it was my turn again for another exhausting intake procedure. During the signing of all the papers and the searching of my cavities, there was an incident in the parking lot out front and the police were called. I found out later in a tabloid article that Tom assaulted my dad and the staff at the hospital called the cops.

At the time, no one would tell me details, but I knew that my dad being here meant he had been notified by someone, most likely Dr. Jolie, that I had been moved without his consent. That had happened several times before, too.

My dad had gone to pick Jessica up from one of these placements once, and the placement called my mom to let her know that my dad had taken her. My mom didn't know the intent. Was he just refusing to be railroaded, taking advantage of his custody, or was he kidnapping Jessica? She called the cops and as my dad cruised calmly away from the place with Jessica in the car, several cop cars got behind him and pulled him over at a 7-Eleven, approaching him cautiously with their hands on their guns.

This happened another time, too, where the police had been falsely told that my dad was armed with an AK, another brilliant suggestion from the lawyers to get the cops to intervene faster and with more concern. It scared the shit out of my dad, who could have easily been shot.

I hoped he was attempting one of these rescues on me, but by now I knew how the system worked. Since I had run away, I was a danger to myself and the hospital could keep me here for seventy-two hours without my consent or my parents'. By then, my mom's lawyers would have it worked out so I'd stay. I surrendered to the fact I'd be here indefinitely and was happy at least that I'd get to spend some time with Jessica.

I asked if I could see her. It was about four a.m. now and one of the staff led me into her room and let me wake her up. There were three beds in each of the rooms. These were the same beds as before: metal frames bolted to the ground, plastic-covered mattresses on top, and a set of white sheets with the blue Angelica trademark printed across it, one plastic-covered pillow and one woven blanket on top of it. If you earned your privileges, you could have someone bring you a comforter from home. They would paw it to make sure no one had sewn contraband into it before letting you have it, which wiped off any comforts of home that might've been attached. No item of comfort was comforting anymore after being handed to you by an orderly.

I stood over Jessica and shook her until her eyes opened and locked on me.

"What're you doing here?!"

"I'm admitted!" I sang, adding some jazz hands.

The problem was that no one liked it when Jessica and I were together at these places. We had the human equivalent of Littermate Syndrome, a phenomenon that occurs when sibling dogs are raised together and bond with each other instead of their owners. They don't listen and they gang up on everyone else. It was much easier to control us when we were apart. We only got to hang out for a few days before it was decided that Jessica would be moved elsewhere, this time to a school in Utah named Rivendell (a *Lord of the Rings* reference).

Van Nuys Psych was a lot different from CPC. The mentally ill adults, mentally ill kids, and drug addicts of all ages shared common living spaces. This made for a lot of interesting interactions. When my friend Dale was admitted, a large woman in camp fatigues yelled at him to empty his pockets, and he obeyed until a nurse interrupted and told him he didn't have to. The woman in camp fatigues was not a staff member but a patient. A large patio connected the separate units, and, although it was surrounded by four giant walls with razor wire at the tops, you could see open sky. This was a game changer for a claustrophobe like myself, and I spent as much of my time as I could underneath the beautiful smog. The patio had several seating areas, tables with umbrellas, a pool table, and about ten ashtrays. We all smoked here. The adult smokers had it easy. They would have visitors bring them cartons that they could just smoke and smoke and smoke.

As a minor, you had to have a parent sign a permission form to be allowed to smoke, and none of them were that excited about doing that. You could convince them that cigarettes were better than the meth you were doing at home, and that it was cruel to expect you to quit everything all at once, but even if you had a signed permission slip, you needed a supplier. You couldn't have peers or anyone else visit without your parents' permission, so that meant no dealers, no best friends, no "bad influences." In other words, no one who would bring you cartons. Parents would sometimes give you a pack, but they were very stingy with their rations.

Option B was to work a deal with one of the adults. That was tricky. Most of them only wanted benzos, and no one wanted to give up their benzos. You couldn't get many cigs for most antidepressants since they worked cumulatively, but a single Ritalin could be worth a whole pack if you could find the right person to trade with. The problem with trading pills is that we had no access to our medications except for the second we were up at the nurses' station taking them. You would have to coordinate some serious mouth calisthenics to make it look like you'd taken your pill while also cheeking it. You had to open your mouth to show that you'd swallowed it which leaves a very tiny blind spot, then you would have to casually saunter away so as not to seem suspicious, and get somewhere you could transfer the disintegrating capsule into your hand to let it dry out. Storing these stowaways was difficult as we had no personal storage space. We checked our toiletries in and out as needed. We had a single small nightstand next to our beds, but anyone could access it. You had to find somewhere better to put them.

I never got the good drugs. I had refused to try medication the whole last year while at CPC because my therapist and I didn't think I needed it. Dr. Jolie once told me my parents were insisting I be put on an antidepressant, but when I said, "Ask me why I'm depressed. I have a thousand reasons and none are chemical," she nodded and didn't press the issue again, which I appreciated.

Now that I was somewhere new, it was decided that CPC hadn't "worked," and I needed more aggressive measures. A psychiatrist named Jamyl was assigned to me. After one minute in his presence, I never wanted to see him again. I know when I'm being patronized, when I'm being overlooked in an effort to appease my mom. He was another savior. He was going to be the One who fixed me. He wrote me a prescription for Prozac immediately, and I lost it. Fucking with my brain chemistry felt like the most malicious attack I'd endured yet, and I shut down completely. I had learned right before our session that Jamyl was just back from a leave to deal with the passing of his mother. I felt sorry for him, but now that he was threatening my brain, he was an enemy, so, trapped, I went for the jugular.

"Be happy your mom died so she doesn't have to watch you put kids on drugs for money," I said. He went silent and white and left, and I don't remember ever seeing him again. I still feel bad about this, but also—do not fuck with my only asset.

For the next two weeks, I cheeked all the Prozac, collected a nice little pile of semi-digested capsules, and traded them to an adult for two cigs. A new therapist was assigned to me. His name was Timmy. He was not a psychiatrist. He was . . . something else. Timmy was, like, seven feet tall, barrel-chested, and red-faced. He wore Hawaiian shirts and thongs with khaki pants, his white hair and eyebrows contrasting with his bright skin and making him look like a sunburned tourist. He ate bee pollen throughout our entire sessions. Timmy never diagnosed me. He never tried to figure me out. He never shamed me. He never mentioned my weight. He didn't force the issue of Prozac. What he did was listen. He listened to every bratty rant I went on. He listened like I was his favorite podcast. He snickered occasionally and sometimes asked me questions that were actually answers. He was a tiny port in the storm, and I loved him.

Now that I had no meds to trade for smokes, I had to move to option C. Option C was to collect all the stale and lip-wet butts from the many patio ashtrays, take them to my room, remove the tobacco, and construct a new homemade cigarette. This was done using the least disgusting filter of the lot, and one strip of a page of either Alcoholics Anonymous's *The Big Book* or the Bible. There was always an abundant supply of these in the mental institutions. Because you can't smoke tape, you'd use a tiny bit of mint toothpaste to hold the paper together and—voila!—a menthol from God.

This was also the place where I learned to do prison-style tattoos using a needle, pen, and thread. I did this with only a verbal explanation from one of the patients from the adult unit who had spent some time in prison, and I gave myself a happy face tattoo on the back of my left hand. It was stick and poke, and it hurt like hell, so I never got past the first dot for the smiling mouth and ended up with just three dots. Two eyes and one mouth dot, which conveniently was also a gang tattoo meaning *mi vida loca*. I mean, same thing, right?

The main difference between my previous placements and this one was that we got to leave the unit a couple times a week to attend AA meetings around town. Not just AA, but CA, Coda, PDAP (which stands for Palmer Drug Abuse Program and is essentially AA for minors), NA, and any of the other Anonymous incarnations. The staff tried to cover everyone's disease at some point, but since we could attend only one meeting at a time, we all had to go to all the meetings. Even though I didn't identify as a compulsive overeater, I was given the title and I dragged all the alcoholics and drug addicts with me once every six weeks or so to an Overeaters Anonymous meeting.

OA was the worst because there were no muffins. There was no cream or sugar for the coffee. The attendees struggled harder than anyone else because they had to face their drug of choice several times a day, actually ingest some of it, *and* stay sober. What a headfuck.

At a Cocaine Anonymous meeting I was attending, the leader was a very famous child actor. He was about nineteen at the time and got up to say "I'm _____, and I'm an alcoholic." We all clapped lazily. I scanned the room to place bets with myself on who was going to report everything he said to the *Enquirer* immediately after the meeting.

As he began to talk about his struggles with cocaine use in the entertainment industry, my sinuses tickled and my nose started to run. I am easily touched and my eyes tear up often, so this sensation was not surprising, but when I used the back of my hand to wipe the snot away, I saw a bright red trail across it. I looked down to confirm that I was really seeing blood, and a deluge poured onto my underdeveloped tits and pooled at the top of my fat roll, where my cleavage was thinking about being. I cupped my hand under my face, stood up, and ran to the bathroom.

The thing about finding spaces for addicts to convene is that they need to be free. These places were usually functional businesses during the day, or churches, or classrooms, or meeting rooms at the mall. They were never stocked for the comfort of the users, and as I leaned over the sink trying to contain the mess, I realized that the toilet paper rolls and paper towel dispensers were all empty. I had no belongings on me. We weren't allowed purses. I figured I'd just stay over the sink until I stopped bleeding. I locked eyes with myself in the mirror and thought God Is Fucking Specifically with Me in Very Me-Specific Ways and This Would Never Happen to Anyone Else. This is the Pentland Curse in full force.

Two adult women walked in, told me they had seen what had happened and that it happens to "all of us," and they dug in their bottomless bags for Kleenex and anything else to help me out. They didn't let me get a single word in edgewise, thinking they were making it impossible for me to make excuses and were just forcing me to see the truth. Well, I did see the truth. And that was that no one else was ever seeing the truth. I said thank you. I left. I found the group of kids from Van Nuys Psych, and I got in the shuttle to go back.

I had never before—and to date have never again—had a nosebleed.

I liked Van Nuys Psych because there were other celebrity-adjacent kids here and I could relate to them in ways I couldn't to other kids. I had a roommate named Merida whose dad was on TV, and we had a lot in common. One day I decided I was going to walk the long corridor of bedrooms with open Sharpies in each hand and draw lines as I walked. I can't imagine why that would have been as thrilling as it was, but that's probably because I now have entertainment options other than live-streamed news about the Gulf War and sewing leather wallets.

When I got busted and yelled at for drawing the lines down the walls, I was told I would have to clean it, so I spit on the wall and rubbed it around with newspaper while Merida watched and giggled. We would burst out in song and kick the walls to the beat. We were little shits. She was my favorite roommate.

Merida and I had a third roommate, a fifteen-year-old girl named Loretta, who was here for postpartum psychosis after delivering a baby fathered by her priest. That wasn't even the most shocking part. Her parents would bring the baby to her three or four times a week trying to get her to bond with it, WITH THE PRIEST IN TOW. Loretta was completely gone. She would walk down the halls slowly and almost catatonically and drop dirty maxi pads out of her pants on purpose. One time she took all my goth makeup, threw it into our toilet, and took a shit on it. I couldn't imagine what she had against me, but after that I was scared to sleep in the same room with her. She wasn't there for much longer than a couple weeks, thankfully.

A few months into my stay, I was allowed to go home for a weekend. Not just any weekend, it was the weekend of my mom's wedding to Tom. Don't let this confuse you. It was in fact their *second* wedding. It's always a great sign when you renew your vows after a year and a half. This time, Tom was Jewish. He had officially "converted," aka donated a large sum to the temple in lieu of taking classes. This time was going to be a proper wedding with lots of guests in a public venue, live music, a huge dance floor, and a ton of celebrities. Only one thing was missing: my mom's family. Things had been strained with them since the first wedding, and no one was talking.

Guests at this ceremony dressed in extravagant outfits with large jewelry and headpieces. I kept my army boots on, but the long white crinoline skirt I wore instead of my Goodwill dress covered them. My sisters and I were bridesmaids, and my brother was best man. I was in hell and made no effort to hide that fact in any of the photos by the line of about twenty paparazzi shooting their cameras off.

Along with my guest Natasha, whom I had befriended in the psych ward and whose dad was a famous musician, I approached them to hand them a business card. It had a picture of a man bending over between his own legs with his entire head up his ass. It said "The problem is obvious" on it and nothing else.

I was stupid to make enemies of these people because later that night, after the wedding was over and we all went to our nearby hotel rooms, Natasha and I went downstairs and hailed one of the on-duty limos reserved for drunken party guests and demanded it take us to the Nuart Theatre to see *The Rocky Horror Picture Show*. I had the driver stop at 7-Eleven and buy us cigarettes, and then wait to bring us back after the show. I thought I was being slick, but the next day my mom told me I had to go back to the psych ward early. A "concerned" paparazzi photographer had followed our limo, taking pictures of everything, and showed them to my mom. I was accused of ruining the wedding, but I believe it was already ruined just by way of occurring.

When I got back to the mental institution, I had to take a pee test. This was mandatory after any off-site adventure if you weren't escorted by staff. I hated it, and was angry to be asked, but there was no way out. If you refused to take it, you'd have the same consequences as if you had a dirty test. I went to the nurses' station and got my sterile cup. It was a nurse, Greg, who handed it to me with a smirk. He knew how humiliating it was to have to carry your pee around and turn it in, and he loved it. We had been in several power struggles in my time here, and the last one had ended with his making a joke about my being fat.

I took the cup to my room and left it on the counter for after breakfast, and I got in the long line of kids and adults getting their food. I took mine and, when I got to the drink section, I grabbed an apple juice. It was the small, half-cup-size plastic kind with the foil on top. It was always impossible to get the foil off, and was maddening until I once saw an adult from across the cafeteria just stick a straw right through the foil. My mind was blown. I put two juices on my tray, ate my breakfast, drank one juice, and tucked the other into my armpit to take back to my room.

In the bathroom, I locked the door and ran the hot water until it was at its maximum temperature, then put the juice underneath it to warm up. I then stabbed the foil with my finger, poured it into the pee cup, and added a little hot water to get the temperature just right. I then loosely screwed on the cap and took it to Greg at the nurses' station. He looked disgusted when I approached him with my filthy fat-girl pee and put on a rubber glove to take it from me.

That's when I "tripped," spilling it all over his face and shirt. I watched it drip from his fingertips and chin and I was about to laugh, but I saw his eyes go black like a cartoon demon. He was going to kill me. Like, kill me kill me. Before I could even enjoy it, I had to scream, "IT'S APPLE JUICE," to save myself. He turned around and, without saying a word to me, left for the day, indicating to a fellow nurse to put me in Obs, which they did.

Later that night from the Obs Room, I asked if I could brush my teeth, and, when the nurse on duty let me, I tucked a pen and some small scrap paper we kept by the pay phone under my boobs and took them back in with me. I wrote limericks all night, most of them about Greg attempting to suck his own dick and shitting himself, and in the morning, I passed them out to my peers. They were an instant hit and were memorized and repeated often, hopefully even after I left.

At some point I was released, with the stipulation that I would attend at least two meetings a week, one OA and one PDAP, and continue my counseling sessions with Timmy at the Daniel Freeman Marina Hospital in Marina Del Rey. It seemed like a fair trade for my freedom, so I agreed.

Sharon would drive me to my appointments, popping her gum the entire time, which was excruciating because of my misophonia, and I would roll into a fetal position and writhe around in the back seat for the entire drive there and back. One day I told Timmy that I'd never actually tried the Prozac, and he asked me if I would. I did for him, and I felt exactly the same, except I was too tired to be mad about all the shit around me. I needed to be mad. If I wasn't mad, I'd have no shield at all and would have no choice but to internalize everything. I knew I wouldn't have lasted long like that, so I stopped taking it.

My mom took me to an endocrinologist, thinking my depression, or whatever it was, could be hormonal. I was almost fifteen and had not gotten my period yet. Add in my weight, and maybe I had a thyroid issue.

I remember the appointment very clearly. I had to pee in a cup again, but also have my boobs palpated and get a Pap smear. The doctor asked if she could talk to me alone, explaining to my mom that I would be more likely to tell the truth that way. Mom left, and that's when the doctor started asking me a million questions. Do you do drugs? Do you drink? Are you sexually active? Are you being abused? After I answered no to everything, she asked me what school was like. I told her I hadn't gone to a regular school in two years and explained what I'd been doing instead. She listened intently, her jaw dropping more and more with each sentence I spoke. She excused herself and came back with an older doctor about fifteen minutes later. My diagnosis: primary amenorrhea caused by stress.

Even though *this* doctor believed that my symptoms were triggered by stress, everyone else still seemed to believe that all my problems were caused by my weight. After over a year and a half of sitting on my ass smoking cigarettes and eating prison food, I, not surprisingly, weighed 230 pounds, the heaviest I'd ever been.

Ironically, another cause of primary amenorrhea is fad dieting. I don't remember what order they took place in, but I was put on every single diet in existence. It's just an eighties montage in my head of consultations illustrated with silicone models of a pound of yellow fat on the table, boxes of freeze-dried foods or pouches in the lobby, and a slew of disgusting things meant to get rid of cravings, like flavored mouth sprays and canned shakes. I'd be on each diet for a few weeks and lose only a pound, so I'd go on another. Nutrisystem, Jenny Craig, Weight Watchers, Optifast, Lean Cuisine, SlimFast, Dexatrim, etc. Nothing worked, of course.

Around this time, the nurse who had been on duty at the residential center the night I ran away with Jill filed a lawsuit against my mom and Tom, saying that she was injured in the scuffle that occurred when they dragged me out of CPC and took me to Van Nuys Psychiatric Hospital. She also said that the injury caused her to lose a baby, claiming to have been hit in the stomach hard enough to miscarry. I was called as a witness and had to testify that there was no way that my mom and Tom could both carry my humongous ass *and* assault another person at the same time. No one was that strong. In front of a jury, I had to answer questions like "How much do you weigh?" and "How many people do you think it would take to carry you?" and "Where were your mom's and Tom's hands as they carried you out?" I was under oath. I couldn't help but feel like this was yet another prank from the universe, and I decided I was gonna get in on this joke as opposed to being the butt of it. I turned on the charm and answered all the questions thrown at me like I was Rodney Dangerfield, if he were a fat goth teen. By the end of my testimony, the jury, the lawyers on both sides, the judge, and the paparazzi who were camped both in the courtroom and outside of it were cackling. I came off the stand like I was coming offstage. The case was thrown out. I had taken some control back, and it felt good.

I can't remember which diet I was on when my fifteenth birthday rolled around, but it definitely did not allow for cake. My mom and Tom threw me a beautiful party. They hired someone to plan it, to send out invites, to decorate the Brentwood mansion. They hired a professional party leader to guide us in games and keep the event structured. He was extremely coked up and irritating, and we could tell he hated us all. He was also kissing my mom's and Tom's asses, and I had had about enough of that.

When it was time for the "cake," the party planners wheeled out a table . . . of fruit. Some of the strawberries were dipped in chocolate, or was it carob? I was humiliated, because all my friends were there and they all knew what it meant. I was too fat for cake. I took a strawberry and ate it, and then I walked over and shoved the party leader into the pool. I laughed and my friends laughed, but the party guy did not laugh. In fact he screamed. He was livid. He had his beeper (google it, kids) in his pocket, and it was ruined. He had no change of clothes to go home in. As he tantrumed, I rolled my eyes and went up to my room. The party was over anyway. A few of my friends stayed behind and followed me, two favorites from the hospital: Merida and our mutual friend Ryder, who was a big eternal child and made everything fun. He told me he had a birthday gift for me, and I was excited to receive it. He reached into his bag and pulled out a rat.

Ryder had a pet rat at home that I loved, and he was giving me a pet of my own. It was the sweetest, most thoughtful gift. He was no street rodent; he was one of the cute gray kind with big black eyes and soft fur. I named him Jughead, because Ryder's rat was named Archie, and I made him a nice nest out of my clothes and turned him loose in my walk-in closet, which would be his home now. Well, for a few days anyway, until my mom found out, made me give him back to Ryder, and sent me to Wilderness Survival.

12.

Death by Survival

The summer I lay down to die in the dusty, hot cactus fields of southern Utah, I was fifteen years old—it was the summer of 1991. My peers were home watching *The Simpsons* and brushing their Furbys' hair while I was out here on "Survival," eating squirrels and wiping my ass with a pinecone.

"Survival" is slang for any number of private programs that lead you on a wilderness expedition with the sole purpose of self-improvement. Some, like National Outdoor Leadership School (NOLS), were reserved for consenting adults, while some, like Aspen Achievement Academy (AAA), were for nonconsenting teens. Teens like me.

The majority of these teen "students" (these places always called us "students" or "attendees" or any other word other than "captives") were spoiled rich kids who were here to be stripped of all luxuries and broken down until they were groveling urchins who would be grateful for a single bowl of gruel. In theory, we'd return home full of gratitude and would beg to do chores and be the middleman for our unhappily married parents in exchange for their subpar room and board. That was the dream the parents were being sold for the low price of sixty thousand dollars.

Jessica had been sent here a month before me and was still out on course when I arrived. We wouldn't see each other, as she was in a different peer group, and much further into the program. I was once again following in her footsteps.

One downfall of being Jessica's successor was being held accountable for her behavior and/or confused with her. The incident with the Youth Transport Service (they called themselves this; we called them bounty hunters; my dad called them ghostbusters; they *should* be called kidnappers) was just the first of many times this happened.

The crew my parents had paid to escort me to AAA were the same bounty-hunting, ghostbusting, youth-transporting kidnappers for hire who had come to get Jessica two years prior to take her to her first placement, CEDU.

The bounty hunters had noted the altercation they had had with Jessica and the kitchen knife she'd pulled on them in their file captioned "Pentland female," so when they came to get me two years later, I was handcuffed in order to prevent *my* ever doing this again.

"Wait! That wasn't me! That was my sister! We're Irish twins!" I pleaded, to get them to take the handcuffs off as I boarded a flight to Utah.

"Every criminal has a twin that 'did it,'" said a man who looked like the lead in a community theater production of *Thor*, as he moved the cuffs from my back to my front so I could sit on the plane. I rode that flight fluctuating between a hysterical laugh and a surrendering cry and was relieved when we landed. Now there was just a long car ride to base camp, where the cuffs could be removed.

Base camp was a warehouse in the desert of Loa, a town with a population of around five hundred that boasted one Mormon temple and one tiny motel called the Sunshine Inn that was probably solely kept in business by AAA students stopping to shower on their way back to civilization. Recently, I learned it was named by a missionary for Mauna Loa, a mountain on the Big Island of Hawaii that I am looking at through my window right now, thirty years later, which feels like another of the multiverse's playful synchronicities.

There were seven duffel bags arranged on the floor of the warehouse, each with a large radius of space around it where the counselors and other adults could pace around, explaining things. Two of them were male and two female, to make the escorted bathroom trips legal.

This is where we would learn the rules. These counselors would bark in some sort of sergeant-speak. They'd use the language of the program, like any good cult workers. If you had been to a lot of these orientation processes, you could see all the parallels between them. They were all basically some form of Erhard Seminars Training (est) during the human potential movement, like that "tough love" horseshit.

I was taken to a duffel bag that had a giant handwritten tag with my name on it. I didn't recognize the handwriting. My name was spelled out in girly script: Jennifer. No one called me that. It occurred to me that Tom had had one of his eager-to-please hot-girl assistants buy me everything off the intake list right under my nose. It always stung to realize that these placements were planned, that I had eaten dinner at our cartoonishly long dining room table for weeks, laughing and joking, while documents were being couriered and signed, phone calls and travel plans made, tickets bought. I was always the last to know.

The duffel was an expensive canvas bag from whatever prepper store was closest to rich Brentwood at the time. Inside were new outdoor clothes: polypropylene long underwear and sock liners, wool socks, a wool balaclava, a wool sweater, a raincoat, rain pants, bandannas, and cotton shorts, T-shirts, and underwear.

I explored the contents further to see what other hideous new things were tucked away inside. I pulled out the pair of custom-made army boots I had been gifted to accommodate my fucked-up feet. I had been unknowingly breaking them in for weeks. When I sat in plaster casts at the podiatrist's office to have these measured for me, I thought they were an apology for not knowing I had a birth defect. I had always wanted Doc Martens but they hurt like hell, and these were the next best thing. I had expected to wear these while sneaking out to do minor crimes! Not to thrash through cacti on some haunted mountain! I wanted to put cigarettes out with these thick soles, not campfires! My shitkickers had become hiking boots, a goth's worst nightmare!

I thought my parents were finally accepting my eccentric style and allowing me to express myself in clothing, something that had been forbidden for the past couple years due to its being "imagey" (a made-up therapy word that refers to any outside thing you use to identify yourself with that might distract from the Real You).

At one point, a typed letter had been professionally framed and hung outside our bedroom doors listing all the rules we children would need to follow in order to live in my mom and Tom's house. Some were easy, like "turn off all lights," and some were hard, like "shower." Rule Number 1 was "No more than one piece of black clothing a day. No dirty or torn clothing. No holes. No offensive logos." Unfortunately it was unknown at the time that my hideous fashion choices were the Real Me and not an image I was trying to hide behind. I think in my forty-three years, I've proved *that*, if nothing else.

Moving away from the devastating flood of realizations brought on by seeing these boots, I put my arm back into the duffel bag and fished around for more things to hurt my feelings. Among the new purchases, I found a Swiss Army knife and a magnesium fire-starter kit. Something in me knew these were not allowed. After two years in the teen help system, my experience with paraphernalia was vast. Paraphernalia is the same across these programs for the most part: sharps, razors, knives, hairpins, Number 2 pencils whose erasers could be extracted, leaving a metal ring to be bitten down on and made sharp, cigarettes, lighters or matches, shoelaces. This one never made sense to me. It was to prevent strangulation, but a lot more damage could and would be done with the simple bedsheets provided. I knew all the things we couldn't have. I also knew how to get them.

One way to get things was smuggling them yourself into your place of confinement. My dad loved to buy all kinds of trinkets and spy gear and miscellaneous Hammacher Schlemmer–ish stuff. He had bought a book about paleontology with the insides cut out and lined with green felt and fitted with a lid. When the book was closed, it looked like any old research book. On a day pass from CPC, I filled it with cigarettes and matches and put a more believable jacket on it—*The Bachman Books: Four Early Novels by Stephen King*—because it fit both the book and my personality. I figured I'd better read it in case one of the intake staff started asking questions. I was hooked and spent my weekend pass reading the whole thing. My favorite story was about a man stuck in a horrific contest where he will die if he stops walking. Some of the characters had just given up and let themselves be shot to death instead of continuing with the game. I couldn't understand this level of surrender. Yet.

I tucked the knife and fire-starter kit inside a hidden pocket in the prepper duffel. Was it intended for seeds? Ammo? Passports? Cipro? Cyanide? I put a bandanna over them just in case. I finished taking out what the staff had told me to take out for the week and packed it into a smaller bag. We were instructed to zip our duffels back up and leave them there, where they would be kept in the warehouse and brought to us weekly to change out our dirty underwear. Fuck. That meant that they would probably find these things and take them. I'd get in trouble for not turning them in and then I'd be here longer or suffer some other consequence. I debated confessing but decided to just play stupid instead. Maybe I never saw the pocket? They could prove nothing. I was in emotional distress. I wasn't paying attention. I let the staff know I was packed and ready, and they let me know it was, once again, time to pee in a cup. After all, they had to know what kind of detoxing to prepare for. These places were set up for a range of mental health issues, but since most kids learned quickly to self-medicate, the Venn diagram of behavioral problems and drug addictions was pretty much a circle.

After filling the cup, I was told to change out of my personal clothes and to put on the supplied outfit: underwear, bra, polypropylene long underwear top and bottom, wool pants, a shirt, a sweater over it, hat, bandanna, socks, and boots. Once we were geared up, we went back to the main room, from which our duffels had been removed, and collected the piles that had been left for us for the week. A large poncho and some parachute cord had been laid on top.

We filed into a van and were driven a distance. When the doors opened and I climbed out, I could see by the light of the van's headlights that there was nothing there. Absolutely nothing. No cabins, no outhouses, no fire rings. Just dusty-ass flat earth. Once the van was unloaded, it turned away and drove off. Those red taillights would be the last sign of a civilized society I would see for fifty-two days.

Before the lights disappeared completely into darkness, our attention was redirected to the fact that we were going to now, in the dead of night, start hiking. I would like to reiterate that this entire story up to this point has taken place in a single day. I woke up to the bounty hunters, traveled in cuffs from Los Angeles to Salt Lake City, got in a car and was driven to Loa, was stripped and humiliated and drug-tested for hours in a warehouse, and now was going to hike in the desert for God knew how long.

At drop-off, we were given a single banana, barely ripe, the kind that leaves an antiperspirant coating in your mouth. Antiperspirant. Remember that? What a luxury that was. We hiked only about a mile, an incredibly short walk for AAA, as I would discover. Short but difficult, as it takes the human eye hours to adjust to low light. At first, it's like being blindfolded, but then, within minutes, you can start making out the difference between the starlit sky and the dim land. An hour after bushwhacking in the dark, you can see a bit of depth and separation between biota and rock. A couple hours later you can walk at a decent pace without running into a tree. This kind of sensitizing is disorienting. When they say silence is deafening, this is what they mean. On high alert, you can hear every sound and smell every smell. This is a good thing for survival in the wilderness, but a bad thing for Wilderness Survival, where you are never more than three feet behind another sweaty teen on the trail. I didn't know what a chicken coop smelled like at that time in my life, but later, when I'd find myself cleaning one, I'd recognized the smell of ammonia, wet feathers, dirt, and asshole.

We finally reached a clearing and were instructed on how to set up a shelter using our parachute cord and ponchos. The poncho was a large rectangle with eyelets all around, including one in each corner. A head hole with a hood was right in the center. During the day, we would bundle up our belongings inside these ponchos, making a very primitive backpack, and at night we would tie the hood shut with the cord and attach it to a nearby tree. The four corners of the poncho were then tied to heavy rocks, making an A-frame shelter. We would lay our flimsy blue foam sleeping pads on the bare ground and put our sleeping bags on top.

That was it. That was our shelter. We were still very exposed to the elements and to bugs or critters that were curious to see what smelled so bad. I woke up more than once with a family of rodents shopping for nesting materials in my semi-dreadlocked hair. We would surrender our shoes outside this shelter every night so the staff could collect them to prevent us from running away. They would sleep with them right next to their faces in their tiny low-profile tent and return them at sunrise. They deserved that fate for leaving us barefoot to pee at night.

Have you ever tried to pee in the woods with no shoes on? You definitely don't want to step on a cactus or wander too far and have to run back in the dark when an elk finds you, so oftentimes I would end up peeing too close to my bed, a slow trickle finding the same path of least resistance I just took, but backward, right into my shelter. Going to the bathroom during the day wasn't much easier, since the benefit was that it was light outside, which also meant more chances to embarrass yourself. You'd want to venture out farther than you did at night, find a suitable place and some plants/moss/pinecones to wipe (if you're using a pinecone, GO THE RIGHT DIRECTION), dig a hole, disrobe from the waist down, do your business, wipe, cover your waste, and dress. To prevent anyone using the ridiculous amount of time this took to get a head start running away, we would also have to sing out loud or whistle the entire time, so that the staff knew we were still there. I cannot whistle. Also, I cannot sing. There was no running water, no soap, nowhere to wash your hands. I will let your imaginations write the next paragraph, which will kindly remain invisible.

Waking up that first morning was brutal. Part of me still thought it might be a dream, though I never fell asleep for long enough to have one. I was trying to tune out every leaf rustle, every cold breeze that blew, every thought of my family, whom I simultaneously hated and missed, and every realization that only six hours had passed and there were fifty-one more days of eternity to go. The hunger pangs, the dry mouth, the feeling of being on the cusp of having to pee, but not needing to badly enough to crawl out of a warmish sleeping bag into the feral night. The only thing worse than being half-asleep is being half-awake.

When you sleep outside, your circadian rhythm resets. You start to get dopey as the sky gets dark, and you wake up slowly with the sunrise. It is, in short, wonderful. The first morning light is medicinal, but it was being crammed down my throat, so I couldn't let on that I found it so completely transformative. No one was going to win my gratitude so long as I was at the mercy of outside forces, not even Mother Nature. She was trying pretty hard, though, with her sunrises and sunsets, clear starlit nights, calico sandstone hills, mountaintop views of the wavy purple and coral expanse that stretched out like an infinite Hollywood backdrop, her springs and carved-out riverbeds, caves, and windbreaks.

I loved her, and it pained me to have to ignore her beauty in order to suffer and make sure that everyone around me suffered as well.

At first light, our shoes were returned outside our tents and we were instructed to put them on. It was time to break down camp. This was a low-impact adventure, meaning we left every site in better shape than we found it, with no traces of human visitors. That meant that any area we cleared had to have the forest duff redistributed over it. Fire pits had to be kicked over, and the charcoal that remained had to be crushed to spreadable ash by way of being smashed between two rocks. Those rocks then had to be cleaned and set back into whatever hole was made when they were moved. We packed up our stuff, finished the last bits of camouflage, and started our next hike. As we climbed in elevation, I was sure I'd see some landmark or sign of life in the land around us, but there was nothing. No roads, no towns in the distance, no tents, no plumes from others' campfires. Nothing. So much nothing, for what seemed like thousands of miles. I felt more alone than I ever had in my life.

The male counselors, Chad and Chris, spent the entire day making inside jokes to each other. They wanted that good-buddy love so badly. This was a type, I found: Young men who still acted as though they were twelve and were not really interested in sexual love, but instead just wanted to play video games or frisbee golf with their buds. There was a woman, too, Laurel, but she was young and distracted and couldn't compete for Chris's or Chad's attention. She was the kind of quiet that lets you know she's here because she is trying to have her own trans-formative experience and you are just a doughy stepping-stone on her path, a path that will inevitably lead to a village in the developing world from which she will take home a souvenir child that becomes her whole identity. Chris and Chad led and the six students marched behind them. I dragged at the back of them all, except for Laurel, who was tasked with being caboose and had to walk behind me, frustrated at my slow pace and doing nothing to hide it.

After the third day of this one banana bullshit, we were made to sit down in a circle and were each gifted a can of peaches. We were embar-rassingly grateful. The staff watched us struggle to figure out ways to open the cans. We tried smashing them with rocks, prying them apart with sticks, and just begging the staff to open them for us. After all attempts failed and we had given up, the staff passed each one of us a simple, wooden-handled steel knife in a leather case. I couldn't believe that these people who took my shoes every night were giving me a knife after only days of knowing me, and even after most likely being told by the bounty hunters that I had threatened people with one in the past. I was confused. Chad took one of the other kids' knives and showed us how to use it to open a can. You might think it would involve stabbing the blade down into the lid, but it was a much gentler motion. The tip of the knife breaks the lid enough that you can hold it with the blade facing up and rock it back and forth away from you. We all sloppily cut into our cans and ate the entire contents in a simultaneous gulp. We drank all the syrup out, some of us carefully and others not so much. We all had tracks out the corners of our mouths where drips fell and collected the dirt on our faces on their way down, like the tears of a toddler who had fallen face-first in mud. A couple of us had small bleeding cuts from the sharp lids. This was the end of the first phase and the beginning of the next one. Primitive, it was called.

Primitive phase had us eating nothing but raisins and peanuts, raw cornmeal we named Yellow Death, and some beans we half cooked each night in a dirty billycan (a recycled bulk coffee tin) that would serve as our only cookware except for the wooden spoons we each carved for ourselves with our new knives. GORP (good ol' raisins and peanuts) was our main trail food, and we ate small amounts of it all day.

One of the first skills we were supposed to master on Primitive was "Getting Our Fire," which meant making one from scratch with a bow drill set. We used our knives to carve a base, a spindle, and a bow. We used a piece of our parachute cord to finish the bow, and the handle of our knives served as sockets for the top of the spindle. We formed "nests" out of roughed-up tree bark that would catch easily when the punk (wood dust from friction that becomes an ember when it gets hot enough) was dropped in and blown into a flame. Upper body strength was a necessity, and I did not possess any such thing. I could not get a fire no matter how hard I tried. One by one, I watched as the other students succeeded.

I also had no lower body strength. Or other kinds of strength. My

body had slowly been becoming my enemy with weight gain and prepu-
berty, and it was really doubling down under these extreme conditions.
I don't know if it was the heat, the hiking, the dehydration, or the constant squinting to diffuse the unobstructed sun, but I had a headache
almost the entire time.

My feet ached and were covered in blisters. My skin was chafed at
the thighs and under my arms. I was covered in mosquito bites. I had
tiny burns from embers popping away from our nightly circle around the
fire and landing on my exposed face and hands. My lips were chapped
and cracked on the outside and on the inside had rubbed on my braces,
covering the backsides of them in cankers. I still hadn't gotten my period yet even though I was fifteen, and that was the only kindness my
body extended me. I was thirty pounds heavier than my peers and way
less in shape, thanks to sitting in a community room in front of MTV
in lockup twelve hours a day for two years. My peers' frustration with
me slowing everyone down was humiliating, and the only way I knew
how to deal with that was to humiliate myself even more, tantruming,
whining, and complaining with every step I took on my deformed feet.

I was relieved when, on Day 16, we were told we would spend the
day solo. They explained that this meant we would be in a spot alone in
the woods, away from anyone else, and would be able to sit for twenty-
four hours. I had never wanted to sit down for an extended period so
badly. The idea of being alone in the woods at night was absolutely terrifying, but my desperation to be alone for one fucking second was so
strong it overcame all the reasons why this was a terrible idea.

Laurel walked me out into the woods. I could feel the psychic buzz-
ing of the other living human bodies getting fainter and fainter as I got
closer to my designated spot. She dropped me off, repeated a few rules,
then left me there. The rules were: No communicating in any way. This
meant no howling, whistling, talking loudly, and definitely no screaming. Easy. I didn't want to talk to anyone anyway. Another rule was no
leaving your assigned area. They had included enough space to accommodate going to the bathroom, so there was no need to wander. She
handed me a russet potato and a single carrot, then left.

Just like eyes adjusting to darkness, my etheric body had to adjust
to the staticless quietude of being without other people. I had noticed by

now that not everyone seemed to be as hideously sensitive as I was to the sound of TVs in nearby houses. Not everyone hated shoes and clothes and makeup and perfume the way I did. Not everyone felt like their skin was made of electrified steel wool. The sound of someone's brother's breathing while riding next to him in the back seat of the car on the way to school every morning didn't send them into a rage, didn't give them that nails-on-a-chalkboard feeling starting with a rumble in their inner ear that drips hot liquid metal down their spine until it pools in their tail-bones, making it excruciating to sit and stay where they were.

After a few hours of being alone on this solo, I could hear ants walking by and the tree sap fossilizing into amber.

A tiny stream about four inches wide ran through the lower end of my site. It was deep enough to stick my top pinky phalange in. When I did, I could feel the sandy and claylike bed. I started digging with my hands to make a dam that I could fill my canteen in without taking tiny handfuls of what I could collect and dribbling them into the bottle clumsily. I had already tried that and, an hour later, I was trying this.

I filled my bottle and I added ten drops of iodine, shook it, and set it aside to sterilize. While I waited, I started making little people out of the clay. I found sticks to sculpt them and I plucked leaves and other forest supplies and spent the hours of the day making a village. Time is so much about the people you are spending it with, and being alone made it nonexistent. When I noticed the sky getting darker, I panicked. I was supposed to have spent this time getting a fire to cook my potato and carrot on! The smoke would keep away the bugs, the light would keep away predators and ghosts, and the heat would keep away the cold. I had fucked up.

Luckily, a couple days prior, we had had a visit from our duffel bags and I had decided it was time for me to sleeve the fire-starting kit. I left the Swiss Army tool, as I much preferred my large Green River knife now. I tucked the kit into my bra and I went about my week like there was not the key to the greatest discovery since the Stone Age tucked against my sweaty boob.

I checked around with my ever more alert eyes and ears to see if there were any signs of staff hiding and spying in the brush. I gathered wood as if I were confident I was going to get a bow drill this time, just in case I was being watched. I got everything ready as if I intended to make the fire the right way. I put my bow drill kit next to me and my nest made from bark and dry leaves. I looked around again and pulled the illegal metal brick from my shirt. I shaved some magnesium off the brick into a pile inside the nest and struck the steel until I shot a wad of embers into it. I blew it gently until the embers turned to tiny flames and then I put down my handful of fire and slowly laid tiny twigs on it. Then I put larger and larger pieces of wood on top until I had a proper fire.

It was dark now and I was too afraid to collect more wood. I was going to have to try to fall asleep before this went out. I hid all evidence of my crime, got into my sleeping bag, and tried to sleep. The silence was deafening, as they say. I could hear the effervescence of my gut, each tiny bone creak, the blood whooshing into my heart and back out, speeding up with each anxious thought, the feel of the tiny lactic acid crystals built up inside my eye muscles grating as I scanned the darkness for other eyes watching me back. Human eyes, animal eyes, rodent eyes, reptile eyes, alien eyes, insect eyes.

All of a sudden, I heard a scream. I recognized it as one of the other kids. It was bloodcurdling. I rolled into a fetal position, awaiting a bear or snake or band of Native American poltergeists. Nothing happened, but I still waited. I stared at the blinding laser show of stars overhead until the sky started getting blue again.

When I got up and moving, I smashed and spread the ashes of my fire. Was this so that I would be the best low-impact camper around? Or to destroy any and all evidence? Only one person knows the answer to this question, and I'm not telling. Laurel came to get me. She saw the remnants of a fire and was confused.

"Wait. YOU got a fire? Out here? Alone?"

"Well, yeah, I just don't do well under pressure, so . . . I probably can't do it in front of anyone."

She was immediately sure I was lying and got down on all fours to dissect the coals and study the earth for clues. I watched, terrified I'd missed a shaving of magnesium. I held my breath. Turns out I'm a good crook. She found nothing. I was so relieved that I wasn't caught! I knew if I had been, they would start the solo all over. I wouldn't be able to handle that. Even though I hated the rest of the group, I didn't want to be alone in the terrifying wilderness anymore.

I started packing up my camp but Laurel stopped me and informed me that the scream I had heard was my peer Kerry being touched by a mouse. She had "broken solo" and now the clock was going to start over. The news was unbearable. I knew Laurel would be watching me more closely now, trying to catch me in the criminal act of Being Warm and Safe, so there was no fire on my agenda tonight. Day 17 lasted a year, and I knew the night would be even longer.

Kerry screamed again that second night. This time, she had witnessed a large elk standing near her site. She said it was "looking at" her. Solo started over. Day 18. I had now spent three days alone save the visits from Laurel to see if I was journaling and self-reflecting. I had eaten the carrot yesterday but was still having a standoff with the raw potato. Halfway through my third solo, it called my bluff and I ate it like an apple.

When solo ended, I didn't believe it. I was sure something else was going to happen and I was just going to live out here alone forever from now on. At this point I had nothing more to write in my journal. Words meant nothing if not used to communicate with others. I had even stopped talking to myself, the way I had been doing on my first day alone. My communications with myself and the world around me now were all telepathic. When the mice got into my hair at night, I simply thought them away. Even though we all returned to group, I never felt the same again. There was a part of me that was just different now.

On Day 19 we were told we were starting the Pioneer phase. We were given a wagon with two large wheels at its sides and a mule bar in the front. The good news was that we no longer had to carry our cumbersome backpacks. The bad news was that we now had to push them in a two-thousand-pound vehicle. It took six people to move it when it was full of all of our gear. Two people pushed from behind, one person managed each wheel, and two people leaned against the bar. Each small rock in the ground had to be navigated, one wheel needing to move while the other was stationary. We never got more than a few feet without a struggle of some kind. A couple times we came up to a gulch that was impossible to cross with the weighted wagon. We'd have to unload all the gear and move it manually, crossing back and forth over the gulch twenty times to get everything, then drag the emptied wagon over the gap, and repack it on the other side. This took hours.

Occasionally, someone would push too hard from the back while one of the two mule people weren't leaning on the bar, and the wagon would tip backward, flinging one mule person up into the air. Toes were run over, fingers smashed. We did get an iron Dutch oven to make bread out of the Yellow Death. We got spices, too, for which we were supposed to be really grateful. Salt was a life changer in these conditions. But I had already figured that out due to a chance discovery.

I had gone to pee once and happened upon a fallow paddock. I noticed what looked like a giant square crystal in the grass. It was obviously unnatural, so I inspected it and realized it was a salt lick. I used my knife to chip off a piece and kept it in my bag among the quartz rocks I had been collecting. I'd sneak a lick occasionally or whittle some off onto a raw potato, changing it into a gourmet meal.

By Day 31, we were entering the next phase, where we got nice backpacks with straps and a few luxuries like salt pork. Salt pork is a hunk of skin-on, mostly fat, cured pig. I don't want you to think I ate this one raw also, but also, I ate this one raw. It wasn't as good as the feral squirrel Chris had killed with a slingshot a week ago. He had asked me to help him skin it, so I held its tiny rodent paw while he sliced a circle around its wrist and yanked the fur back like he was taking a compression stocking off a grandma. He traded me a leg for my service, and we cooked it on a tiny spit. I ate my little morsel the way Pee-wee eats baby corn. It tasted like . . . chicken.

Each phase was meant to earn us new privileges and luxuries, but privileges and luxuries are just heavy responsibilities and dangerous liabilities in lingerie. Though things seemed to be getting easier, I was getting more and more exhausted. My head constantly hurt. My whole body ached. I was full of chafe and blisters made worse by my damp shoes and socks. We had just spent three days hiking through a storm and all my gear, including my sleeping bag, was wet. I hadn't slept deeply in weeks.

One day, we were hiking through some thick trees and I just . . . was done. It wasn't an angry, reactive done, but a calm and otherworldly done. I had decided.

I needed to find the right place, though, so I kept on. We finally came out of the dimness into a bright mesa. The sun was shining and everything was beautiful and warm and dry. A breeze was blowing tiny glowing dandelion seeds around. I felt my solar plexus tingle like I'd swallowed a nine volt. I was dumbfounded and hypnotized by the spectacle around me and, in admiring it, was floating even farther behind the rest of the group. My slower pace meant I had no momentum, and it wasn't long before I was just standing still watching their dirty asses full of pinecone dingleberries and GORP skid marks struggle into the bush ahead until they disappeared behind a mountain. A mountain. I'd climbed one of those before. Not my favorite. Don't really need to do it again.

I understood the people from the "Long Walk" story now. They knew there was only going to be one winner and it wasn't going to be them, so they opted for a merciful death instead. I surrendered. This was going to be my final resting place.

You might wonder why a young girl with endless potential, with her whole life ahead of her, the daughter of a rich Hollywood celebrity, might want to die. Well, I thought I was going to spend the rest of my life as the middleman in terrible family conflict, constantly disappointed and always disappointing. A fat, gray sheep in a family of black and white ones. I had no real aspirations or goals, no plans for the future. I thought I would always be unhappy, uncomfortable in my own skin, terrified of abandonment, and crippled by anxiety. I was tired of being a pawn in a very stupid game of chess. I felt like an unloved commodity, a product whose selling point was how fucked up I was and/or could get, to those who gained access to my fantastic Motion Picture Health and Welfare insurance.

I thought about my family at home. My little brother Jake, just twelve, would be spending his entire summer reenacting the JFK assassination using his BB gun to take out several diet Yoplait containers he had lined up on the cement-block wall outside my dad's new bachelor pad in Topanga Canyon. He would film this with the camcorder our dad had used to film himself eating cheesecake with before sending us to Fat Camp. Jake would save the best takes on labeled VHS tapes to rewatch several hundred times in slow motion, trying to prove his second-shooter theory. I missed him like a mother misses a son. I had always been his protector, and now that I was gone, he was turning into a yogurt-sniping, conspiracy theorist Incel.

My dad's biggest burden was his love for us kids, and I'd be doing him a favor freeing him from a third of it.

Jessica would be on her way to another est-inspired boarding school, this one in northern Idaho, her fifth placement in two years. I was fully aware that that would be my next stop if I kept going, and I wasn't real excited about that prospect.

My mom was dealing with her runaway career and all that came with it, indentured to keeping that good insurance and making money to provide therapy for us kids forever. I knew from day one where her relationship with Tom was headed, and I didn't want to witness any more of it. My extended family had been ostracized and cast out by Tom, and the rift felt irreparable.

I knew I was never going to catch up to everyone else. I was never going to get my period or lose enough weight to be lovable and impregnable, and I would never have those babies I desperately wanted.

I sat down. When the others had completely disappeared, I took off my pack and lay down in the dust. I let the sun hit my face. I breathed deeply for a while, put my arms and legs out and maximized my surface area to collect all the elements like a solar panel made of flab and stink. I heard the birds above and imagined them being curious, but then losing interest in this huge prey they could never carry. I wondered if there were vultures or buzzards nearby. I listened for their less birdlike, more pterodactyl cries but instead I just heard coyotes. Meh, that would work.

This was perfect. I hadn't felt such calm since I was a little kid lying on the warm sidewalk-chalked pavement outside my house the first weeks after a long Colorado winter. Something about the air smelled exactly the same. Nothing tumultuous was happening. The only chaos around was various kinds of tiny life finding ways to survive, and, ironically, I felt like I was doing the same by lying here to die. I was keeping alive the untouchable part of me by removing all that threatened it. I had to hurry before it was too late.

I wasn't sad. I wasn't angry. I was happy and at peace for the first time in forever. It was okay. I was okay. The people I loved knew I loved them. I forgave all perceived sins against me, and I forgave myself for all the things I had done. I started to drift off.

I heard scrambling steps coming out of the brush. I hoped it was my coyote, but it was Chad.

"Get up, Jenny."

Oh! He didn't know that I was serious. He thought I was still playing one of my dramatic little games made to test his patience and punish him for choosing a career exploiting fucked-up teens. Of course he did. I had changed a lot in the last five minutes and was different now, but there was no way he could know that. It wasn't his fault. I decided to gently enlighten him in a final gesture of grace.

"It's okay, Chad. I'm happy and at peace and I'm ready to go. Please tell my sisters and brother that I love them very much and I will watch over them . . ."

"GET UP."

I figured his insistence was a test to see how badly I really wanted this so that he would feel no regret having respected my last wishes.

"I'm okay. I promise. Just let me go. "

He seemed to finally understand as he took some steps away from me. I relaxed into the heat as it evaporated the remaining water from my body. I squeezed my eyes shut, content that Chad was on his way to deliver my messages. I couldn't hear his hiking boots dragging through the cacti anymore. I started to fall into that high-on-the-beach sleep where you get heavier and heavier until you enter a fairytale slumber. Not sleep, but slumber.

I was almost gone when I felt what I assumed was a buzzard swooping into the side of my face to tear off a hunk of cheek meat for lunch. Though I was expecting and welcoming it, the pain still startled me and began to wake me. Coming through the subconscious layers back into consciousness felt like it took hours. My eyes struggled to focus on this buzzard. He was large and looming, his wing extended. He was . . . wearing a Patagonia windbreaker? Wait. This wasn't a bird of prey. That was not a wing. It was an extended arm with an open hand. I felt my cheek. It was still intact but stung from Chad's sweaty-palmed slap.

"GET UP!" he ordered. I shot up drunkenly in a double daze from the sun and the smack.

"Don't you ever—EVER—put your hands on me aga—" I began to growl.

Thunk. He slapped me again. In the same place. Same force. I felt lava pouring from all my chakras. I jumped to my feet.

"I AM GONNA LIVE BUT JUST LONG ENOUGH TO TAKE YOU DOWN," I yelled. "I'M GOING TO TELL EVERYONE WHAT YOU DID."

I marched along the path toward the group, who were an hour ahead of me now. I was going to tell Mark, the psychologist who made weekly visits to us at our campsites, that Chad had hit me. "You'll be fired and put in jail for assaulting a minor. . . ."

Chad followed behind me, carrying my pack in his hands. I had left it behind in my hurry to destroy him. I had no use for earthly possessions. They didn't matter anymore. I had one sole purpose on the Earth. I had never hiked this fast. I continued to threaten him from steps ahead until he finally ended my grumbling with, "Who do you think they're gonna believe? Me, or a fuckup?" I was stunned into silence and even angrier than before.

In my very humble opinion, I was not actually a fuckup. I had never so much as touched a drug except the one time I was dressing up in my parents' closet and smelled a strange yet identifiable smell that I tracked like a truffle pig until my nose rested on the pocket of my mom's bathrobe. I reached my hand in and pulled out a half-smoked joint. I couldn't believe my parents had drugs! Who were these people? What other secrets were they hiding? I put the joint to my mouth and pulled stale air through it, tasting ashtray with a hint of flower. The taste instantly took me back to the sickness I felt after smoking a Merit cigarette Jessica stole from my mom's ashtray when we were seven and eight. I put the joint away, as I did the memory of the experience, to throw in my parents' faces later.

I hadn't been drunk since the time Jake and I polished off a bottle of Manischewitz on Passover, falling asleep under the dining room table among the swollen ankles and too-long toenails of our extended family.

I had never been in trouble with the law.

The main complaints against me were that I didn't respect authority and that I was fat. I was a mouthy fat little bitch, but I was not a fuckup. In my mind, everything I did was in reaction to someone or something unjust around me. I never sought out trouble on my own, though maybe I had made a few bad decisions to impress friends.

This asshole had hit me twice and called me a fuckup after thwarting my plans for a peaceful death, and now he needed to be destroyed. When we got to camp, he took my knife and shoes and made me sit away from the group and the fire. I used the time to plan what I was going to tell Mark—how I was going to reveal in a dramatic way what Chad had done. I wanted him humiliated before being fired. I wanted him to hear a superior say, "What were you thinking?" while I stared at his face.

When Mark came the next day, I waited for the other six kids to have their meeting with him first, since I was sure what I was going to say was going to create such a huge commotion, no one else would be able to get their weekly session or letter from their parent. When it finally came to my turn, I was shaking and emotional and losing my nerve, but I kept reminding myself how my cheek stung after being jarred back into this pudgy corpse against my will, and I forced myself to.

"Chad hit me," I said, trying to stay angry so I wouldn't cry.

"Why?" Mark asked.

Why.

I wasn't prepared for this question. I started crying and turned slightly so Chad couldn't see my face from across camp.

"Well, I was lying down on the trail and he wanted me to get up. No one else was around so he hit me. *Twice.*"

"I'll talk to Chad about that." His tone was more dismissive toward me than reassuring.

Chad was right. In everyone's eyes, I was a fuckup, and that alone *made* me a fuckup. And that made Chad a saint of a man who chose to spend his time on Earth helping out fuckups. He was the hero here, no matter what transpired, and I knew it. I knew he knew I knew it. But I absolutely refused to let him intimidate me into being silent, and that was going to have to be enough for me.

"Good," I said loudly, as I shot Chad a glare to let him know I had told on him.

The last couple weeks of survival were monotonous, but we got a lot more rest than usual. We were in the final phase, which was more about reflection than it was about hiking. We stayed at one campsite for a few days at a time before moving to the next one, which was only a couple miles away. There was time to dry out my clothes and sleeping bag and do a lot of journaling. As my body recovered a bit, so did my will to live. Eventually, I started to find tiny bits of pleasure in the privileges of the last phase. We got toilet paper. No more pinecones! This was great until we realized the main disadvantage of combining toilet paper with low-impact camping: having to keep the used pieces in a ziplock to burn in the fire at night. We had been desensitized by the small brown paper bags the girls would have to set alight when they had their periods, the paper disintegrating in the flames long before the tampons did. This was the first time I felt grateful for my late period. We did this after cooking dinner, at least.

We also got a doughnut. Remember how we ate a can of peaches only days after our last meal? Imagine then what ensued after two months. This doughnut cannot be described, but I will say that, as it hit the sweet buds on the back of my tongue, I forgave Chad and figured he had done the only thing he could do, and I felt grateful to him for this extra moment on Earth. Don't worry, though. The second I swallowed the last bite, my contempt returned.

It was almost over, and most of me had survived.

The day before Run In (the equivalent of a graduation ceremony), I tried one last time to complete a bow drill fire. I got closer than I ever had, but as the punk started smoking, my arm gave out. Chris saw how close I was and jumped on my bow with me, going so fast my arm fat-slapped against my sweaty armpit. We made a tandem ember and I dropped it into a nest and gently blew it into flames. We counted that as a success. My peers all cheered for me, able to be supportive now that they knew they'd never have to listen to me whine or see me again after tomorrow. I played along with their cheering, but I was indifferent. Though I was the only one who knew it, I had already showcased my survival skills weeks ago on that endless solo and had already Gotten My Fire.

13.

"Freeze! Police!"

Immediately after the Aspen Achievement Academy's graduation ceremony, I climbed into Tom's rented luxury vehicle and headed to the airport. He had volunteered to pick me up since my mom was too busy. I will never forget what sliding into the cushioned leather seat felt like after two months of sitting only on rocks. It was like my body was flooded with opiates and all my weight was distributed perfectly. No sharp corners dug into my tailbone. No nerves were pressed. I sank into the marshmallowness of it and ran my hands all over the clean interior. I caught my face in the rearview and was shocked. I hadn't seen my reflection in months, and I looked completely different than I did last time I had seen myself in the base camp bathroom as I handed my piss to a staff member.

I was thinner. I had lost about twenty-five pounds, but it looked more like forty, since I had gained muscle. I was tan, but I couldn't tell how much of that was a thick layer of dirt. My hair was sun-bleached and filthy and, juxtaposed against the rich cream interior of the car, I looked absolutely disgusting.

I couldn't get on a plane in this condition, so we stopped at the tiny motel nearby and I took a shower. For the past two months, the only bathing I had done was in freezing cold rivers. We had no soap, just a bandanna to scrub as much dead skin and forest duff off our limbs as we could. To have a constant stream of hot water running over me while I used actual shampoo made me feel like Cinderella after her marriage. I had taken everything for granted since I had been born, and I started making a mental list of these things while I watched the very dark water swirl in the drain. Ice, toilet paper, doors, *electricity*, cooked food, *cheese*. I kept washing and washing until the water ran clear. I realized I was going to be able to sleep in a bed that night and was overcome with joy. Maybe survival had been good for me, even if it was only for the perspective of how bad it had been and the fact that it was over, not because of the primitive skills I had acquired or the therapeutic program I had undergone.

Pretty soon after arriving back home, Jake had his Bar Mitzvah. He had been taking classes while Jessica and I were locked up. I guess that was how they kept him busy as the only child in the home. Now that Tom had converted and we had a relationship with the rabbi at our local temple, it only made sense that he should become a Bar Mitzvah. Jessica and I were lost causes by this point, and I doubt we would have been allowed the daily Torah and Hebrew classes needed in our institutions, so all the family's Jewishness fell on Jake.

The party was at the same temple where Tom and Mom's second wedding had been held. It was a serious extravaganza, with live music and elaborate decorations and food. Jake's favorite comic at the time, Kevin Meaney, performed, though he made it obvious that he was not thrilled about the gig. All of Jake's friends were there. He had a beautiful cake that took up a whole table and had chocolate sculptures and elaborate paintings on it. No carob-covered strawberries for this genetic lottery winner! At the end of the party, an assistant drove a brand-new Jeep into the room with a bow on it. Jake was thirteen, so it would sit in storage for two years, much as his sisters had.

Suddenly it all became too much for me: the joyful celebration, singing and dancing, the Jeep, the fucking cake . . . I wasn't feeling jealous or resentful, just sad. I had been disenfranchised from Jake's life for so long that I didn't recognize most of his friends, and that broke my heart. I felt like I couldn't relate to anyone anymore. I slunk out of the party and went to find somewhere to cry.

I walked down a long hallway and discovered an office with a bathroom next to it. There was no one anywhere near, so I went in, checked that I was alone, and started weeping. After about ten minutes, I realized that my lower abdomen was aching and cramping. I had never felt anything quite like it and figured I was finally about to get my period. Maybe I was having a Bat Mitzvah after all, here alone in the rabbi's bathroom. The thought made me laugh, and I collected myself and went back to the party.

I was exhausted when we got home later that night, and I passed out in my clothes. When I woke up the next morning, I went to pee and saw that I was bleeding. I had become a woman in my sleep, after weeping my way through a party. For some reason, that made sense to me. I sat for a moment thinking about what this meant—how long I had waited and how desperate I had been to start my period a couple of years before. But now, I did not want one single more thing on my plate.

I said, "Fuck," dug through the under-the-sink cabinet, found Jessica's tampons, and put one in. That was it, the big moment I had been waiting for. I went back to bed.

Another year of school started just a few days later. This time I went to a continuation school right across the street from CPC. A couple of my friends from the fucked-up kid circuit were there, and that made it less awkward. I was doing okay and making friends and getting decent grades. The classes were short and the pressure was low and the art studio was full of supplies and covered in amazing canvases. I liked it there. I met a boy named Ricky who came to school on a scooter every day and we started dating.

He saved money for months to buy me a bottle of White Diamonds perfume by Liz Taylor, and I reluctantly wore it to make him happy, even though it gave me instant migraines, because that is what love is.

A few months into the year, and I was in trouble again. My dad had randomly seen me riding on the back of Ricky's scooter and he busted me. I had a helmet on, so I wasn't in as much trouble as I would have been, and my dad didn't know that I had been on that scooter many times before.

One of those times was to go to a motel on Pico Boulevard, a tiny, filthy little pit. Ricky saved up more money and instead of buying me perfume, he rented us a room. I knew what happened in motels and I was terrified but excited. Now that I'd had my period for a full four months, I was ready for my next step into womanhood. Ricky went inside the office to check us in, and I stayed outside smoking a cigarette. I wasn't sure we were going to pull this off. I was fifteen but looked twelve, with my pudgy, makeup-less face and my baby fat, but apparently those kinds of establishments don't care about that much.

Once inside the room, we sat on the bed and both immediately rolled into the concave center of the deteriorated mattress. We laughed and kissed and lost our virginities for the most part. Then we packed up and got on the scooter, and he took me home.

It was anticlimactic, as was getting my period and, I would discover over time, everything else, too. Later that week, when my mom and Tom were away and the live-in nanny, Sharon, was watching us, I decided to sneak Ricky into our house for another shot. I gave him detailed instructions about how to bypass all the gates and alarm systems of a proper Brentwood celebrity's home. I turned my TV to the channel with the correct security camera feed and waited the twenty minutes it took for him to drive from his house to mine. This was clearly before cell phones, so I could do nothing but watch him and cheer him on silently. I waited to see him approach the gate and punch in the code, and then I watched him walk through.

When he got to the front door, I switched to another channel to watch him punch the next code in. I couldn't see his hands, just his shoulder, and I watched them jiggle a bit until he disappeared into the open doorway.

I heard the beeping of the alarm inside the house, and then I heard his clumsy attempts to turn it off. Over and over. I knew you only got three attempts and he was already on two, so I ran to the panel on the second floor just in time to hear him make a third attempt. The alarm started screeching and echoing down the hallways. I was trying to shut it off from the panel on the second floor when Ricky ran by me. I told him to go to my room and hide and I'd take care of it. I typed in the right code and the wailing stopped. Now I just had to wait for the alarm company to call and ask for our password. That would stop the police from coming. The next problem to solve would be Sharon. She had been sleeping downstairs but was wide awake now, terrified that we were being robbed. I feigned calmness as I answered the alarm company's phone call and gave them our password. I told the man on the other end that I had set the alarm off by going outside for a cigarette and apologized. He did not give a shit.

I showed Sharon that I'd handled it and told her I was going to bed. She stared suspiciously at me for a minute and then went to bed, too. I was proud of my acting and believed she had bought my story.

Ricky slept over and we had sex, and then he sneaked out early in the morning. The problem was, Sharon had not been as convinced as I thought she was and had reviewed the security camera footage from the night before. She pieced together the truth and told my mom and Tom, who confronted me the next day.

I tried to lie about it, but they had hard evidence, so I had to admit that I had sneaked my boyfriend in. I didn't tell them that we'd had sex, but I didn't need to. Why else would a teen girl sneak a boy into her house and keep him there overnight? They were pissed. I would have to lie low for a while if I didn't want to get sent away again

For Hanukkah a few days later, Tom gave me a humongous stuffed gorilla from FAO Schwarz, and as I was dutifully thanking him and cuddling it, he said, "Now you don't have to sneak anyone into your room when you want to hump something." I was humiliated and mad and stormed off, wondering if the jokes would ever end.

Later that week, we went to visit Jessica in northern Idaho at Rocky Mountain Academy to celebrate Christmas with her. This was another CEDU school like the one Jessica had escaped from in California a couple of years back. This campus was also tucked into the mountains, but ones that bordered Canada. It had the same Synanon-based philosophy and curriculum, but it was much harder to run away from since it was so much farther from any true civilization. The closest town, Bonners Ferry, was seven miles away and boasted a ski resort, a movie theater, and a police station . . . Oh! And the Aryan Nations headquarters. There might have been a Subway or McDonald's, too, but I didn't see them.

We found out later that an employee of RMA had been fired for plotting to kidnap Barbara Walters's daughter (Barbara Walters was the one who had suggested CEDU schools to my mom) and Clint Eastwood's son, and any other "high-profile kids or Jews," hold them for ransom to fund white supremacist activities for their KKK branch, and hide them at a stocked base at the bottom of a nearby mountain. That was the beginning of the infamous Ruby Ridge incident where the apocalyptic fundamentalist and white separatist Randy Weaver was surrounded by FBI agents in his cabin and shot at; his wife and son were killed. The standoff lasted almost two weeks, and all the students at RMA had to wear reflective orange vests while doing their chores in the woods until it was over.

I had heard that Jessica was doing great and loved RMA, that she was a new person, and I was relieved. I couldn't wait to see her. This would be the first time in a while that Jake and I would get to spend some time with her, and it felt the way Christmas should feel.

The campus was beautiful and snowy. The wooden buildings, all constructed by students over the last twenty years, looked cozy and warm, with smoke pouring out the chimneys. Inside the Family Area, as they called it, there were about ten different seating sections with a few couches and chairs in each. To the left was a huge room full of wooden picnic benches, where the students ate three times a day. The kitchen was open and busy with local women making fresh bread and granola and meals that, with the giant wood fire in the middle of the family room, made the whole building smell like heaven.

When we finally were reunited, we jumped up and rushed Jessica to hug her, and she hugged us back. She looked great. She was wearing normal, Midwestern mountain clothing and her hair was its natural color. No more black hair in her face, no more corpse makeup. I truly believed she was doing better and was hopeful she would be able to come home soon. I didn't understand that this place was a two-and-a-half-year program, though, and when I heard that, I was devastated. She would be eighteen by then and obviously would go out on her own. We would never live together again. I thought, This is it! We'll just be going our separate ways from here on out.

Jessica got permission from staff to spend some alone time with me to apologize for the ways she had treated me back home. Was this real?! I had been waiting for an apology since the first time she peeked over the side of my bassinet with the look of murder in her eyes and tried to knock me out of it. She kept up her perfect little amends-making prin-cess ruse until the moment we were on our own.

"Give me any money you have," she demanded. Oh no. It was old Jessica in disguise. She was still there scheming, and "doing better" was part of the act. "I'm running away in a few days with my friend, and we need money for food."

I was instantly defensive, since I'd been warned a million times that she was going to manipulate me and that my idiotic codependent ass would be unable to say no to her, and she would use me to do dumb shit that would get her in trouble and jeopardize her life. I was told how to handle these interactions. I was supposed to Refuse to Be Manipulated and stand up for myself and tell on her. I said I couldn't give her any money and I told her running away was dangerous and I was not going to be a party to putting her in harm's way. She grew silent and stared into my eyes, hypnotizing me.

"You know they're sending you here next month, right?" she asked me in a low and serious voice. "They're just waiting for me to advance a group so we're not in the same one. They've signed all the paperwork." I refused to believe her and told her that was a low blow as far as ma-nipulating me, but somewhere inside I thought she might be telling the truth. I gave her all I had, which was twenty dollars and my mascara and lipstick, and I went home the next day, confused.

Guess what happened the following month? I was told I was going to RMA. Because Jessica had warned me, I was mostly resigned, and all my fight was gone. I wouldn't mind being near that wood-burning fire eating those fresh rolls and hanging out with Jessica, and because it was a long program, it would be my last. I wouldn't have to wonder when the bounty hunters would be coming next. I wouldn't be locked in some tower with no fresh air. At least there was a farm with chickens and sheep and pregnant horses and crops.

The night that my mom and Tom told me I was going to RMA, I had a scheduled PDAP meeting at a nearby church with several friends, like Ryder and Merida, and staff from Van Nuys Psych. I was going with the intention of saying goodbye, but as I sat outside telling Ryder and Me-rida where my fate was taking me, I got so sad. Merida said, "Nah, let's run away instead," and so we did. We left before the meeting was over, about twenty minutes before Sharon was due to pick me up. Merida was sixteen and had a car, so we climbed in and drove from Beverly Hills to the Valley. We crashed at her friend's place for the night and then, in the morning, decided we needed to leave her car behind. It was exhilarating, but I don't like being exhilarated. I was on high alert, knowing that our parents would have called the police by now, and we weren't taking any chances. We walked from the house to a bus stop and mapped out how to get to Venice Beach.

Our friend Lucas lived right near the Santa Monica Pier. His mom had been one of our counselors at Van Nuys Psych, and Lucas was also in the program. There were a lot of families that had multiple members in recovery. One person would get sober, inspiring a kid or parent to get sober, too. Whole families were in the program together. There was usually one sibling among them that was in treatment for codependency. Although Lucas's mom was very cool, I knew she'd do "the right thing" and turn us in. I also knew she would be at work and that Lucas would be home, and sensitive to our situation.

We got off the bus and walked to his place. Merida knew where everything was, thankfully, and easily maneuvered her way through the small beach town streets. I have always managed to befriend people who make up for my navigational shortcomings, especially while crime doing. When Lucas answered the door, he told us that everyone was looking for us and that Tom and my mom had called and threatened everyone at the PDAP meeting the night before. We asked Lucas if we could stay with him, and of course he said no. He didn't want to get in the middle of anything, especially anything involving my mom and Tom and their limitless resources. He did help us look in the phone book for a nearby shelter that took teens off the street with no questions asked. We wrote the info down and he gave us each an apple as he escorted us out of his apartment.

Merida and I followed the directions to the address we had written down, and stopped a couple blocks away from it to sit on the curb and enjoy a cigarette. As we sat there smoking, cars passed us by, their drivers eyeing us with pity and fear. We looked like street kids. I was avoiding their stares by looking down at my own feet, and that's when I noticed the very shiny bumper of a car pulling up just a little too close. I looked up to see Tom behind the wheel of his Bentley that my mom had gifted him. I hated this car. It was uncomfortable and beyond tacky and cost enough for a family to live comfortably on for five years, ten if they lived like we had before my mom's fame. Tom had once volunteered us to feed homeless people on Thanksgiving at a local shelter, and he drove this fucking ridiculous car there. Jessica made him drop us off a block away before we walked in to help.

Now that it was pulled up to my shin, I hated it more. I turned to look at Merida, and she jumped up and just ran. I would have, too, if I hadn't been so out of shape. Tom got out of the car and approached me with a wild look in his eyes, and I panicked and wrapped my arms around a lamppost and started screaming, "HELP! HELP! I DON'T KNOW THIS MAN!" Tom was yanking on me, trying to get me into the car, but not before my knight in shining armor could rescue me.

A man about five feet tall and covered head to toe in tattoos (long before that was a thing) came running out of his apartment screaming at Tom. I was so relieved. Until I realized he was screaming, "FREEZE! POLICE!" He had tucked his pointed forefinger like a gun into the waist of the boxers he wore with nothing else. I could tell his bare feet were hot on the asphalt as he ran like Yosemite Sam across the street to save me. Not super-believable, guy. You could have just presented as a high-as-fuck gang member, and that would have been scary enough, but, if you're out there, I appreciate you trying. No one else tried to save me. You're still my hero for that.

Tom was fixated on bringing me to my mom like a trophy animal, and since Merida was gone and I had nowhere else to go, I let my arms slip off the lamppost and I got into the back of the Bentley, swearing like a sailor.

The ride home was awful, with Tom bragging to me the entire way about how he had outsmarted me by threatening Louie. Louie had called Tom the second we left his apartment and gave us up without so much as a tiny, time-buying bit of small talk. Being friends with people in recovery was a crapshoot. Sometimes they would be your ride-or-die, and sometimes they'd transform into your concerned parent. This had more to do with where they were at in their recovery than where you were at in yours. It was hard to tell who to trust as a runaway, and I had chosen wrong.

I woke up the next morning with the familiar bounty hunters in my house. Sharon turned my plane ticket over to them and they offered to carry my luggage. It was far more cordial this time. We were old pals by now. We flew to Coeur d'Alene, Idaho, with no drama. Once we were off the plane, a van met us and drove us the two hours to Bonners Ferry. I was handed over from the bounty hunters to the school administration, where I started yet another intake procedure.

I didn't fight. I was happy I would get to be with Jessica again. That is, until she ran away with the money I gave her a few days later and got sent to a different place. She came back, though, and over the next two years we were together more often than we weren't.

A girl I had seen with Jessica when I came to visit greeted me as soon as I was escorted from the admissions building to the House, the room we had met in a few weeks before. She said, "Oh, you're here now? Your sister told me that was gonna happen."

"Yeah. She told me, too. I didn't believe her." Her name was Beckie and she told me the reason she didn't have eyebrows was because she shaved them off after smoking pot and watching Pink Floyd's *The Wall*. We became immediate friends.

After Jessica ran away and I realized that that was an option, Beckie and I and a girl named Mia decided we were going to run away next. We decided to meet in the wood corral at dusk, the place where we chopped whole trees down into various sizes of wood for all the stoves in all the buildings on campus.

Mia and Beckie made it, but I got caught immediately, and they were forced to leave without me. A counselor took me upstairs to an office and grilled me on the details of our plan. I played dumb. Suddenly I was aware of my aloneness here and I started to cry. I cried for hours and couldn't stop. I was tired of being left behind. Thankfully, they were gone only a few hours before the cops brought them back. They were put on Booths, which referred to the hard wooden booths in the dining room they would have to sit at for six hours a day doing writing assignments instead of participating in the regular daily activities. On a Booth, you could talk only to students preapproved by the staff, and you were on Bans (actively banned) from everyone else. This meant no sign language or eye contact or note passing or anything. Booths lasted anywhere from a day to a week and were the mid-level consequence for misbehaving. If you Broke Bans, or Broke Agreements while on a Booth, you were punished further with a Full Time. Full Times were the more serious punishment. They were mainly the same thing as Booths, but longer and with more restrictions. These punishments usually lasted weeks. On both Booths and Full Times, you had Work Assignments, which meant that, instead of school, you did manual labor alone somewhere. This was anything from logging to landscaping to building rock walls by stacking rocks you collected around campus, to cleaning and organizing nooks and crannies, or Working the Toolshed, which meant you were in charge of checking tools in and out for other kids on Work Assignments.

Occasionally a Work Assignment would be something with spiritual intent. I was ordered to build a rose garden once because I "had to create a beautiful space to make up for the negative spaces I had made." There was always meaning attached to everything, and the rules were malleable for that reason. It was up to the staff member who knew you best, your Family Head, to curate your course of treatment.

By the end of the two-and-a-half-year program, you were so indoctrinated into RMA's particular brand of therapy that you spoke a different language than everyone else on Earth. Part of the therapy was extreme confrontation, which was mostly done in Raps. These were intensive group therapy sessions that lasted three hours, three times a week. There were also seven longer versions throughout the program that went anywhere from twenty-four hours to seven days, called Propheets.

In these Raps, your friends, enemies, Family Heads, or other staff would indict you. Being indicted was scary. You had no idea it was coming until a person you knew you had wronged or hurt got up from wherever they were sitting in the giant circle of chairs and switched seats with whoever was directly across from you. They would then say your name and the reason they had requested you. "Jenny, I requested you today because you made me feel unsafe last night when you talked about wanting to smoke cigarettes."

Sometimes the indictments were trivial issues between dorm mates, like someone didn't take their clothes out of the dryer as soon as they were done, and so the other person had to do it for them and felt disrespected.

Other times, they were hysterical, hyperventilating, primal-scream sessions where the indicter would Take Care of Their Feelings about a friend doing something scary like Splitting and OD'ing. These would start with a confrontation of the other person, but would turn into an internalized struggle during which the indicter would process their own feelings about having been scared or hurt. They would lean over their own legs and look at the ground while Running Their Shit.

This meant giving voice to all the dark thoughts in your head and letting them out so they wouldn't fester and control you. While Running Your Shit, you would often drip snot and tears, and the person sitting next to you would grab a box of Kleenex and lay five or so tissues out under the snotfall. When you were done, you'd grab the stack of wet tissues and clean up your fluids, then sit back to collect yourself, exhausted. A staff member or facilitator would gently move the group's attention away to the next person.

Screaming so hard you pour snot out of all your face holes with no self-consciousness was cathartic as fuck, and even though you'd feel a slight sense of shame for the deep vulnerability you'd exposed, you would be too exhausted to care. It felt much the same way that you felt as a child when you wept until you had diaphragm spasms. You released everything and then would sleep so peacefully afterward.

Staff were able to indict students, which seemed cruel at times, since the line between adult and kid was blurred by our shared emotional vulnerabilities. Students were able to indict staff as well, but if you confronted staff for shady behavior, one of their golden children or, as we called them, Look Goods, would defend them. There were some fucked-up dynamics I don't have time to break down. I'll let the several cult documentaries, whistleblower websites, Facebook survivor pages, nonprofits, tell-alls, and the very excellent CEDUlegacy.org website made about these schools do it, and you can either spare yourself or look into it further if you want.

My experience of RMA was unique for several reasons, but the most obvious was, once again, having a celebrity mom. Everyone always wanted to appease my mom, which, at this time, meant appeasing Tom, who was her mouthpiece. CEDU schools were originally set up as an alternative to the psychotherapy world, and medications weren't allowed here. If someone needed to be medicated, then RMA was not the right place for them. Tom couldn't accept that there was more than one way to get sober or deal with emotional problems. The cults of AA, psychiatry, and Synanon were colliding, and Jessica and I were the pivot point. Tom hated that I wasn't seeing a psychiatrist, and he threatened to sue the school for malpractice if they didn't hire one. To appease him, I was sent outside the school to a psychiatrist in town, a man named Dr. Walden.

As soon as I walked into Dr. Walden's office, a cold chill went through me. I have felt the coldness I felt in his presence only a few times in my life. He was a vacuum. A black hole. His eyes were like Third Reich medals. He asked me questions, and I refused to answer them. He wasn't answering any of my questions; why should I answer his? Minutes into our appointment, he said he believed I needed medication. I asked him what made him believe that, and he looked at me with such disgust and disdain that I snapped and started yelling at him.

"You don't know me! You don't know shit! You're trying to appease people at my expense, so fuck you!" I got up and stormed out. I was put on Lithobid, a form of lithium, and after having my blood taken two weeks later to see if there was any damage to my liver from the new medication, it was discovered that I had been cheeking the pills. I tried to blame the lab to buy myself time, but instead they switched me to a liquid version and watched me swallow it and then open my mouth. There was no way around it, and within days, I was a shell of myself.

I felt like I was under a spell, like I was someone else entirely. My sense of humor was gone, as was my desire to be around people I loved. I lay in my bed refusing to do the day's activities, only moving when the urge to destroy myself outweighed my apathy. I punched the wall over and over until my hand was numb and my knuckles were raw and swollen. I was like Frodo when he wears the ring too long. The bad guys had gotten to me and I was sick. My Big Sister (not Jessica, but an assigned older student) came to try to talk me into being alive again, but when she saw the state I was in, she just hugged me, walked out, and told my Family Head that I probably needed to go off the meds, and somehow they helped me make that happen and let me quit seeing Walden. RMA did not want me on medication, either, but they had to at least prove that they had tried.

When Tom heard this, he was furious that I was allowed to manipulate my way out of yet another treatment plan, and he called the school and demanded they hire an on-site psychiatrist. The school was adamantly against this, but to avoid being outed as alternative therapy and sued into oblivion, they settled on a psychologist. He was hired and had an office in the school administration building and was there three days a week. He only had two patients: Jessica and me.

It seemed like the addition of this new element tore a hole in the CEDU fabric, and soon after, the psychologist started seeing some of the other kids. The school split into two, and my beloved farm was turned into a separate school called Boulder Creek Academy that allowed for kids on medication. Now there was a strange segregation, and no one knew where I belonged. I was sent from RMA to Boulder Creek Academy just hundreds of feet away, but a universe apart. I was again with strangers. After I begged, Beckie was allowed to come visit me for an hour, and when I saw her, I realized I had to get out of this situation. This time, I did manipulate. I pleaded. I charmed. I pulled out *all* the stops. A week later, I was moved back up to the RMA campus, where my friends and my sister were.

My mom and Tom came to visit me during this time. Our visits were different from everyone else's. We were sequestered in private rooms where the other parents couldn't gawk. That also meant that Mom and Tom didn't have to complete any of the group therapy parts of the program that were intended to bring self-awareness to the role that parents played in the conflict tango. They were also meant to create empathy and understanding for the work we kids were doing, but Mom and Tom were exempt. We also had a private security guard to stand outside the room. Our visits lasted hours instead of days because my mom had to get back to her shooting schedule. All of these special circumstances made our time more like prison visits than the kind of family weekends everyone else had.

I was worried about my mom. She seemed a shadow of herself, completely withdrawn, but I thought it was just me: she was done with me, and her apathy was my fault. I had pushed too far. I wasn't worth the pain I caused. She didn't look like herself at all. She had had several plastic surgery procedures that had transformed her into a goth Russian version of herself, and she read way too much into everything I said. I had witnessed her slow retreat in the small ways I could when I was around her since the divorce from my dad, but I thought she was just overwhelmed with work and paparazzi stuff, and I didn't know how to help. I figured that letting Tom take over aspects of her life was her only way of coping, so I played along where I could.

I had limits, though. During one of these visits, Tom told me he'd like to go for a walk with me so I could get some exercise and we could bond. I was reluctant because these things always ended in disappointment, but also I was positive that, at some point, a spontaneous understanding of me would come over my parents, and they would all of a sudden just love me. I wasn't going to stop trying until that happened. I still wanted their approval and their acceptance, even if I would die before admitting it. It was always just out of my reach. Maybe today was the day. I agreed to go, and we walked down to the farm, which took about fifteen minutes each way.

There was small talk at first. Tom asked me about the things he knew I was interested in. What was the art studio here like? Did I enjoy the pioneer-esque crafts? Were there any boys I thought were cute? Were Jessica and I getting along? The questions were personal enough that I let myself think they were expressions of actual interest and I let my guard down, ready to sing like a bird at the next question. He must have felt that, and so he cut to the chase.

"You really jeopardized my life back in LA. You know that, right? When you refused to get in the car and screamed that you didn't know me when you ran away."

"How so?"

"Well, that guy that came out to help you had a gun in his waistband."

Tom had been trying and trying to make this canon, but unfortunately I suck at being gaslit, and I had been denying it every time he tried.

"No, he didn't. He was wearing boxers and ran across the street. How could the gun have stayed in the elastic if that were true?"

Tom kept telling the same version over and over like the hypnotist I used to see to lose weight. Jedi mind tricks.

I now knew there would be no true bonding. This wasn't about my best interest. This was about him being vindicated. I was mad now and I shouted, "WE WERE BOTH THERE!"

As soon as I yelled, I lost. This was me being out of control. This was me being resistant. This was proof I had not grown. This was disrespect, an inability to communicate calmly and rationally. He didn't have what he came for, but he had something.

He said we should go back, and I agreed. When we did, he reported to my mom and counselors that I was defiant and verbally abusive, which made me defiant and verbally abusive, proving his point. They cut the visit short and went home. I wept for days while I watched everyone else's parents roam the campus learning the lingo, and when I wasn't weeping, I was staring forlornly out the nearest window. I had lost my chance at being loved. I hated myself for being so stubborn. I should have just said I was sorry.

My peers would bring their parents up to introduce Roseanne's daughter to them. I tried to be gracious, but I was so fucking empty inside. Some took my sorrow for aloofness and acted as if I was a spoiled brat who was ungrateful to meet the people who had put my mom up on that pedestal from which I had benefited. Some would gush and gush and not see how deeply it hurt me. Some would go out of their way to let me know they weren't interested. Some would ask me about episodes of the show.

"I don't know. I haven't seen it. We don't have TV here," I would tell them.

Jessica got the same reactions, but instead of brooding like I did, she would act out. She would be more daring and more fun. All my friends always wanted to hang out with her. Pretty much right after this visit, Jessica won the privilege of going on a Town Trip. This meant being able to go into Bonners Ferry with a couple of friends for a few hours. What seemed like privileges were sometimes tests to see if you could Handle It. Handle It meant two things: (1) handling real-world situations in responsible ways, and (2) not giggling uncontrollably when someone said *boobs*.

When evening came around, I had a horrible feeling for no reason, and I went to stand outside and see what I was picking up. I call this zombie-ing, because there is an electrical impulse at the base of my brain that takes over and I will just kind of go to the place where I need to be. I'm smart enough not to try to figure it out, other than just feeling grateful and saying thank you, though I'm not sure who I'm thanking.

As I stood outside, I saw Scott, one of the two friends Jessica had gone to town with. He was pacing frantically on the porch of the administration building. He was alone. He looked really scared. My heart dropped and my knees got wobbly and I went to walk toward him, but a staff member collected him before I could. I went to my sister's Dorm Head, Allie, and asked where Jessica was. She wouldn't answer me and I finally got it out of her that her Family Head, Carla, had demanded no one tell me anything. Why the fuck would she do that? Mostly because she was a sociopath who preyed on kids and existed on drama. I backed Allie into a corner with questions, and she said, "Carla wants to wait for a Rap tomorrow and she's gonna tell you in there." This girl was brainwashed and it was no use trying to get info out of her, so I decided to go to Carla's house, which was on campus. I don't remember walking over to her house and I don't remember how my Big Sister Katie ended up with me, but I was glad she was there. I banged on Carla's door, and when she answered I lunged forward, but Katie grabbed my sweater and held me in place.

"Where is my sister?"

Carla didn't answer. I assumed she was sizing me up to see how much danger she was in, and when she looked in my eyes, she backed down a bit. Her control was lost.

"WHERE IS MY SISTER? YOU DON'T GET TO NOT TELL ME."

"She OD'd." This was her way of getting the upper hand back, not saying immediately after that Jessica was alive and in the emergency room and stabilized. She took her time telling me that part.

She was like this, a special branch of predator. Predators were attracted to places like this because the kids were already half-groomed for them. Neglected. Wanting attention. Removed from parents.

Carla had been a student at CEDU before she was a staff member. She knew the system like the back of her hand, and she manipulated it for maximum entertainment. Had she never been entangled with CEDU, she would have been a mentalist or a hypnotherapist or a cult leader.

I sensed her predatory nature pretty quickly after being enrolled at RMA, and I had never liked her. She made sure to get all the mean kids on her Family Team, the alphas and others who were perceived as more valuable than us fat uglies. All the pretty skinny girls and all the buff jock types were in her group. They all worked out together. It was like picking teams in gym class. Jessica was in Carla's Family on account of being skinny and pretty and mean, and also because she was a celebrity's daughter. Carla wasn't going to let anyone else get Jessica.

When I was enrolled, I was told that Carla would probably be my Family Head, too. She came to meet me, and I was immediately placed on Bruce's Team. I was not cool enough for her. She largely ignored me after this, except to ask me personal questions about my mom, the answers to which she collected like baseball cards. Everything she did was for power.

Bruce's team was full of artists and animal lovers. They were mostly very gentle, and I liked them. However, Bruce was a gorgeous cowboy with black hair and the kindest blue eyes, and I could not even look at him due to my horrific crush on him. I did not want to blow snot on the floor of any room he graced. I did not want him talking to me about my bad attitude or fatness, so at some point, I transferred to another team.

No one knew where I fit and neither did I. Because of the inability to categorize me, my short temper, and my sharp tongue, everyone was always a little bit afraid of me, even the untouchable Carla. She averted her eyes from mine as I stood winded on her porch, both of us wondering if I was going to kick her ass. Katie still had ahold of my sweater but it was a loose hold. I was so fucking angry but so scared and so tired and it was all too real. I turned around and walked back to my dorm, where I lay in my bunk bed praying and crying.

I found out the next day that Jessica and the other girl on the town trip, Gianna, had taken a bunch of bronchodilators to get high. Trucker speed, as it was nicknamed. It was available over the counter at most truck stops and kept truckers alert on their long drives. The prescribed dose was a single pill, and they had each taken a handful. They went to watch a movie with Scott, who had luckily noticed they weren't well and called an ambulance, saving their lives.

Both girls had their stomachs pumped and their bodies flushed with charcoal. Gianna went into cardiac arrest and was harder to stabilize, but both of them were going to be okay. I wanted to see Jessica's face so badly just to guarantee that the nightmare was over and that she had indeed survived. I didn't trust anything anyone told me if I didn't see it with my own eyes. I heard she was transferred to a nearby drug rehab center later that night, where she would stay for a month. I'd have to wait.

In the meantime, I was assigned another Big Sister to help me deal with Jessica's being gone. It was Jessica's close friend, Angela, whom we all called "Shmee" because that was her childhood nickname. A lot of people went by their childhood nicknames here to connect them to their innocent beginnings. Shmee was hilarious and sweet and had a heart of gold and repeatedly told me that Jessica would be back soon and would be fine. Between her and Beckie, I was doing okay, but the reality check that Jessica had almost successfully killed herself with drugs would never leave me.

Fifteen years later, Shmee would be the one to die from an overdose, sending Jessica and all their mutual friends into a collective tailspin. I would draw a line later with an adult Jessica after watching her do a bump of coke from my minivan key. For now, I was mad at Carla. It was her fault, the system's fault, my parents' fault, fame's fault, the media's fault. I was pissed off at everything and everyone, and every experience was sinking me a bit deeper into the quicksand, but the promise of my nearing adulthood, my freedom, kept me going.

Every second of suffering and every struggle was getting me a little closer, and my fantasies and plans for cake, sex, and babies were just enough to keep me wanting to live.

13B.

The Difference Between Jokers and Jesters

There are jokers and there are jesters.

Jokers lie in wait, running everything through the fine combs of their brain to pick punch lines out like lice. They have to scrutinize everything to consciously live like this 24/7. They require constant praise to counter the universe of criticism they live in. They don't see themselves or anyone around them clearly because they have to bend reality to get to the joke. They cannot live in the present. Getting a laugh is their top priority. They are always mocking someone and victimizing someone to get that laugh. They have the best one-liners, and the worst relationships. They are exhausting. They are bullies. Jokers always think they're Jesters.

Jesters are truth-tellers. They make fun of thought patterns and zeitgeists. Their work is loving and merciful at its core. These are people who can see through bullshit and want to destroy it so we can all live in truth. Jesters love humanity. They want to contribute to its conscious elevation. They know the best way is through laughter. Their jokes are a nudge toward awareness. They are terrible at following social rules that protect Bullshit. They are always in the present. They are philosophers and philanthropists, best friends and role models. Your favorite grandparent. They are few and far between and should be treated like gold.

14.

I Was Mine Now

Just a few days after Jessica's overdose, Beckie decided she had had enough of this emotional growth bullshit and packed to run away. I could not have this. With Jessica gone, Beckie was my one and only, so I followed her ass on the seven-mile walk to town, begging her not to leave me, to come back, to wait out the next year or so until we graduated and could move into an apartment together. Beckie was a five-foot, eleven-inch Amazonian blond goddess of a woman, and I was not about to let her get nabbed and murdered by the pervert truckers all us kids had been warned about. Right before we got to town, a police car rolled up, and I flagged the officer down and asked him to take us back to RMA. He took us to the police station first, where Beckie tricked him into getting us ice cream before making his report and driving us back.

When we got there, I was very proud of myself for having saved Beckie's life, which is why I was so confused when I was treated like I had run away as well. I was put on a Booth and given writing assignments and told that I was manipulative and a liar and that I needed to admit that I had run away, too, even though Beckie corroborated my story.

The counselors almost believed me, but my mom and Tom didn't. They reminded the school of how convincing I could be, and just a day before my seventeenth birthday, I was punished by being sent to another survival program, this one in the nearby mountains of Montana. I was driven by an RMA staff member and dropped at a base camp. It had four or five canvas teepees and a giant mess tent out in the middle of nowhere on the bank of a small creek. I watched a couple kids my age walk down to it with five-gallon buckets filled with water. There were also some kids inside the mess tent cooking on primitive kitchen equipment. Some were reading quietly by themselves.

I was assigned a teepee to sleep in and went to set up my sleeping bag around the wood-burning stove in the center. From base camp, hiking expeditions would go out for a week at a time. I would have to wait two days for the team to return before the next one, leaving just enough time for me to celebrate my birthday with a thick emergency candle stuck into a PowerBar. Kids I didn't know and staff I didn't like sang to me. I blew out the flame, thinking about the fact that this was my last birthday as a minor. No matter how bad it would be, it would be my last year in captivity. Every miserable thing that happened after my next birthday would be mine. My choice. My fault. My problem. I was in the final year of my countdown to freedom.

The next day I witnessed a twenty-five-year-old staff member take down and restrain an attractive young girl because she called him a name. I could feel the perverted abuse of power, so I called him out while he was on top of her, and he jumped up, screaming at me, and told me that I was interfering with staff discipline or some shit. I was put on a solo a hundred feet away from camp. There would be no comfortable teepee for me. I got a familiar poncho tarp, some parachute cord, an insulation pad, a sleeping bag, a journal, and a pen and was sent into a bramblebush to spend the next two nights. They had taken my shoes away so I wouldn't run, and the first time I went to go pee, I realized that the ground was covered in thorns. My feet were full of tiny puncture wounds and, having squatted, I had also peed down my legs. I used my water bottle to clean myself and then I got straight to work making myself a pair of shoes. I sharpened a stick on a rock and crudely cut six inches of foam from the bottom of the insulation pad. I cut that in half and had two soles. I used a plant to make cordage the way Leroy had taught me on my last survival experience. I braided it into two lengths, punctured holes in the foam, and made a pair of slippers. I then urinated like a human being.

When the staff brought me dinner and saw I had invented shoes, they asked me what my plan was for running away. I was just trying to pee, I explained. They Refused to Be Manipulated, and here I was again. It was decided that instead of finishing my solo, I would immediately be put on Course, which meant hiking and sleeping outside with a group, like my last survival experience. I spent the next five weeks in the same loop of negativity I had been stuck in on other Wilderness Survivals: whining, having headaches, feeling like I couldn't do it.

Once, while traversing a rocky hillside, I slipped and turned my ankle. I couldn't walk, especially not with my sixty-pound pack, so I just sat down and cried. A boy named Brian came over to me and said, "I'll take your pack." How? He couldn't have weighed more than one hundred pounds himself, and our two packs together would outweigh him.

Well, he was going to hike miles to camp, drop his pack, hike back, and get mine.

I couldn't believe a person would volunteer to do this horrid fucking hike twice just to help me. He seemed to genuinely care that I was suffering, and to understand that all my dramatic whining and crying was just to have someone show me they cared about my suffering. For some reason, the gratitude I felt at his offer, maybe because no staff forced him to, made my mind do a flip and my entire perspective shifted.

I didn't feel hated or judged or alone for a second. I felt nurtured and free, and I clung to that like a lifeline. I limped to camp and thanked Brian over and over, which he seemed to be indifferent to. My ankle was much better in the morning and I resumed hiking. That same day, a new kid joined our Course. He was whiny and stuck in his head, tormenting himself. I had always been the lagger on the trail, but this kid was behind me. He cried the entire time. I turned around and saw myself in him. I wanted to tell him to focus on the beauty around him, that someone loved him and that, at the end of the night, he would be at camp, that he could and would do it. He didn't need to torment himself. I wanted to hug him and enlighten him and carry *his* pack and hike the trail twice willingly. I was seeing this situation from another side and the hill in front of me shrank. My steps found a rhythm and I suddenly and spontaneously Got It.

That night around the campfire, a staff member told me they noticed a change in my attitude and asked me what had happened. I told them that I realized I was making things harder with my negativity and attitude, that I couldn't help anyone else from a place of lack like that, and I didn't want to live like that anymore. The next day, I was returned to RMA. Cool. Now that I wanted to be out here in the woods, I couldn't. As they were discharging me, a staff member said, "You were only supposed to be here for two days to teach you a lesson and get you to confess to having run away, but your attitude toward staff was horrendous, and then you tried to run away again."

K.

I tried to stay in the headspace I had been in the day before, but the continuous misunderstanding about who I was and what my intentions were was wearing me down. I wondered if I would ever actually be *seen*. I fantasized about adulthood constantly, about autonomy and the ability to create my own reality, as opposed to living inside everyone else's. Those daydreams of a monotonous life of diapers and dishes kept me alive. I couldn't wait to be the world's most boring housewife with hours and hours of tedium to tend to. I wanted to weave and can and sew and darn a sock.

When I got back to RMA, I threw myself on Beckie. Jessica was back from her rehab and this was the first time I'd seen her since her OD. It hurt me to look at her and feel how sad I had been not seeing her for two months, and how I had almost never gotten to see her again. I was torn between absolute joy and rage. I requested her for a Rap and I moved across the room from her and I told her what I had been through that night and begged her never to do that to me again. It was harder for me to be honest with her than it was with any other person on Earth. Everything hurt more with her.

Now that I was not in trouble anymore, I got to go on a home visit. This time I again went to our house in California for a few days. I was able to see Jake for the first time in a while, and was shocked to find him, as a fifteen-year-old, basically living with his girlfriend at the time.

I remembered her from his Bar Mitzvah. She was tiny and beautiful and quiet and ate 24/7. She was also on birth control since she and Jake were doing it.

I was not mad at Jake, but imagine coming home from a reform school you were sent to for sneaking a boy into your house for one night to find your brother, who is that same age you had been, *living* with his girlfriend in the same house, with the same parents. I was confused.

A few days later we flew to Tom's birthplace in Iowa. My mom and Tom were huge there. They were the biggest celebrities to set foot in Ottumwa, home of the famous Hormel slaughterhouse.

Tom was always very proud of his roots and wanted a second home near his large family. It was a lot like our home in Denver, but even more farm-friendly and rural. He and my mom thought that opening a restaurant and creating jobs in this otherwise underemployed town was a good way to give back to this community that Tom loved. My mom had fallen in love with it, too.

This was the main reason for our visit. It was the grand opening of Tom and Roseanne's Big Food Diner, a fifties-type greasy spoon restaurant. We were also checking on the construction of their home. They were in the middle of building the largest residence in the state on a several-hundred-acre parcel they had purchased. The mansion was going to have an indoor swimming pool and a bowling alley, but until it was completed, the only place to stay was a large mobile home. There was a small pond right out front that wild animals would sometimes wade out into the middle of and die. We had ATVs and dirt bikes and dogs and pigs and horses and trucks and land. I was allowed to drive on the property and was asked what kind of car I wanted. I said, "Hearse," and lo and behold, one was delivered. I wanted to love it here. On paper, it was the low-key heaven I was pining for, but something just felt wrong about it all.

Maybe it was because my mom and Tom fought the whole trip. Their fights were intense and seemed to be growing bigger every day. Everything was tense. Tom's family was tense, the diner was tense, every car ride was full of thick, tense air. There was no possible way for me to understand what was going on. I was out of the loop and only understood what pertained to me. I just wanted to enjoy my time in the real world. I waited tables at the diner on the day of the grand opening and tried to have a good attitude. Tom's brother Chris was my first customer, and he ran me ragged on purpose and then left me a quarter for a tip. It was funny, but I couldn't help feeling like everyone in town thought I was some spoiled little rich bitch to whom they were trying to teach a lesson. Mostly because people would literally say to me, "I thought you were going to be a spoiled little rich bitch, but you're not that bad."

Thanks?

I found a photo album in the mobile home where my mom had recorded the stages of recovery from multiple plastic surgeries she had had while I was away and it shocked me to my core. Seeing her face swollen and bruised and bloody made me scared for her for the first time. I had never seen her as a vulnerable person. She had the strength of an actual goddess, but life was chipping away at her, and I could see that clearly on this visit. I was worried about her.

And she was worried about me. My mom's discomfort with my weight was at an all-time high, and any time I ate in front of her, I could tell she was bothered. When she decided I had eaten enough, she'd pour my soda on top of the plate so I couldn't eat more. She'd micromanage what I ordered or change my order right after I'd placed it. I had gained more weight at RMA and was close to 250 now, which was a cause for concern, and I think that my mom felt powerless to help me. Her powerlessness was what troubled her most. She had entrusted my care to professionals out of love and her fear of not being able to help me, and even they couldn't fix me.

I was disgusted with my weight, too, and felt like everyone else was also disgusted by me, either for being a spoiled little rich bitch or for being fat. The only people who were nice to me were the ones trying to get insider info on our family or to get close to my mom, and that seemed even more the case here in rural Iowa. Aside from my time dirt biking alone and sneaking out with Tom's nephew to get a tattoo in someone's garage, the trip was miserable. My mom had to fly back to Los Angeles on business a few days before I was supposed to do the same. I had plans to spend a week with my dad before returning to RMA.

My dad was supposed to pick me up from the airport, but when I deplaned, the only familiar face I saw was my mom's bodyguard, Ben.

It only took me a second to put two and two together, but when I did, I knew I wasn't going to see my dad or go back to school. I started yelling, "NO. NO NO NO NO NO," until the whole airport was staring at me, wondering how to react. I hoped someone would interfere and help me, but I'm sure I was a terrifying sight, and no one wanted to get involved.

"WHERE ARE YOU TAKING ME?" I demanded. I screamed that if he touched me I would kick his ass using nothing but my metal lunch-box purse. He very calmly reminded me that he was a martial arts expert, and that he was authorized to cuff me. He very nicely asked me if I would be willing just to get into the limo and skip all the embarrassing drama, and made it sound like a good idea. I agreed, but refused to sit in the back with my mom, who had been waiting curbside with special permission from the airport to park in the loading zone. I sat in the front with Ben instead, asking questions from a safe distance.

"Where am I going now?"

"UCLA. They have a great eating disorder unit there," my mom said from the back.

Jesus Fuck. I clenched my jaw and fists and stared out the window attempting to burn the city down with my eyes. I could not fucking believe this.

We pulled up to UCLA and were greeted at the loading zone by a nurse who would escort me upstairs. I stared catatonically as the rage swirled in my guts and I endured one more intake procedure, the same as all I'd done before. I was assigned a new therapist and a room (with no roommates at least) high up on the tenth floor or so. I had the bolted bed, the plastic mattress, the bleached Angelica sheets, the bulletproof tinted glass, and the single pillow with nothing else. The industrial laundry smell brought all the memories back and made me feel sort of at home. A few days in, and my mom came to visit with some comfort items, one being a life-size inflatable doll of Edvard Munch's *The Scream* figure. I put it in my window facing out, wishing the paparazzi would take a picture of that and print it as an SOS. Maybe the friends I had left behind in LA a year and a half ago would see it and come rescue me.

I was weighed daily and had my food monitored and attended meetings and individual therapy and group therapy and occupational therapy, strangely with the same occupational therapist from whom I had stolen the awl to run away from CPC. She seemed less than thrilled to see me again as I had tormented her before. I did my best to apologize to her and tell her I had grown, and she seemed to accept my apology, which was very generous of her, considering. That was a nice feeling, making amends. I considered maybe calling Dr. Jolie or Dr. George and doing the same thing, but nah.

After two weeks, my assigned therapist took me for a session. I was nervous, as I could tell by her mannerisms that she had something to tell me; historically, these meetings never worked out in my favor, but I had to stay calm to prove that I had matured, just in case this was a test. I was racking my brain trying to think of ways that Tom and my mom could have worked around the law to keep me incarcerated for the rest of my life. Would they suggest ECT (electroconvulsive therapy) or something else with permanent consequences? Maybe I'd be transferred to another country, where there was no legal age of adulthood. Maybe I would be turned over to the government. I had literally no idea and started trembling.

"You don't belong here."

"I know," I said, bracing myself for her suggestion of an even more terrible place where I did belong, one that would petition to keep me after my eighteenth birthday, one that would lobotomize me or do experimental tests on me. I didn't want to focus on my birthday anymore because I thought that if They felt me looking at it and wanting it, They would take it. That was my last lifeline, and losing it would be a death sentence.

"What do you think the best course of action here is? Do you think you should go home?" No one had ever asked me what I thought was best. This must be the test, I thought, and considered which chess move to make.

After running a bunch of scenarios through my head, I decided I wasn't calm enough about the subject to play chess with it, so I just told the truth instead.

"I think I should go back to RMA. I have good friends and my sister is there. I have less than a year left of the program and I've invested a lot of energy and time and I honestly would like to finish *something*." I sat for a moment while she scrawled on a paper and then she said, "Okay, then. That's what we will do." I waited for more, but there was no more. I wanted to divert my eyes so as not to draw too much attention to the shock and joy in them. For sure that would set off her prey instincts, and she would renege on everything.

I wouldn't believe it until the next day when I was on a plane back to Jessica and Beckie.

Although it would most definitely not be smooth sailing from here on out, I felt extremely grateful to be spending my last months as a captive among people I loved in a beautiful, natural setting. Jessica was already eighteen but my mom had gotten Extended Custody of her based on her OD and some other things, so she couldn't leave until her graduation in December 1993, when she would be nineteen. A few months later, in March 1994, I graduated from RMA with Beckie.

My dad picked me up from school to take me back to LA, and then dropped me at my mom's house, where she let me know that she was separating from Tom. I was happy to hear it, but I was concerned for her. She was even more a shell of herself than she had been while visiting me in Idaho. She seemed meek and scared, and it didn't help that there were paparazzi everywhere. The news was full every night with stories about her and Tom. I had forgotten what Los Angeles was like while I was tucked in a secluded corner of Idaho.

A day or so after I got back, my mom had an appointment with her lawyers, and I was alone in our Brentwood house. I heard a knock at the door. I went to answer it, and it was Tom's assistant. She said Tom had left a few things. He was standing about ten feet behind her. I told them that I was the only person here, and they both agreed that it would be the best time for him to collect his stuff. I didn't know that my mom had filed a restraining order against him, and seeing his face made me sad even though I was still very angry at him. A part of me loved him because of our intense history together, and so I let him in. He went downstairs to the vault in which we kept photos, cash, and security tapes. He was down there for a while, and when he came up, he told me he loved us kids and was sorry for how things were turning out, and then he left.

When my mom got home, I told her what happened, not thinking anything was wrong with his getting some of his things. She was mad but not at me. She knew that Tom had manipulated me. He had been watching the house and he took advantage of the situation. I thought he was just getting his passport or something, but he had taken all their wedding photos and videos and also a fat chunk of cash that was stashed for emergencies. She told me about the restraining order and my heart sank. She told me she couldn't take the paparazzi right now and wanted to go to Europe. She was leaving soon. I should go stay with my dad for a little while and she would send for me and my siblings when it was safe. She gave me a car, an older Mustang convertible, and I moved to my dad's bachelor pad in Topanga Canyon.

Reporters were camped outside our gate full-time. They followed us everywhere we went, and we made a game of it. My mom's assistants, Jake and I, and whoever else we could rope into our shenanigans would take the paps on wild-goose chases. We would use the empty limo to make it look like my mom had already left the house, and then we would sneak her out in the back seat of her assistant's car, covered in jackets so she could have some space.

We loved doing things like bringing bouquets of flowers to the Beverly Hills Hotel, where Tom was reportedly staying. Once there, we would just sit in the lobby and eat snacks while the undercover reporters walked around pretending they weren't eavesdropping on our conversations. We would plant little seeds of lies and see which ones bloomed in the tabloids that week.

They tapped our phones, dressed in costumes, blatantly lied about who they were, and did anything to try to get information about the separation. They attempted to blackmail everyone around us for info. They were relentless, and it was exhausting. My mom fled to an island off the coast of Sardinia and took Ben Thomas, her bodyguard, along as her personal security guard. She wasn't there very long before a boat full of *Enquirer* paps and Tom Arnold pulled up to her private island. She was terrified and fled as soon as she could to a villa in the Italian countryside, where no one could find her. She couldn't tell anyone, including us kids, where she was, but she sent for Jake and me in mid-May. We had to make sure we weren't being followed on our two-day travel journey, and we were relieved to end up in the beautiful stone castle–like house in Italy.

It was stunning. I toured the house to choose the best room before

Jessica could get here and take it. She had been invited to come with us, but since you couldn't bring drugs on a plane, she politely declined. Since getting home from RMA in December, she had cultivated a lovely speed addiction that took priority over all other things. We had both been staying in Topanga at my dad's, but the only times I really saw her were when she called me into her room to ask me if the lights outside her window were police cars or UFOs, or when she tricked me into driving her to get more drugs.

I found the room I wanted and put my stuff down, and then I went on to look at the rest of the place. I found my mom's room and went to look at the master bath. That's when I noticed that both my mom's and Ben's things were in this room together. Good Lord, they were doing it. Next to their bed was a fax machine that spewed endless ribbons of legal documentation mixed with handwritten pleas from Tom. I went downstairs and immediately made fun of her for bedding down with her security guard, but in reality I was extremely happy that the Tom nightmare might really be over.

I had always liked Ben. He was stoic and calm. Years ago, I was in the back of the limo with my mom and we got into a fight. We were stuck in traffic on Wilshire Boulevard, and I jumped out of the car screaming and walked barefoot across the hot asphalt and ran off. The entire city was staring at me but I did not care. After about a half hour of my walking nowhere, stepping on any patch of grass I could to cool my soles, a motorcycle pulled up. It was Ben. He handed me a helmet and said he was giving me a ride. Fine. He took me home. Our family and everything surrounding us was so dramatic that it was nice to have someone around who didn't get involved. Ben had grown up with a dynamic mother, and he knew how to handle us.

We left the house in the country and went to Venice to meet up with Brandi, my oldest (but also newest) sister. This would be the first time we got to hang out since meeting in the mental hospital five years ago. We bonded immediately and laughed the entire time, hooting from the balcony of our rented flat at the gondola rowers below us, while drinking straight from a bottle of wine.

At midnight on May 28, 1994, the ten-year countdown to my eighteenth birthday, to my autonomy and freedom, came to an end on that balcony with that wine. I sat alone, knowing that no one but I could understand what this meant to me. I finally did it! I made it to adulthood! This is what I imagined inmates being released from prison might feel like. I suppose it was essentially that.

I was mine, now.

My eyes welled up with tears, but I was too happy and relieved to weep. I could grieve the last few years later. I had to start thinking about what future I wanted to create. The daydreams I had been living on for the last eighteen years seemed a bit ridiculous to pursue right now. I had just gained my independence. I didn't want a husband and kids this minute and, who knows, maybe I didn't even want those things at all. Maybe they were just a defense mechanism my brain had invented to keep me from wanting to quit and die. Maybe any vision of any future at all would have been enough and maybe I wanted to be a spy or a baker or a doctor instead, now that I could enjoy my freedom to choose.

The next night, my mom, also enjoying her new freedom and her return to self, decided she had to have chocolate and talked Brandi and me into going with her to find some. We made sure the very protective Ben was asleep and sneaked out. We walked up and down the cobblestone streets until we found a bakery. It was late at night, around one a.m., and though there were people inside baking for the next day, it was closed. My mom walked up to the window and knocked and a woman inside shook her head no. My mom kept just saying "chocolate" over and over to the lady and she kept shaking her head. My mom took a hundred-dollar bill from her purse and held it against the window, repeating the word *chocolate* until the lady rolled her eyes and opened the window. She passed us four chocolate croissants. My mom gave her the money and we stuffed our faces in the dark alleyway.

A man approached us saying, "Beautiful ladies, come to my house!" and I froze, half in terror and half in consideration that maybe I should go home with him. My mom did not seem afraid and said, "No thanks." The man put his arms over my shoulder and kept trying with me. My mom lost interest in her croissant and charged at him, getting within an inch of his face. "DO YOU WANT TO DIE?" she growled at him.

"No, Mommy. No, Mommy. I'm sorry."

"THEN GET YOUR FUCKING HANDS OFF MY KID!"

He retreated, and so did we. We went home, laughing the whole way. Ben was awake when we got back and calmly let us know that what we had done was Not Smart. We didn't care. We got to spend this night together after years and years of estrangement, both physical and emotional, away from the watchful eyes of the press. We were free to be our true rabble-rousin', dangerous selves alongside one another as peers. It was a handsome reward for surviving it all together. Plus . . . chocolate.

14B.

Full Circle Cafe

After I graduated reform school and my younger brother Jake turned eighteen, my dad was free from the obligations of joint custody and decided to move back to the small mining town of Georgetown, Colorado, where he and my mom had met twenty-some years before. He and his girlfriend, Becca, bought a little Victorian house near Main Street and settled into the quieter life of a small town.

Some of the people he had known years before still lived here, and not much had changed. There were new names and new signs on some of the buildings, but the inside of each store looked exactly like it had not just twenty years ago but at the beginning of the century. The houses that surrounded the center of the town were all restored Victorian homes painted in vibrant color combinations that made them look like toys. Aside from the modern cars parked out front because the driveways were too small, the only signals that this was the end of the twentieth century were the chain-link fences that held everyone's dogs and kids in their yards.

The people who lived here were gaunt and afflicted by poverty. If not for their modern clothing, you'd never know you weren't seeing the ghost of a mistreated miner. There was also a crystal meth problem that added to this sickly energy. At night, when the Red Ram closed, the people stumbling home in the dark could easily have been covered in soot, coming home from a whorehouse after pounding homemade whiskey for dinner.

My dad and Becca decided they wanted to buy a business in town. They chose a restaurant near the Red Ram, the true center of everything. They purchased it and named it the Full Circle Cafe to represent my dad's journey and return. He and Becca busted their asses to make the cutest greasy spoon diner you've ever seen. It was homey, warm, and kid-friendly, and the food was simple and comforting. The walls had shelves full of really cool novelty gifts hand-selected by Becca. There were a few booths, several tables, and some stools that sat up against a bar. There was a TV playing cartoons for the kids. They had a machine that made that special capsule-shaped ice that is imperative for a diner to provide.

After my dad was all set up, Beckie and Jessica and I, and Jessica's pit bull, Rufus, drove Jessica's sedan to Georgetown, each taking turns at the wheel while the others rested. I folded the back seat down, put my legs in the trunk to stretch out, and watched the familiar Colorado landscape rush by like it did when we would drive to my grandparents' house when I was a kid. We smoked pot and fueled up on gas station junk food, Diet Coke, and Camel Lights while switching between the Pixies and Grateful Dead cassettes. It was exactly the plan we had made in our late-night whispering bunk to bunk at reform school. It was perfect.

It was a short visit, but it was really nice to see my dad moving on from Hollywood and all he'd left behind. One of my favorite memories was going to the antique bar and drinking (yes, I was underage—it was a different time). After a few drinks, he asked me why my brother Jake had a collection of name tags in his Volkswagen bug. Our whole family were avid true-crime fans, and we all knew that collecting tokens and driving white Volkswagens were basically prerequisites for being a serial killer. I knew where my dad was leading with his questions. I also knew the answer was that Jake had found a name tag once and pinned it to his visor so he could joke about being a serial killer, and then his friends got in on it and started collecting more name tags for him. I took my sweet time telling my dad that. I wanted to hear him actually say the words so I could tell Jake that Dad thought he was a serial killer. My dad doesn't remember this, but Jake and I both do. We still laugh about it.

My dad loved his "new" house, a cozy little Victorian he had filled full of antiques. It must've looked just like it had a hundred years before.

The only thing I didn't like about that house was the upstairs. Specifically, one of the two bedrooms there. The rooms themselves were identical, but I could not bring myself to cross the threshold of the Green Room. I could sit for hours in the room just three feet away, but the Green Room was different. We found out later from historical records that a very young girl had gotten sick and died in that room.

It seemed as though everywhere you turned in this town, there was some sort of paranormal activity. I didn't mind that and was excited to go back again during the summer and spend more time here. My dad and I would talk weekly to catch up, and he started telling me stories about strange things that were happening, like water faucets going on by themselves and pictures hanging on walls being thrown to the floor. Becca started having more and more strange experiences when she was alone late at night counting money or doing dishes. Once, she turned around in the kitchen and saw a man in a full-length apron standing there. He was transparent but also very visible. He had a mustache like a hipster, and Becca instantly recognized him from pictures she had seen of the restaurant when it was a fish store back in 1900. One night, she was sitting on a stool at the counter, and something spun her around. She was alone and immediately gathered her stuff and went home. Later that night, she posted her story in an online forum about ghosts. A TV show called *Sightings* reached out to her a couple days later wanting to set up a time where they could come film a segment. They specialized in hauntings and would bring their secret weapon, a medium named Peter James.

The show sent a scout to see if there was potential for an episode, and after a few days of talking to townsfolk, they had several stories they wanted to investigate. They sent a crew to Georgetown to film Peter James investigating the café, along with a former whorehouse and another restaurant down the road. Skeptics thought my dad was bringing his Hollywood bullshit to their tiny community and were vocally judgmental about it. They figured he was just trying to drum up business, which was frustrating for my dad as that was very much not the case.

Between the skeptics, the small pool of available non-meth-addicted employees, and the ghosts, the café was losing its romance for my dad. Only a few years after deciding to settle down there, he and Becca decided to trade it all in for a Class A RV and hit the road as "full-timers," or people who lived in their RV full-time. This would be the case for the next twenty years.

15.

What Does Armageddon Have to Do with Me?

After Italy, we went to Spain, where Jessica finally met up with us just in time to detox off speed. That was a fun trip. Jessica seemed to mix her detoxing and family vacations often. It was efficient, really. However, it wasn't that much fun for the rest of us. Jake somehow got food poisoning the same week and was walking around in a robe sharting himself while Jessica writhed around on the couch like Regan from *The Exorcist*. I sat outside on the stone wall that kept the ocean from flooding our villa and tried to lock eyes with any man who might want to be gifted the privilege of dicking-down a newly legal plus-size queen. No one in Europe seemed to be into fat chicks, though. A true missed opportunity for all.

Despite my attempts at getting laid, Jessica's detoxing, and Jake's sharting, my mom seemed to be having a good time. She had gotten long blond hair extensions before our trip and was mostly unrecognizable unless she spoke. Being able to fly under the radar, along with her freedom from the press, her freshly divorced status, and her new, protective boyfriend, she could let loose for once.

Though she had hired a historian named Francis to escort us on daily trips to all the great tourist destinations, she would wake up every morning, have him take us to a nice breakfast restaurant, and then tell him to take us back to our flat for a nap.

"What about St. Mark's Basilica? Don't you want to see that?"

"No. Go to the gift shop and buy us the book. Bring it back here with some cake," she'd tell him. He *hated* us.

One day, we decided to go along with him on one of the tours, mostly because the destination was a restaurant. We reserved a limo boat with a bar and drove up a canal. We were all pretty tipsy when we pulled up alongside a giant yacht full of people. My mom turned to them, lifted her shirt, and exposed her naked boobs to the group. They all started cheering and clapping and we kids laughed our asses off. That is, until we realized that the yacht was docked at our destination a few minutes up the canal. Oh well. No one recognized her here, so we'd just be another group of white trash tourists who won a trip on *The Price Is Right* or something.

When we walked in the building, the whole group came up to her one by one and said, "Thanks for the show, Roseanne." Turns out it was a boat full of Middle American retirees. We had fun.

We got back from Europe and the press was still following us and camping outside our Brentwood house, constantly shouting out questions about the divorce. Brentwood was a rich area, but it was relatively off the radar of the Maps to the Stars–type vendors and tourists. It was quiet and green and like a country of its own tucked in a hard-to-access cove where the canyons and the beaches met. There was no reason to stop unless you lived here. There was one grocery store and some smaller expensive restaurants and an amazing weekly farmers' market, but it was not a place to Be Seen. It made it all the more irritating that we were being followed around.

A few days after we returned from Europe, two people were found murdered in the courtyard of a nearby apartment building. As soon as one of the victims was identified as Nicole Brown, the ex of O. J. Simpson, Brentwood lit up with paparazzi and ambulance chasers, and a chunk of the parasites outside our house moved west to camp in front of O. J.'s house, a mile or so away. It was an unfortunate reprieve for us until the tourists who started coming to see the nearby crime scene and the home of the suspected murderer decided to take detours to honk at our house on the way. This lasted for years.

My mom would try to go outside to garden or drink coffee, but each time she did, someone would shout at her from the street or peek their head through our fence or use the call button on our gate to communicate over the speaker.

I had to get out of there. I knew it was time for me to buckle down and do something. RMA was not an academic school by any means, so when I graduated the program, I was short half a credit and could not get my diploma. I had several credits too many in PE from my time on survival courses and not enough credits in government. Beckie's situation was similar, so we decided to move to Ocean Beach together and get GEDs. Beckie moved in with her boyfriend, Gavin, who quickly became her fiancé, and a few pot dealers to offset the rent.

I, however, would be moving into *my* new place, a shanty full of roaches in San Diego, close enough to the beach to excuse the vermin, but not dilapidated enough to excuse the guy who shit on my porch, wiped his ass with his own T-shirt, and threw it too high into my tree to ever get down. It hung like a terra nullius flag. I spent the remainder of my year living on Taco Bell bean and cheese burritos (extra beans, extra cheese, no onions, no red sauce) until Beckie and I finally got our equivalency certificates.

I didn't love living alone, so when my friend Jerrie from RMA asked me if she could come crash on my couch, I said yes. She forgot to mention she'd be detoxing from heroin. Fortunately my experience with hospital roommates and Jessica meant that I was old hat at detox. My house was the catch-all for any spurned spouses, addicts, or transients, and I was always cleaning up broken glass, spilled bong water, vomit, or pee. It's one thing to potty train a toddler and another entirely to beg an adult to please aim for *inside* the toilet. I was not ready for motherhood, especially when all my children were older than me and on drugs.

One night, I had a dream so strange that I woke up and wrote it down over and over and over for three days making sure it was all committed to memory/Akashic records. It lasted the entire night. I know everyone *loooooves* dream sequences, so I'll keep it short:

I was in a room that was completely empty aside from a tiny box (Rubik's cube–size) stuck on the wall. I walked over to it and I heard a voice tell me to open it. I turned around and saw a man I barely recognized from a single photo I had seen of him. It was Ben's dad, Buck Sr., who had passed away before I could meet him. I looked at him and turned back and reached out and opened the box. A small monarch butterfly flew out, an important symbol to me. As it flapped its wings, it started to grow until it took up the space of the entire room, its wings whooshing louder and the wind they generated becoming more powerful, until I was completely engulfed. I heard Buck Sr.'s voice tell me that only good things were going to come to me now, as if I had paid off a karmic debt or something. I didn't know this man or have any emotional ties to him, and couldn't explain what it meant. All I know is that I woke up a different person.

A few days later, my mom called to tell me she was pregnant. She had been on a mission to conceive a baby with Ben, a project she had tried with Tom five years before without success, thank *all* the gods. Her fertility treatments had finally worked, and she was going to have Ben's baby/babies—three embryos had implanted, though over the next month, two would disappear. One was holding strong, though. My mom married Ben in a big ceremony when she was eight months pregnant. Her wedding dress was a red velvet gown handmade for her and embroidered with cherubs down the long train. She and Ben looked like the cover of a plus-size romance novel.

I finished my GED testing and decided to move back home to await the birth of my sibling and work for my mom until I had adjusted to society enough to get an outside job and live a normal life. This was a lot harder than it sounds, having spent my teen years in various cultlike schools. My sense of reality seemed to be completely different than that of everyone around me. I could relate only to people who spent their days immersed in emotional turmoil, turning the events of their lives over and over in their heads and being unable to exist in the accepted model of society that included activities like holding a job or talking without crying. I could have a three-hour-long, mutually life-changing conversation with the lady living in the Canter's Deli parking lot, but I couldn't order food from that same restaurant without my voice quaking from nervousness. There was no way I could handle a job interview.

Another reason I was moving home was to have gastric bypass surgery. At this point in my life, I was close to 280 pounds, and my mom was increasingly concerned. One of the writers on *Roseanne*, Carrie Snow, had had gastric bypass surgery and lost about a hundred pounds in the past year and seemed to be doing great.

I wasn't sure I wanted to assume the risks associated with the surgery. No one my age had done it. It was a relatively new procedure and was invasive as fuck. You were essentially filleted and your organs were rearranged and no one knew what the long-term effects would be. I was resigned, though, knowing that no crash diets or lifestyle changes were going to help me. I had tried everything over the years and nothing worked. I just wanted to be the skinny, hot girl I knew I was inside, and I did not want to suffer through five hundred more crash diets to get there. I was mostly convinced, but Carrie wanted to take me for sushi and quell whatever remaining fears I had. At lunch, she told me how happy she was, how the difficult recovery was worth it, how she appreciated my mom so much, and how she would do it a million times over.

I was convinced until, as she was driving me home, she had to pull over to vomit the expensive sushi we'd just eaten into a gutter. After her fifth time vomiting on Melrose Boulevard, she had cleared her pouch and we were good to go. I was not sold on the idea anymore, but I ended up having the surgery mostly because I didn't believe anything else would ever work. I felt that this was my final option before just surrendering to being buried in a piano case after choking to death on a fried chicken bone.

Halfway through Season 8, my mom gave birth and named the baby Buck, after Ben's dad. The morning we went to meet him at the hospital, I felt changed. The last ten years had been a whirlwind in which there was little joy, but his birth brought a new dynamic of hope to our family that was much needed. I remembered the dream I had in San Diego, and I felt like I understood what it meant. The message had decoded itself upon my hearing the baby's name. My mom had a nursery set up in her dressing room so that a nurse could watch him there while she was on set. We all thought it was hilarious that Buck's life would start in a trailer like our older sister Jessica's had, but with completely unforeseeable differences.

When Buck was almost a year old, I underwent the gastric bypass surgery. I wasn't afraid, but hopeful. I was ready to finally be free of the struggle with my weight and everything that meant. It would be like poison on the root system of my pain going all the way back to Matt in grade school calling me Fat. It was going to fix my self-esteem issues in ways that the live-in therapist never could. It would heal the shitty power struggle with my mom over her concerns with my weight. It would make all of Tom's commentary part of my past. All my issues with men and sexuality would drop off me in tandem with the pounds. Every cruel thing ever said or done to me would be moot because that girl wouldn't exist anymore. I hesitate to say that all those things happened because of the surgery. I know that is dangerous, but, for me, it was like a pebble tossed in a pond whose ripples not only went forward, but also backward, severing that timeline completely. I woke up from the procedure and, though I was the same size for now, it was as if I had come out of a fifteen-year fog. The thing that had most controlled me was a nonissue now and I could finally start my life.

Brandi had moved out to Los Angeles to be near us and to work as an assistant stage manager on *Roseanne*. Jessica and I were working for *Roseanne* now, too, but lacked the maturity needed to have actual titles. We were banished to my mom's office at the now-defunct production company she had started with Tom, Wapello County Productions. We had been tasked with opening my mom's fan mail, which was like a college course in forensic psychology. I was fascinated. Most letters were legible and short, "I'm a fan, please send a signed photo to . . ." but others were filthy, with vague threats scrawled all over them. A lot were in German or other languages and I quickly learned to translate them enough to know what to send back. We would share the craziest of them with my mom's bodyguards and agents and, at times, we would frame the extra-craziest ones and keep them at home or in the production office, sometimes quoting them to each other. One way Jessica and I kept ourselves entertained was imitating the styles of the most notable fans and sending our own fan mail to our favorite celebrities. Jessica sent many letters to Keanu Reeves, while I sent mine to Jack Nicholson.

> Dear Mr. Jack Nicholson,
>
> I hope to here back from you. Please send me a letter to (address) and if you cannot send a letter please come say hi in person just nock on my door and i will open it and we can say hi. I know that once you see me you will understand. I tried to come say hi to you before but people did not understand. Once we say hi to each other they will understand and i just need to look you in the eyes and when you look back you will see why i want to say hi.

Etc. It was two pages full of typos in a nearly illegible, smeared pen. I wondered if Jack's assistants framed it and put it in their office.

A few months later, when Season 9 started taping, Jessica and I were given jobs as writers. None of the other writers wanted us in the room. To them, we were essentially teen spies with no experience who were being handed an opportunity they had worked their asses off for. We desperately wanted to participate, but felt the discomfort we were causing and opted to spend our time in producer Allan Stephan's office smoking all his pot, scarfing all-you-can-eat buffet sushi from down the street, and sending personal assistants out for impossible finds like Yak's Milk Frappés with Brambleberry Syrup. One writer, Cindi, took us on and taught us a little bit about creating a storyline and writing dialogue. Jessica was a natural, but I was too busy trying to sleep with the cute production assistant to take it seriously. I was petrified of failure and creative vulnerability and couldn't even bring myself to try. I spent a lot of time smoking joints and walking around the fake city streets on the lot.

I'd ride my mom's golf cart over to the old *Gilligan's Island* set, which was now the Greens Department, the place where all the plants were kept and nurtured for set design, or go nap on the grass behind the house. It was a surreal place to be insanely high, as you would walk past celebrities all the time and catch snippets of their very odd conversations or see them pacing about the forested areas reciting lines. This was before Bluetooth, so it was an extra-unusual sight to see someone walking alone while talking to themselves out loud.

Since the restraining order, Tom was not allowed back on set, but he *was* allowed back on the lot so long as he kept a specific distance. There was a show that Tom was part of that was filming a few stages over. Once, I ran into him. It was awkward. I was angry at the things my mom had told me, and angry about the past five years, and angry that he had separated me from my extended family. I couldn't look him in the eye. He tried to say hi, but it infuriated me further.

I have never been good with vengeance. My anger never makes it very far, and I talk myself into understanding the person long before I can ever fully retaliate. I am always for the underdog, even if they are the underdog because they completely fucking deserve it.

During all the press about the divorce, my mom and Tom were slamming each other to the public. My mom's go-to was that Tom had a three-inch penis and I knew that bothered him, so I found out what stage he was taping on and made a large gold star nameplate with a drawing of a tiny penis on it and a ruler that said "3 inches" and went to stick it on his dressing room door. My plan would have worked, but unfortunately the door was not latched all the way, and the pressure I applied opened it slowly until I locked eyes with his assistant. I took off running. I hid behind Brett Butler's *Grace Under Fire* trailer and watched security drive by on their golf carts looking for me.

When the coast was clear, I ran back to the *Roseanne* set and found my mom in the wardrobe room where she always hung out. I told the girls what had happened. That's when we heard security come onstage looking for me. Some quick thinking, and I was dressed in a movie-quality Santa Claus outfit. No one here fit Tom's assistant's description. Aside from a scolding from my mom's lawyer telling her Tom's lawyer had called and she had better not have had any involvement in the situation, I got off scot-free.

Later, I worked on my mom's side project, a sketch show to rival *SNL* called *Saturday Night Special*, in a production office across the street. At that time, Tom was starring in a movie whose production office was directly above us. One night, I stayed late waiting for a ride and a courier service came to drop something off. I signed for it and then realized it was meant for the other office, Tom's office, and it was addressed specifically to Tom.

It wasn't sealed. It was a script. A menacing flush went over me and I knew what I had to do. I took the script to a writer's assistant, who spent the night rewriting it and changing all Tom's lines to some version of "I have a small penis" and then we re-grommeted it and I dropped it off at Tom's dressing room. Later that week, when we knew the show was taping in front of a live audience, some friends and I went to a sex shop, bought one hundred tiny penis toys, and passed them out to the live audience waiting to watch Tom's show. That was enough. I could move on now.

Season 9 of *Roseanne* wasn't doing all that well in the ratings. I knew it was because my mom wanted to spend all her time with Buck and was sick of doing the show. She was ready to settle down and be a mom again. She started tying up loose ends in the scripts and figuring out where to go next with the storyline. She knew how she wanted to end it. After all, the show was based on our lives, and she wanted to keep it that way. She added the storyline of the Conners winning the lottery so she was able to talk about what having money does to people, what being a writer is like. That would be the final season. Well, for twenty years, anyway.

After the show ended, with her four eldest kids now adults and a toddler at home, things were calmer, but none of us would ever put our guards down completely again. We were still followed everywhere we went, with paparazzi trying to get pictures of Buck, people shouting my mom's name trying to get her to turn in the direction of their cameras, store managers calling TMZ to say Roseanne Barr was inside, shady motherfuckers trying to get a piece of my mom's money, or, worse yet, her time and attention. This was also the time my mom's quest for spiritual guidance was peaking. The show was over, and the last ten years had been a whirlwind of mental health disasters. My mom had a friend who introduced her to the Church of Scientology and she had weekly meetings in her own home with a guy named Bob from the Celebrity Center and whatever handful of spiritually transient celebs were available at the moment.

I was rapidly losing weight from the gastric bypass and, within a year, was one hundred pounds lighter. I didn't weigh myself but used the metric of male attention instead. The fact that men who would have just dumped all their emotional baggage on me before were now trying to impress me with their knowledge of pop culture was unbearable. I acted out a bit by sneaking into bars with Jessica and flirting for free drinks. Occasionally, I'd make out with someone and then lose interest once I'd thought about how they would have snubbed me a year ago. Once I took a guy out to his truck and had him disrobe but keep his cowboy boots and cowboy hat on. Then I thanked him, got out of the truck, and went back into the bar, leaving him naked. I don't know why. I was partly angry, but mostly I was feeling naked and vulnerable and didn't know how to live without armor.

Ford Models, who had a plus-size division and represented Mia, the daughter of Steven Tyler from Aerosmith, took a meeting with me. They wanted to put Mia and me together as the chubby daughters of celebs, and I was unsure, but I had to take photos for a portfolio anyway, so we set that up. I met two ladies in a park in Venice Beach and spent the most awkward day of my life. I did not have it in me to follow directions or pose or be generally humiliated. After twenty-four hours of having a modeling contract, I quit. I destroyed the pictures when I got them back. It was too much for my dysmorphia to handle after losing so much weight so fast.

Aside from my experiences with Ricky years ago, and a minor slipup or two in my San Diego beach house, I was basically a virgin. I was approaching adulthood with nowhere near as much experience as my libido thought I should have.

Ten years before this, when the first 976 number was established, I had started making daily calls to party lines. They were like a dollar a minute, but it was worth it to thirteen-year-old me, who would not be paying the bills anyway. I figured my parents were too busy to notice that I had been making adult male friends over the phone, but I was wrong. After a several-hundred-dollar phone bill, my parents were on to me and eavesdropped on the kitchen phone while I talked for hours, lied about my age, gave out my address, and made plans to run off to New York with a stranger. My parents called the phone company and had all 976 numbers blocked from our line and lectured me about my stupidity, but all I saw was that I was not going to get to have sex after all.

Trying to have sex in lockup was not worth the trouble. Sex during

Wilderness Survival would have been like rolling around on a public bathroom floor. Sex wasn't an option for a lot of years, but now that I was free and an adult, and the Lord had blessed me with the internet, AOL chat was my new lifeline for trying to get some ass. This future was glorious. No nudity and no touching, talking, breath-smelling, misophonia-inducing dinner dates . . . I could still explore the depth of my sexual being without having to hear someone scraping their metal fork over a porcelain plate. Men were paying attention to me in real life now, too, and I was conflicted. On the one hand, I wanted to sleep with all of them, but on the other, I did not want to sleep with any of them. It was a very confusing time.

We were all coming out of the black hole of the last decade, mostly by pretending none of it ever happened and just being grateful that the worst was over and the dark cloud seemed to be dissipating. We were all free, alive, and together, and getting along as best we could. My mom loved every minute of her fifth and final miracle kid and spent her time doing things with him she hadn't had time to do in years, like shopping and growing spiritually.

I ended up getting talked into taking some "classes" at the Scientology Center one night when I went over to put Buck to sleep. I came into a living room full of mingling seekers walking around like Sims, trying to force eye contact with me so they could tell me why I was bad and they were good. I had nothing in common with these people because I wasn't looking for anything. I had spent half my life in self-discovery of all kinds and didn't have room for any other doctrine at the moment.

Every successful business has a famous spokesperson. That was the ticket to the mainstream. All you needed was one good celebrity endorsement, and you could put a down payment on that old building in the heart of downtown and call it The Center. From there, it was easy. The Fat Hairies would eventually come seeking the Great Knowledge that these Wise Hotties had somehow mastered to obtain happiness (money, power, and sex).

They would pay handsomely to figure out how to make money.

They would devote themselves completely to the belief system to learn the secret to manifesting all their hopes and dreams (the secret is devotion).

They would spend all their free time trying to learn the formula to making enough money to have free time.

All these programs and places were very much like the Lion looking for Courage and the Tin Man looking for a Heart.

I get it. I'm a seeker. I read *A Course in Miracles* and *The Secret*. I just learned that the *actual* secret of *The Secret* is that your Higher Self—the mama bear bitch who is not having any of your shit, the one forcing you to grow—*she's* the one in charge of manifesting. Not your low-level crotch chakra self who wants a Lamborghini and someone to pay for your new tits.

Mom had bought me a package of twenty lessons, of which I took two just out of morbid curiosity. I had all the intel I needed to decide they weren't my thing, as much as anything that calls anyone who disagrees with them "toxic" is not my thing. The first class took place at the Celebrity Center. As someone who was already so sick of the starfuckers that abounded everywhere around me, I couldn't stand the fact that there was an entirely separate "church" for elites. Also, having stomached so many intake procedures in the last five years, this was by far the creepiest. I don't think you were meant to notice that that is what was happening. They called it an interview, but I was a master of decoding manipulative language at this point. It was an intake.

One of their procedures was having you sit in a classroom facing the front with other student-member-participants, which immediately threw you back to your youth. They gave you a workbook full of Dick and Jane–type drawings of people in different social scenarios, with lined spaces to answer questions about the drawings. There was something so nostalgic about the smells and setting, the paper, the way the Number 2 pencil glided above the lines, the ass pain from the hard plastic chairs. It was hypnotic. During my induction, after completing the workbook, I was escorted to a basement office where I sat across from a clearly Capricorn woman in a pencil skirt. She had a computer in front of her on which she recorded the answers to the questions she had asked me. Some questions were meant to make me feel shame. I was beyond that. I decided this was not for me, and I never went back.

A year after I declined their invitation to another class, they started calling my house daily. I finally snapped and screamed, "I AM WAY

TOO FUCKING HIGH TO DEAL WITH YOU. DON'T EVER CALL ME AGAIN OR I WILL CALL THE POLICE." Did that work? No. I'm still receiving calls and mail twenty-five years later despite having moved twelve times and called them ten-plus times to tell them to stop. Every piece of mail I receive after I expressed my clear disinterest feels like a threat. That's about twice a week.

I tried telling them I wasn't interested, that their ideology didn't match with mine, that the only thing we had in common was a distrust of pharmaceutical-prescribing therapists, but they hadn't listened to any of that, so I hoped my being on drugs would be reason enough for them to lose interest in me.

When my dad and Becca first got serious about each other, they rented a tiny two-bedroom house on the inland side of Topanga Canyon, only miles from the bachelor pad he owned, where Becca could live and sleep when they weren't riding Harleys or eating out. Becca has restless legs and my dad snores like a woodchipper, so they were a poor match as sleeping partners. This house was left vacant when Dad and Becca moved back to Georgetown, so to help Jessica and me get on our feet, my dad let us move in there together and he continued paying the rent. He sent us small amounts of money for food when he could, too. It wasn't much. We spent most of it on weed and alcohol, and then, with whatever change was leftover, we bought seven-layer burritos. He had bought Jessica a VW Squareback and let me use his antique Mercedes-Benz as my car, and probably hoped we would use them to find jobs.

Eventually the limited budget took its toll, and I decided I did need to look for work. I didn't know what I would be qualified for, both experientially and emotionally, but when I saw an ad looking for employees at the mystical bookstore from which I had been buying stuff since I was eight, I knew I had to apply. My application was accepted. I found out later that this was because the owner recognized my name and knew my mom and dad as customers and also celebrities. Plus I had zero experience and so would be easy to train. There had apparently been more than six hundred résumés turned in for the job.

I loved working there, besides the fact that it was minimum wage at seven dollars an hour. It wasn't too labor intensive and we were indoors in a darkly lit, air-conditioned environment. We had access to all the books I remembered from my childhood, and there were so many more now. I picked up *Behold a Pale Horse* and realized that, even if this guy was nuts, there was a lot more going on in the universe than we knew. I became obsessed with ancient astronaut theory and got some books on that to supplement my white witchcraft library. I spent the days straightening books and dealing with the teenage girls who came in looking for love potions or spell kits after watching the movie *The Craft*. We had a separate table near the front register with all the campy bullshit these kids were looking for. It was a distraction to keep them from our cherished oils and Qabalistic Crowley books in the back.

One of the reasons the bookstore was so popular was because it kept two to three psychics on duty at all times. You could call or walk in and get a reading from someone who had been FBI-background-checked. Some were channelers, like the lady you could hear slowly growling through her curtain. Some read cards or palms, and some were astrologers who did birth charts by hand before computers took over.

I met a lot of cool people there, including Sagebrush, who had his natal chart tattooed on his belly, his south node extending to the tip of his penis. I was crushing on him immediately, but I was never going to tell him that. Being separated from males for the formative teen years had taken a toll, and I had no idea how to act around them. I was awkward and aloof for a long time, but I eventually started to feel safe with Boyse, what with his understanding of divine feminine energy and his passionate pursuit of awakenedness. We ended up sleeping together, and afterward I completely shut down. He tried to talk to me about that, but I was terrible at communicating. I realized that my fear of vulnerability was crippling me, and I decided I was going to make an effort to work through it, but I forgot to tell *him* that. Before we could get any more serious, he slept with one of the psychics. I was crushed. I quit the bookstore and filed for unemployment. No more of that vulnerability horseshit for me.

And thus began my promiscuous stage. I started sleeping with people I met at the bar so long as I didn't like them. That was my type—guys I didn't like. I started resenting anyone who paid any attention to me. After all, they would not have given me the time of day when I was fatter. I also resented the ones who didn't pay any attention to me. Couldn't they see how funny I was?

A friend brought a group of boys to my house one night, and I seduced one of them. In the morning he apologized for taking advantage of me, and I laughed in his face. I couldn't believe he thought that was what had happened. He got mad and left, but his friend Clive stayed behind and we hung out all day. He ended up coming over all the time.

A couple weeks later, Jessica went nuts and charged at me with a beer bottle. She had a hair trigger at this point due to her new addiction, fen-phen. Everyone wanted to be skinny, and there was a new miracle drug that could help. It was a combo of two tiny pills. One was fenfluramine, and the other was phentermine. Both were appetite suppressants, but one was basically legal speed. Dr. Quacky, as the women on the set of *Roseanne* had named him, had prescribed the pills to Jessica to lose weight. They were meant to be used for six weeks, but Jessica had been on them for six months. One of the best assets in Hollywood is a doctor who will prescribe you anything. It's not just who you know in the entertainment industry that matters, but who you know in the medical fraternity. Once someone found a doctor willing to prescribe anything they wanted, word of mouth would spread until we all went to that doctor, trading stories and pills within our new community.

Jessica chased me around our living room. I stopped her arm as it came down at me with the bottle, and I put her on the floor and sat on her. She gouged my leg with her nails just like old times, and I grabbed a handful of her hair and pushed her face into the carpet. She kept gouging, so I kept smashing her head, and then she told me she couldn't feel her legs. She was paralyzed and needed medical attention. She continued to play possum until I finally agreed to call an ambulance. When I told them how she became paralyzed, they informed me that the police would have to come, too, as it was a domestic dispute. I said never mind, but it was too late. I let Jessica know the cops and the paramedics were on their way, and she immediately and miraculously recovered enough to try to clean up the paraphernalia that our little rental was covered in. Just then, Jake arrived to introduce his new girlfriend to his sisters.

When they walked in, Jessica and I both launched into monologues about what had happened, and then there was a knock at the door. Jake went to answer it. It was the police. They screamed at Jake, "NEVER APPROACH AN OFFICER!"

I heard him whimper, "But . . . you knocked," as he was pushed down onto the beanbag by a flashlight to his chest. One cop grabbed me and handcuffed me to a chair while they asked Jessica what happened. Another cop walked around looking over the place. He didn't mention the SMOKING POT IS ILLEGAL IN A POLICE STATE bumper sticker on Jessica's bedroom door, but he *did* ask us where the drugs were.

"That's what we wanna know," Jessica said.

I laughed from my chair and the other cop said, "They're around here somewhere." Jessica replied, "They're not. Trust me, I checked."

I wondered why I was the one cuffed, as blood ran from the fingernail marks on my calf to the kitchen floor.

After about ten minutes, the cops asked Jessica if she wanted to press charges against me. She took a way-too-long pause and then said, "Nah."

They left, the paramedics left, and Jake and his new girlfriend also left.

We decided we should live apart.

On moving day, I recruited Sagebrush and Clive to help me. I rented a box truck and backed it into the driveway. Jessica got mad at me for *something* and charged at me with a broomstick, but Boyse stopped her. He was insanely calm, and that made Jessica go even more crazy. She took another chunk out of my arm with her nails and started hitting Boyse. I told him to come with me and we walked away down the street.

There was a liquor store nearby and we stopped in to buy some American Spirits. I noticed I was bleeding and asked for a paper towel. The clerk seemed concerned and asked me if I was okay. I said, "Kinda," went outside, and lit up a smoke. That's when I saw Clive driving his car toward me and Boyse. Jessica was shotgun and she had a look in her eye I recognized from my childhood beatings. Fuck.

Before I could run or do anything at all, Clive pulled up right to us and Jessica unloaded an entire large fire extinguisher directly into Boyse's face. The street filled up with a giant white cloud the size of a building. As soon as the fog cleared, a powder-coated Boyse began to take shape. He was standing totally still and holding his breath, his fingers touching in a Shuni pose, the yoga mudra for patience and discipline. He had remained calm and was using this experience to strengthen his spiritual development, and that made Jessica even more insane. She took the empty extinguisher and threw it at him. Fortunately she has the arm strength of a T. rex and didn't hit her target.

I started screaming at Clive, "WHY? Why would you drive her here?!" to which he said, "She asked me to!" Clive was an actor and in constant pursuit of situations to draw inspiration from, aka a drama lover. His loyalties to both of us were equal, since we had known him only a short amount of time, although he and I would get super-close over the next year, spending a lot of time together, sleeping in the same bed, snuggling. He would become my best friend. But not until after this. After he apologized.

I then noticed the whole street had come out to see what was happening. I put my head down, turned around, and nonchalantly walked a powder-coated Boyse home while Clive drove Jessica back. In the five minutes it took me to get home, Jessica had thrown a mug through the window of the box moving truck we had rented. There was glass everywhere, and a little snippet of conversation from the day before played over and over in my mind.

"Are you sure you would like to decline the insurance?"

"Yes. I can't afford it," I said.

I swept the shattered pieces off the driver's seat, finished packing my last few things, got in the truck, and drove back to the rental place.

I asked the guy on duty if he'd be willing to forge an insurance agreement from earlier so I wouldn't be liable for a seven-hundred-dollar window replacement. I told him what had happened, and he took pity on me and thought about it before asking me how much cash I had. I was just grateful he didn't ask for a BJ, and I gave him my last fifty dollars. I filed a claim, then drove to my new home a few miles away, where I would now live, hopefully peacefully, with Brandi.

We had a very sweet, married Jewish couple named Susie and Ron as roommates, whom Brandi had known in Texas. They were so normal. It was a much more suitable situation for me, since I was pretty much a granny in a young 'un's body.

When Buck was one, my mom took a job playing the Wicked Witch on Broadway and moved to New York for six months. I went to visit her and she offered me a job as Buck's nanny. I was always hovering wherever he was, so I accepted. It would make it less weird that he was the only person I wanted to hang out with, plus I could go off unemployment.

Now *this* was my kind of job. The nanny experience was transformative for me, and Buck was easy, aside from the demands of his dad, who handled his chaotic early life by being extra-organized and in control of everything. He had basically raised himself since he was born and needed everything to be dialed in. We had a baby log we were required to fill out daily in the first person, detailing Buck's adventures, playdates, meals, and bowel movements. If you could get past being asked to wipe Buck's hands and face after every bite he took, it was a great job. Most of my days were spent playing with him and going shopping with my mom, which was the most time I had spent with her since I was eight. I was also tasked with taking Buck on playdates, which are horrible anyway, but much more so with celebrities and rich people.

I was still his nanny when my mom decided she wanted to do a daytime talk show. It wasn't long before we were in production again. My mom wanted me to work on the show and so found another nanny, Linda. We joked about my mom being older and needing her own caretaker soon and suggested that Linda would just shift whose ass she was wiping when the time came, and that's basically exactly what happened. She's still with us, refusing to let us sweep our own homes and miss out on the calorie-burning cardio she could be getting. A favorite thing Linda says is, "I love to have diarrhea," because it means you're losing weight.

I started working in the production office and, aside from receiving more of the glares I had learned to cope with on the sitcom, it was fun. After fighting the network over their hiring pool's lack of diversity, my mom won permission to hire Ellen Cleghorne and Paul Mooney as writers, along with producers of color. It was a great and diverse group of smart, deep, and funny people.

But gimmicky daytime yip yap was not my mom's thing. Her interviews were dark and deep, and no one knew what to do with her. Our family's favorite show was *The Richard Bey Show*, and it was like that mixed with some Diane Sawyer and also *Pee-wee's Playhouse*. Her guests were eccentrics, and she had them on as playmates, not interviewees.

She hired many other comic geniuses as writers and performers, but none of them had experience in daytime TV; most of their pitches could only be shown on late night, when the kids had gone to bed. My mom indulged herself a lot and would interrupt guests and talk over them. Not even her own staff realized that she was doing a character, and they fought to make this an Oprah-type, overproduced, run-of-the-mill, basic-ass daytime TV show.

If anyone understood what she was trying to do, it would have been the best show on TV, but they didn't. CBS and King World weren't really taking the show seriously, thinking she could just get by on formula and name alone, and didn't advertise, save for one single billboard in Torrance. They moved the time slot around every few weeks until anyone who liked it gave up trying to follow. My mom was frustrated, and so she became difficult, and everyone else followed suit.

The majority of producers were working for CBS, and not my mom. They were following procedure for the most part, mimicking what they had seen work on other daytime shows. They were great at their jobs, just not at taking risks.

The producer I worked under asked us one day to brainstorm ideas for the next few weeks. It was late 1999, so I suggested we do a show on Y2K and Armageddon theories. She looked up into her skull as if she were trying to convince me she was actually "seeing" it, and could also see that it was bad, and then she said that the housewives who were home watching the show would be thinking, What does Armageddon have to do with *me*? You know what I'm saying?

I stared, stood up, and walked out of the meeting. I went straight to my mom's office and asked to be transferred to the art department, which was one of the best decisions I ever made. Crew is where it's at. That's where my favorite people were. It was all the creatives with no pressure or desire to exploit, making things in a basement full of art supplies. Like kindergarten, but with cigarettes and whiskey.

I had been dating the show's accountant, Barney, who was ten years older than me. He was a film major and bought me the latest edition of *VideoHound's Golden Movie Retriever*, seemingly just to explain every word in it to me in detail. That was before anyone cared about movies, but I was ahead of my time. He liked to lord his intelligence over me and scoff at everything I said. He corrected me a lot about which movies and songs were good and which weren't. If the *Actually* . . . trope were a person, it would be Barney.

Toward the end of Season 1, Jessica, who had just started working as a production assistant, and I were fired. Nepotism has benefits but also risks. Like, yeah, your mom can give you a job, but she can also take it away if you perhaps, say, decide to use your positions to get VIP press passes for the Cannabis Cup in Amsterdam instead of coming to the yearly Thanksgiving family gathering.

I was still dating Barney, though we weren't working together anymore. Since I had more free time now, I was spending a lot of it with Brandi and Jake and Jake's best friend, Jeff. Brandi and I were roommates, and Jake and Jeff would come over almost nightly. We would cook and sit and talk for hours about Kabbalah, mysticism, aliens, quantum physics, and our other collective interests, or just laugh and play board games.

One night, Barney came over and mocked Jake and Jeff's Trivial Pursuit skills, and I got fed up and dumped him. I wasn't very nice about it because I was on the Pill, which makes me insane, and my Achilles' heel is anyone making fun of people I love, which made me realize that I felt fiercely protective of Jeff because I loved him. I was single for about two hours before I tricked him into giving me a back massage.

The massage turned into more, and we slept together that night. I was nervous about Jake finding out that I had slept with his best friend, but Jeff promised he'd handle it . . . which he did the next day by abruptly saying, "By the way, I fucked your sister," as they walked to their cars together. We've been together ever since.

15B.

Barr Girls (and the Pentland Curse)

Out of the three of us Pentland kids, I was the most Pentland. This was agreed upon by all of the Barrs. Although there was an Ashkenazi overlay on top of my Gaelic features, I was green-eyed and sported the giant forehead of a Pentland. I also inherited the pear shape, whereas my Barr family were all shaped like apples. I was more agreeable and didn't mind casseroles. I liked being outdoors. I could handle small talk. I could chat for hours with relatives I hadn't seen for a while. Also, I shared the namesake's curse.

Anything I attempted to do seemed to be met with hurdles placed by an antagonistic fallen angel with a taste for black comedy. Any money accumulated was immediately lost, or had to be spent on unforeseen events. Any light at the end of the tunnel was the headlight of a train. Any gains were illusive. We were like Wile E. Coyotes in a universe made up of Road Runners, but people liked us Pentlands anyway.

Jessica and Jake were Barrs, it was noted. They had deep brown eyes, were introverted, hated small talk, liked Mediterranean food more than sugar, had darker body hair, olive skin, and Lithuanian features, and would rather be in their rooms than at the table during a Christmas dinner.

I remember feeling a bit left out being labeled a Pentland. Although I loved my Pentland side very much, I did not want my Barr Girl–ness overlooked. I, too, was hilarious and weird. I talked to God and rolled my eyes when adults told me not to trust boys. I liked chopped liver and could be deep when necessary. I could see through people, even if I chose not to in order to get along with everyone. I had a mustache, too, even if I had to get into exactly the right light to flaunt it.

Barrs were powerful and unbending. They took no shit and didn't play into all the social norms. They called out whatever sexist, racist doublespeak they encountered, told people not to touch their kids' heads, and sent a lot of meals back to the kitchen for being wrong. No one liked us.

Barr Girls were a special sect. A Barr Girl is someone who is both of Barr lineage and a girl. She is often warned that men are just trying to sleep with her, while every move she makes is a seductive web to trap one. She is usually pulled aside in elementary school and "talked to" about kissing other kids on the playground. She may have to be reminded to go to her room to hump things when she is young. She might have to be put on a leash because she will sit on the laps of strangers. She may have to have her phone provider block all party-line numbers.

The Pursuit of Dick is our mission, nay, our calling. Male attention is valuable, but that's not the point. There are many girls who pursue men because of the perceived value of their attention, but Barr Girls do it to explore their own subconscious minds and souls and to balance the powers of the universe. We love the men, regardless of their obsession with power. They are smart and kind and solve problems. They grow and open and realize things that unlock the secrets of the universe for other men. They create beautiful rituals and functional art. Realized men are an asset to humanity, evolution, and femininity. They are the conduits of the vast mystical wisdom of women. Of course there is another side to masculinity, but we all see and know about that as we and the Earth die of capitalism and ego. The degree of destruction they are capable of is amazing, but that spectrum has another end, and we Barr Girls wanna hump it.

My bubbe is the original Barr Girl. This means that several men offed themselves when they realized they couldn't be with her. Following my grandpa's passing, she had boyfriend after boyfriend and was going dancing every week and getting free meals. Even at eighty-seven years old, there is a line to be in her company. She is charming and hilarious and, as Jeff says, hot.

I liked being half and half. I am like a centaur, a magical cross between legend and human. The legend of the Barrs was born out of our destroyed records, burned by the Nazis. I'm sure that, if proper documentation existed, we would be as basic as any old Pentland, whose lineage my dad's mom was able to trace back to King Charlemagne c. 700 AD and also show that we were distant cousins of Princess Diana. But the history of the Barrs who came before Bubbe's mom—their real name, Borisofsky, was shortened at Ellis Island—was all word of mouth. They were the great healers in the Kohanim tribe, the Davids, the ancient kabbalistic Jews who elevated consciousness with their hands and minds. The Barrs were direct descendants of God. The Pentlands were direct descendants of kings. Who would want to choose?

16.

The Pee Cup
Is Half Full

The night after Jeff and first I hooked up, he told me he wanted to take me to dinner and made reservations at a fancy Italian restaurant up the road. I didn't want to go, but I didn't want to hurt his feelings either. It was the winter of El Niño. The streets were flooded and rain poured constantly. Parked cars would float and drift away. It was dark and heavy and cold outside. I just wanted to be in pajamas on my couch, but I put on some sort of an outfit. At that time I was wearing a lot of long chiffon peignoirs with matching nightgowns, or fifties dresses. I applied some makeup and we went to dinner.

The whole thing was extremely awkward. Jeff went through all the motions of the fifties movie stars he had seen being romantic on the only TV shows he had been allowed to watch as a kid. He did all the right things, opening doors for me, pulling my chair out, having the waiter light some candles on our table, ordering wine, letting me choose whatever I wanted, etc. I was miserable.

For a long time, I thought I was not a romantic person, but I am. I am so romantic that I cannot stand expected gestures. Romance to me is personal. It's when someone sees you or parts of you that you don't even see. It's being understood, or even better, being *not misunderstood*. I'd rather someone know my exact Taco Bell order than ever buy me flowers.

I made that night so uncomfortable, and I felt guilty knowing how hard Jeff had tried to make it nice. When we got home, I apologized to him and we talked about the awkwardness and he really listened to me. I wasn't used to someone actively trying to hear what I had to say, and it was intoxicating. I haven't shut up since. He actually modifies his behavior to reflect his love and inspires me to do the same (he's much better at it). Crazy, right?

Brandi and I and Jake and Jeff were all on unemployment, and we spent our free time taking classes at the Kabbalah Center in Beverly Hills. We decided it would be easier to move near the center than to drive over Friday nights for Shabbat services, so we found a two-bedroom apartment in Los Angeles and Brandi, Jeff, and I moved in. Eventually a bunch of our friends moved in next door or upstairs. It was like Melrose Place, with more pot and less sex.

A neighbor girl, Rachel, greeted our U-Haul as we were moving in. I recognized her from temple and said hi. She was eight, and she told me that I would like this neighborhood. It was quiet and safe. She invited us over. I accepted her invitation and met her mom, whom I also recognized. She was baking challah for the week and told me to come sit and have a snack and some tea. Her Spanish-style apartment had stucco walls and archways and terra-cotta tiles. I felt like I had stumbled into some sort of seventeenth-century cottage, and I loved it.

Rachel asked me if I wanted to see her fairy village, and there was no way to say no to her. She walked me down the hallway and opened her bedroom door. The wall next to her bed was lined with tiny ceramic houses that were painted to look real.

"I used to make those!" I said. I walked over and picked one up and looked at it. I remembered painting every single detail around the windows and trying to keep the glitter only on the white snow and off the red brick. As I studied it, I realized this was mine and tipped it back to see my own initials on the bottom. I was sure I had slipped into some sort of alternate reality warp. Was I Adjacent-Rachel? Was she Adjacent-Jenny? Was she my future daughter who had inherited my wares? I lost my bearings for a moment, not helped by the smell of fresh baking bread tickling my cellular memory. Rachel was kind of unnerved at my silence, which shook me out of it enough to ask, "Where did you get these?"

"My mom got them at a garage sale at the temple."

"I made these. These are my initials!" She didn't know if I was angry or what. "I'm *so glad* you have them! Thank you for loving them," I said, still totally confused.

Doing further research, I found out that Ben had done a major overhaul on my mom's storage facility in his endless pursuit of order and had gotten rid of everything that wasn't his, my mom's, or Buck's. That meant all my childhood keepsakes, all my journals, all my scrapbooks and yearbooks—everything I had saved or made in the past twenty-one years. Same for all of Jessica's stuff. He gave it all to the Kabbalah Center to sell at their yearly fundraiser. Rachel's mom had purchased them there.

I have never been a materialistic person and after years of moving around with a duffel bag full of strange things, I hadn't felt an attachment to anything except my journals. They had gotten me through, and they knew more than anyone else. I wanted to be able to read them in my forties and laugh about how ridiculous things had been while I gazed out over the pages at my idyllic life. Maybe those journals would have just reminded me of sitting alone in my cold mental institution room, though. Maybe the universe was giving me this opportunity to let go of my past. Seeing a young kid from my temple, where I had taken classes about forgiveness and tikkun (or karma), getting so much joy out of these things felt like a lesson too obvious to deny.

Everything felt that way after taking classes at the Kabbalah Center: everything was tikkun. That of course included my relationship a few years before with their resident palm- and face-reading rabbi, Elijah. We started dating when I was twenty-one. He was ten years older than me, but only physically. We got into our first fight when he accused me of being a materialistic social climber while I helped him get ready for a three-month-long trip to read faces in New York.

"You just want to use me for status," he said from his seat on the aged, stained mattress he slept on on the floor of the community apartment above the temple as we were packing his three pairs of hand-me-down pants into his borrowed suitcase, getting him ready to leave for New

York because the Rav (head rabbi) had told him to. Gimme some of that good status, babe.

I helped him fold the pants and placed them into the suitcase, where I saw a stack of papers with my name on it. I lifted it out and saw that he had had the temple's astrologer draw up a birth and progression chart for me. The only problem was, she had my birth info wrong. The chart was completely incorrect, and I let him know it. In my correct chart, it seems I'm actually attracted to transient philosophers who play Leonard Cohen songs for me on acoustic guitar, so we made up and continued our relationship long-distance for a few months, talking on the phone every night. He kept pushing the learning-Hebrew issue, and I kept feeling like I was being fast-tracked to wig-wearing mother of eight. A few months later he moved back to LA and I went to visit him. At that point, I knew we weren't going to work long term and was waiting for the right time to tell him.

He was busy reading someone's palm, so I decided to go get him some pastries from the kosher deli nearby. My friend Debbie worked in the bookstore there, and she asked me where I was going. I told her I was going to get Elijah some pastries, and she rolled her eyes. They did not like each other. "Well, don't get him the ones with chocolate inside. He won't eat those. He doesn't like the jelly ones either. Oh, and don't even try to get him to eat the sesame ones. He's impossible," she said, exasperated. Oh. She's in love with him, I thought. I broke up with him pretty quick after that. They have several kids together now.

I still enjoyed taking classes over the next couple years. Brandi and Jessica and I would attend together, and Jake and Jeff would show up, too. After one of the sessions, a classmate said, "I love the way Jeff looks at you."

"Jeff who?" I asked. There were several. She pointed to my future husband, and I was shocked. "Him?! No. We're just friends!" It was only a couple months later that we hooked up. We continued our courses together after that.

I loved the teachers and rabbis at the center, but the Rav was getting older and there seemed to be a shift away from true spirituality to whatever that slow ectoplasmic bullshit is that's always waiting to choke out goodness and replace it with capitalism. Part of what we all loved about the temple was that we were all equal there. Fame and status didn't matter here. We all had to follow the same rules. My mom was spending a lot of time there, too, and she really was at peace for the first time I could remember. Then came the day when I watched the Torah being brought out for Ashton Kutcher to touch, as people who dedicated their whole lives to this congregation were held back to make room for him. Ugh. Another Celebrity Center. (Ashton has little fault in this. Whenever I criticize celebrity culture, I can feel other people's contempt for the individual celebrities but—spoiler alert—they're not the problem.)

I started working as a nanny for a family at temple that had two-year-old triplets. The mom was also pregnant with a single child (two years after this fourth baby, she went on to have twins), and they agreed to pay me cash to start. I didn't want to lose my unemployment. It was a hard job by nature, but my body had been doing something weird that was making it even harder. At the end of my workday, when Jeff came to get me, I could hardly walk. I felt like I was dying. I had missed the deadline to apply for COBRA so, without insurance, I thought the way any twenty-three-year-old would: wait and see/die. Turns out it was life-threatening anemia caused by the gastric bypass I'd had at nineteen, which was being exacerbated by a human living in my womb.

Season 2 of the talk show had just started, and though I had been fired for going to Amsterdam instead of Thanksgiving dinner, I would still come to tapings whenever my mom had a great guest on. One day, she was interviewing one of our rabbis (not the one I dated, but a close friend of his), and I came onstage during a break and whispered to her that I was pregnant. Jeff and I had been together only six months, and I was barely twenty-three. She feigned joy, but I knew her well and could tell she was upset. I was glad I told her at a time when she couldn't react immediately in the way she probably wanted to.

"This doesn't mean I'm going to take care of you for the rest of your life," she said to me later in her dressing room trailer.

Although I understood where she was coming from, I was a bit put off, since Jeff had been a great provider from day one, starting with insurance. He had been working in the entertainment industry as a set dresser like his grandpa and his great-grandpa before him. He got into the union when he was nineteen, which was unheard-of. He probably would have gotten in sooner if he hadn't been so busy being a volunteer firefighter in Van Nuys from sixteen to nineteen, which he would have done sooner if he hadn't been busy being a candy striper at Valley Presbyterian Hospital at fifteen. He had forgone a social life as a teen in order to take care of his mom, who was ill, and their house, which was slowly preparing to be a future episode of *Hoarders*. Jeff was capable.

The talk show wasn't getting great ratings. I loved it, but it didn't fit the daytime-TV mold, and the time slot had been moved so many times trying to find its target audience that no one knew when it was on. When my mom realized the producers weren't really invested in it, she decided to go rogue, and it took a turn toward *Richard Bey*. She would wear whatever she wanted and sing with her guests or lie in bed with them for interviews. She hired me to be her makeup artist and had me paint eyes on her forehead or style her hair into horns.

One of my favorite things to do with my mom is to announce our current situation as a chapter title. For example, say I'm in a dressing room trying to yank a spandex body shaper over her back fat—I will say, "Chapter 17: Helping Mother with Her Girdle." The more the fictitious title summarizes the ridiculousness of the situation, the harder my mom will laugh.

» "Chapter 8: Mother Marries Bodyguard."
» "Chapter 11: Mother's Geriatric Pregnancy."
» "Chapter 6: Mother Sings with James Brown."

Mother interviewed psychics and writers and singers and regular interesting people on her show, and it was a good show, if self-indulgent at times. It was a really fun way to spend my maternity.

While I was working on the talk show, Jeff proposed to me on a cliff overlooking the ocean in Malibu. I refused to descend to the area he wanted me to since I was pregnant and would then need to get back up the cliff, so the event ended up happening close to the side of Highway 1. He had two white-gold bands he had purchased for two hundred bucks each. He asked, "Will you marry me?" I answered, "Of course I will, stupid. Now get this baby and me off this fucking cliff."

Our engagement was only days long, so I barely had time to be formally introduced to his parents. And even if there had been time, they were less than excited about our situation and refused to meet me.

I'm sure it had something to do with the fact that Jeff had called his ailing mom weeks earlier to tell her that he had been taking Kabbalah classes, and that he believed her lupus and heart disease were symptoms of negative thinking that could be cured with positive thinking. When she got frustrated with him, he said, "You need to get better. We're pregnant." In hindsight, maybe that wasn't the best way to give her the news. His tone was accusatory and cold and dismissive, which his mom, Diana, had had enough of from her doctors. She hung up the phone angry, but not before telling Jeff to get me an abortion.

I had to remind Jeff that what he really meant was, "I love you," and that maybe he should have just said *that* instead. I asked him to drive me to his parents' home in Van Nuys, and I refused to leave until they came out to meet me. His dad, Mike, finally appeared, but just to tell me that Diana was not going to come out. I told Mike that we were sorry for our phone call and that it was out of line and that we were getting married and wanted them to be there. I made fun of the way Jeff had handled the call, and Mike laughed. He went inside and got Diana. She came to the door but refused to come outside. I talked to her through the screen for a minute and told her I knew how things looked but that Jeff and I loved each other and always had. I apologized to her for how Jeff had broken the news to her and saw her soften a bit when she knew I wasn't trying to trap her son or ruin his life. They agreed to come to the ceremony.

Two weeks later, Jeff and I had a shotgun wedding in Vegas, the seven-hundred-dollar package a generous gift from Mom's husband, Ben. A soon-to-be uncle at four years old, Buck was a perfect ringbearer. I had yet to meet Jeff's brother, Doug, and his fiancée, Angela, who had been planning their own wedding for the past year. Angela was studying law, and Doug was paying for her schooling by working full-time in the studios in the same union as Jeff. They had everything planned out for the rest of their lives, including the unisex name of their first child, who wouldn't be conceived for another six years. The first time I ever spoke to them, I was walking down the aisle in my two-piece, off-the-rack dress. I waved at them and yelled, "Hi! I'm Jenny!" across the pews. Anything for a laugh. They giggled and waved back and said hi to me, and they are two of my favorite people on Earth.

Jeff showed up only a minute late to our thirty-minute window of chapel time and rushed in looking gorgeous and put together in his rented tux. I hadn't known if he would pull it off since, the night before, he had been to a strip club with Jake and Ben and had come pounding on my hotel room door at three in the morning, tinted green. I'd put him in a cold shower and listened to him cry about how he hated strip clubs and hadn't wanted to be there and just wanted to come home to me. *Awwwwwwww*, except I'd wanted to sleep before the wedding.

After Vegas, I continued to work on the talk show until it was canceled in my ninth month of pregnancy. Jeff started looking for apartments of our own, which displaced Brandi. There was no way to afford living in LA without roommates and a good job, and Brandi ended up moving back to Colorado soon after we moved out. I was sad about it and felt guilty, but I didn't know what else to do. Thankfully my guilt was dissolved later when Brandi met her husband, Will, in Denver and produced my very smart and handsome nephew, Ari.

Jeff was right that we needed our own space. He found us a gorgeous 1920s apartment right by the temple. It had hardwood floors and stained glass and molding and piping detail work. It was a proper home, and we turned the back room into a nursery. Jeff spent the majority of his free time at Home Depot buying fire extinguishers, carbon monoxide detectors, axes, first aid kits, and safety paraphernalia. Ours was probably the first OSHA-approved nursery in the United States. I made fun of Jeff constantly, as did all our friends and family, but that didn't stop him.

I was forty-one weeks pregnant and my doctor had scheduled an induction for July 11, 2000. The night before, we were at Home Depot. Jeff left me in line alone to run back and grab some sort of electrical tape, and the guy behind me took the opportunity to ask me if I'd "actually felt my hips spreading" during the last nine months. I was tempted to say, "Only when I was takin' it, you know, bro?" Elbow, elbow . . . I have never gotten used to being community property the way pregnant women are, no matter how many times I've done it now.

My induction went as planned. We showed up at Cedars-Sinai hospital early in the morning and had yet another intake procedure. I peed in a cup for the one millionth time in my life, but this was, by far, for the best reason yet. I happily handed over the golden chalice this time, without being tempted to spill it on anyone.

My labor was progressing, but not fast enough for the doctors, who probably wanted to go home, so they told me the baby was stressed out and I needed a cesarean. They told me I was only seven centimeters and needed to dilate to ten to push, but that the baby was distressed and might not last that long, as they shaved my pubic bone. It felt wrong to me, but try to tell a doctor no, because of a mother's intuition, and see how far you get. They told me someone was coming to wheel me into surgery, and I told them to wait ten minutes and I would finish dilating. They rolled their eyes but humored me, probably because that's how long it would take someone to get me to surgery anyway. When the nurse came to transfer me, I told her to check me again. I was ten centimeters. There was no time for a cesarean. Fuuuck you alll. Thank God for my stubbornness, because my bloodwork had come back showing severe anemia and my bleeding during surgery might have killed me.

I had a pretty strong epidural and couldn't feel my legs, so a team of people, including Jeff, were holding me and telling me what to do and cheering me on. Jeff, of course, was making comments that most people keep inside, such as, "You're so hot!" as I sprayed the doc with diarrhea. I pushed for an hour. I tore, but upward toward my clitoris, and the doc gave me an episiotomy to prevent it from getting worse. I pushed again and saw my baby in the doctor's hands. He handed him to me and I looked at him all bundled up in the white bleached Angelica linen I knew the smell of so well. I knew him. I had known him forever. I was never not his mom. History had been revised. Everything was for this moment. It was worth any struggle and any pain.

I sank into bliss while Jeff took the baby to the nursery. I lay there trying to come to terms with this unimaginable metamorphosis, and after what seemed like both a few seconds and many hours, I realized I was not yet holding my baby. I didn't know how long the nursery process usually took, so I calmly asked a nurse who was cleaning up where my baby was. "Oh, I'm sure they'll be right down." Her tone was too singsongy, and my gut flipped.

"*Where's my baby?*"

She told me she would call and find out, and she picked up the intercom phone in my room. "Jennifer is wondering when she can see her baby," she said. She was silent a millisecond too long, and I sat up on the stretcher.

"Bring him to me right *now!*" I started to panic.

"Your husband is on his way down here to talk to you," she said.

My legs didn't work or I would've been halfway down the hall before she finished that sentence. I threw off the sheet covering me and tried to get off the bed. Jeff stormed into the room as the nurse was pushing me back onto the stretcher and exasperatedly said, "*He has a hole in his head.*"

Maybe because Jeff was not calm, maybe because intuitively I knew my baby would be okay because I had "seen" him as a man, maybe because I had never trusted doctors, maybe because the stakes were so high—I had to become calm. I centered myself outside of space-time and I just knew it was all okay.

"He's fine. Trust me," I said. "Tell me what the doctor told you."

Jeff told me that there was a hole in the roof of his mouth, in the soft part of the skin. My complete obsession with medical information and my previous medical experience with sick dolls paid off. "Oh," I said. "He has a cleft palate. It's only in the soft part?" I was grilling Jeff, but he was too distraught to deliver proper medical info, evidenced by his words "he has a hole in his head" rather than "he has a cleft in his soft palate."

Right then, the doctor walked in and told me in medical terms the same thing Jeff had told me. The baby had a cleft palate in the soft part. It didn't affect the hard palate, and it didn't appear to be serious. The only concern was that he also had a small chin, and this coupled with the cleft could be symptoms of a disease called Rubinstein-Taybi Syndrome, a condition that could include an intellectual disability. Or . . . he could just have a small chin from being a tall boy tucked into a young uterus. We'd have to wait and see. In the meantime, we'd have to meet with a geneticist, a craniofacial team, and several other doctors.

The baby could latch, but he couldn't maintain enough suction to draw milk out of me, so we were assigned a lactation consultant. She gave me a heavy-duty breast pump and fondled me a bunch and talked about every aspect of nursing. I had been extra excited about nursing because I wanted that bond, and also because it was a loving act of subversiveness. I couldn't wait for the first person with balls enough to make a comment to me in public. I had retorts locked and loaded for most situations I could think of, such as, "You're the pervert who wants to fuck a baby's breakfast. Don't put that on me." Or "Take it up with your God. This wasn't my idea." Or even "They're not just for titty-fucking!" I would have to wait for my next kid to use these.

The lactation nurse asked me if I knew what I would name the baby, and I told her we had several short-listed but hadn't decided on one yet. She then proceeded to say to the baby each of our top three names, although I had never told her which names we were considering. She told me that Ethan was the one that suited him. I decided that she knew something I didn't, so we legally named him Ethan, which is the Americanized version of his Hebrew name, Eitan. (Years later, I would attend his third-grade parent-teacher conference, where his teacher would inform me that he was going by Eitan now. She had asked all her students what names they preferred being called, and that's what he told her he wanted. I asked him after the conference if he wanted everyone to use his Hebrew name, and he said yes, so I've called him Eitan ever since. Some family members still call him Ethan fifteen years later. He doesn't mind, but it makes me a little mad.)

After three long days in the hospital, we were allowed to go home. The drive was only about seven minutes, but it was the longest and strangest seven minutes I've ever spent. This was a completely new world. I sat in the back seat of our 1992 Honda Civic feeling like an airbag around Eitan's car seat. Everything seemed threatening and dangerous. I swore at all the tailgaters and speeders and was relieved to finally get home.

The next few months were a blur. Pumping took forty-five minutes, and then it took Eitan an hour to eat, and then it took fifteen minutes to clean the machinery. Since he was eating every two hours, I was tied to the pump 24/7. I slept while I pumped. At our first checkup, the doctor gave me a Haberman nipple to feed Eitan with. This is an extra-long nipple designed to basically clog the cleft to help the baby suck. It didn't. You had to squeeze the bottle and time it so that he was swallowing as you were squeezing. If he changed his rhythm, half my precious breast milk would come out his nose as he choked down whatever he could.

I decided I was going to invent a bottle that worked for him. I went to the store and purchased one of the flat oval Playtex nipples and cut a slit in it like a coin purse. Instead of laying it on his tongue flat, I turned it sideways so he could use his jaw to control the flow. Instead of sucking, he chewed now. He had full control and stopped choking and spitting up and started to thrive. We lived like this for six weeks until my nipples were so trashed that the amount of blood in my milk upset his stomach—and mine, for that matter. I stopped pumping and put him on formula, which squashed my dreams of nursing and made me sad. I knew it was the only option now. The formula made him smell like boxed mashed potato flakes and I still love that scent now.

Jeff continued his work in the industry. His hours were long, twelve hours most days, and so I stayed home. I mean, I *really* stayed home. I was in no condition to do anything, being as I was so anemic.

The times I did leave the house, I regretted it. People were very judgmental of my perceived age and were constantly commenting and criticizing me for extremely innocuous things, like how I held Eitan in a sling or how I put his sock on. Granted, most of my outings were on foot, as Jeff had to take our only car to work. We were Beverly Hills–Adjacent, so I was basically entering Atlantic City in *The Walking Dead*, but instead of murderous brain-eating zombies it was all Jewish bubbes who crave giving unsolicited advice, limping around in half circles to get to you, arms out, tugging at your clothing and blankets, gurgly, breathy, fixated. One would tell me it was too hot, and the next would tell me it was too cold, and the next would say he was too young to be out, etc. Not to mention the superstitions about haircuts and nail clipping and spitting between fingers and . . . etc., forever.

I hadn't been wearing a wedding ring because my near-death state meant my size-five ring was too loose, and I could see people looking at my finger and my baby and my baby face and drawing their own conclusions. I finally bought a white onesie for Eitan and wrote LEGITIMATE on it in iron-on black velvet letters. I couldn't easily keep up that level of contempt and rebelliousness on what little bit of blood was in my body, so I put a mattress on my living room floor, drew the curtains, and lay in front of the TV for four months watching *Fight Club* over and over. I finally started treatment for anemia, which meant getting iron infusions at the cancer center. If I thought I hated the looks of judgment I was getting as a pregnant "teen," I didn't know about their much more crushing cousins, looks of pity. I had to sit next to cancer patients with my baby in a sling across my chest and deal with "You look great and still have all your hair!" Or, even worse, I had to tell concerned cancer patients that I was okay, just anemic, as they sat there vomiting into trash cans. I still have to do these infusions twice yearly, and I cry every time.

When Eitan was about a year old, he had corrective surgery for the cleft. We were assigned the best surgeon, who had the most giant hands. I wondered how he planned on reaching them into the back of this tiny birdlike baby's throat. He managed somehow, and after the scariest four-hour wait, I was allowed to pick Eitan up from post-op. The strangest part of the whole thing was that I didn't recognize his cry anymore. I walked right past him in the recovery room.

Around this time, I got a phone call as I was sleeping. I'm anxious when the phone rings at odd hours. I jumped up, grabbed it and said hello.

"Jenny?"

It was my bubbe's voice. Loaded with emotion, soft, careful. We hadn't spoken to or seen each other in more than ten years, not since our family's falling-out during the Tom era. She didn't know how I would feel about her calling. She had been told a lot of things, but not by me.

"I just wanted to let you know that your grandpa has passed away. I don't have your mom's number." She was holding back so much, her words were like a cold cement dam. I let her know that I would relay the information to my mom and then she tried to say goodbye, but I shouted, "WAIT! . . . I have a son!"

After a pause, she somberly said, "I know."

Apparently my dad's mom had been keeping Bubbe up to date on us kids, which I am so grateful for now. I kept Bubbe on the phone, and we talked very slowly, calculating each word and its consequence, trying to avoid saying the wrong thing. By the end of the call we had a promise to talk again soon. I called my mom to tell her that her dad was gone and threw in that I had talked to Bubbe and that we all wanted to get together at some point. It was a lot for one call.

My mom handled it like she handles all devastating news. She said, "Oh. All right." Then got off the phone. It would be two more years before we got together with my bubbe for a reunion. It was awkward, but I wanted my family in my life, even if it meant overlooking the suspicion and contempt, judgment and pain that had festered over the years in each of us. The bottom line now was that there was no one trying to isolate my mom from people who would tell her the truth or stand up for her, so we could all move on and heal in whatever way each of us needed to. Beanie and Steph had six kids between them whom I had never met. My mom's brother Ben's daughter Melissa was married. Everyone was grown.

Eventually Eitan started to walk. We lived on busy Olympic Boulevard. My mom didn't like this and offered to help us buy a house. I have always been wary of taking gifts because it seems there are always strings attached, doubly so when those gifts are from a mother to a daughter. Plus, next to a kidney, a house was the biggest gift I could imagine receiving. I remembered my mom saying a couple years earlier that she didn't intend on taking care of me forever just because I was pregnant. I had no intention of being That Daughter, but when Eitan was fifteen months old, he figured out the baby gate lock, and I found him standing on our porch. I told Jessica and Jessica ratted me out to Mom, and then Mom called me demanding I accept her offer.

"The house is NOT FOR YOU, DUMBASS. It's for my grandson."

I conceded. I couldn't say no to a safer place for my son because of my pride. We couldn't afford anywhere near where we lived, so we started looking in the more affordable area south of LAX airport. After viewing three hundred houses (I looked at only the first two before realizing that Jeff was going to be impossible to please, and told him to let me know when he had seen one worth my precious time), Jeff finally found one with, as they say, good bones. It was in the up-and-coming 1950s suburb of Manhattan Beach. We chose it for its highly rated school district and the wonderful neighbors. It was idyllic, with a Trader Joe's on the corner and a preschool at the end of the street. It was a community, not just a neighborhood. The couple who lived next to us became an extra set of grandparents for our kids. The husband, Cliff, was known as "the Mayor," and his wife, Joanne, made the best cold-brew coffee on Earth.

They came to all our parties, and on warm evenings they would all sit in their driveway and all the neighbors would come down with their kids to play and chat. It was far from Jeff's job, but it was worth the long commute. Over the next seven years, almost every small house on our block was demolished and replaced with a McMansion. Cliff did not like that, and neither did we.

16B.

Uses for Bodyguards

After my mom sang the national anthem, we were never without a retired police officer bodyguard as we carried on with our lives. At one point, we had three in the house, but only two were on duty in the small office that held the monitors for all the cameras.

The third was Ben, the retired bodyguard who had been promoted to baby daddy when Buck was born. He was a busybody, a workaholic, and a perfectionist. He was either upstairs micromanaging the housekeepers and nanny or in the garage futzing with his toy collection. He had grown up riding ATVs around central California deserts and loved all his new toys. He had an RV, dirt bikes, quads, full-body gear, and a Hummer my mom had painted camouflage and given him for a wedding present.

I'll never forget the day Jerry Garcia died. Ben took Jessica and me in the Hummer and drove around Brentwood and Los Angeles blasting the Grateful Dead through the megaphone that was attached to the roof. He used the CB mic to pay homage by saying, "We love you, Jerry! Rest in peace!" as we went up and down the streets. A proper goodbye.

After my mom and Ben's marriage ended about eight years later and she was single and ready to mingle again, the bodyguards weren't just for protection from the public. We kids would ask these guys to use whatever resources they had to look up any guy my mom was showing interest in. We stayed on top of it pretty well.

My mom had told me she'd been talking to a couple of men online. One was a writer whom she'd met on her website, Roseanneworld, where she kept a blog and spoke personally with her fans, and one was just a regular old Joe from Salt Lake City. I asked my mom if I could check into these people, and she rolled her eyes and said yes. I got their names and passed their info to one of our trusted security guys, who came back a few days later and told me that neither guy had "checked out."

He told me that one of her suitors was using an alias, and that the other did not even exist. I freaked out and told my mom, and she stopped talking to the nonexistent one. It turns out that the one using the alias was very up front about it. He was a musician and was going by a stage name. My mom already knew that. Okay, then. Maybe this other guy had just as good of an alibi?

It didn't matter, though, because my mom was already really into the musician guy, and they had been spending hours a day talking, not just online but on the phone, too. They had plans to meet. They met. They fell in love. Cut to eighteen years later and they're still together.

But the other guy . . . *was not a guy at all. He* was not only a *she,* but she was twenty years older than my mom *and* was one of Bubbe's neighbors and friends. We only found out because she confessed to Bubbe that she had intentionally misled my mom so that she could single-handedly repair the rifts in our family! As a mitzvah? Thanks, but . . . no thanks.

17.

"Aloha" Means Goodbye

My mom was unemployed and restless and also newly single. She and Ben had been having problems and decided to get divorced. Before they broke up, Mom had already decided to buy a small space in El Segundo, where she owned a home near Buck's school, the same one his dad had gone to. She wanted her own place to create content without the oppressive bullshit of a network, and she wanted to work for herself.

She turned the space into a small production studio and needed staff to run it, so she offered Jeff and Jake jobs there. They both accepted, quit their current jobs, and outfitted the studio with all the equipment it needed.

Along with furnishing it as a creative space for herself, she also hoped to rent it out to the influx of newly loaded internet entrepreneurs to offset some of the expenses. In the middle of prepping it for small commercials, infomercials, PowerPoint presentations, and training videos, my mom decided she was going to star in a reality show and use the studio as its production office, so Jake and Jeff had to switch gears. They were excited, though, because they believed the exposure from the reality show would get them more business, and that was the direction in which they expected to continue.

She met with producer R.J. Cutler and came up with the idea to do a show about the making of another show, a cooking show. It was a way for my mom to talk about her crazy experiences in entertainment. She was angry about how everything on the talk show had been handled and wanted to reveal the inner workings of Hollywood. She's always had a Joan of Arc–level boner for exposing hypocrisy.

Before the show started production, my mom had started seriously dating Johnny, the musician she had met online in a writers' forum. He moved to LA from Arizona to write and to be part of the reality show.

The reality show crew followed my mom for months as she went about her life producing and starring in the cooking show, which had its own producers and crew. If there had been a third crew filming the pretentious second crew and the tornado of horseshit around them and the first crew, it could have been so good. My husband and brother had been sucked into it and were doing their best to play along with the agenda, while I was doing my best to avoid it. At one point in filming, though, one of us kids found a piece of paper that we weren't supposed to see. It was a character breakdown of all the cast, listing the names and character descriptions of everyone in my family.

- » *Roseanne:* has-been celeb doing a cooking show, crazy but a genius
- » *Johnny:* freeloader musician internet boyfriend
- » *Jessica:* voice of reason
- » *Buck:* rambunctious 7yo
- » *Jake:* Tweedledee
- » *Jeff:* Tweedledum
- » *Jenny:* daughter, SAHM mom, Jeff's wife, mother of Roseanne's grandson

Rude.

For obvious reasons, this pissed everyone off. Well, except Jessica. Jeff had been great at his previous job as a set dresser on several big productions like *Once and Again* and *Turbulence*, where reputation was everything. He had always left the door open to go back to work in the studios because it was good pay and had great benefits. It was the reason Eitan had had such excellent medical care when he was born. We needed this option to stay open for our family, and he felt like having his reputation threatened could close that door.

The cooking show part of the new sitcom was filmed across town in an actual studio. They had barely pulled together three episodes by the premiere date and were planning on seeing what the response was before committing to making more. My mom was already over being followed and mocked, and she was sick of the show's producers, who kept forgetting that we were human beings.

The family hadn't watched any of the footage, but we felt the same. The only thing we had seen were the three crew members who followed my mom everywhere, and a couple of the hot young assistant girls who were so-so at their actual duties but excellent at making the men feel powerful. When we were told there was going to be a viewing party of the premiere episode, I pictured one of these guys' home movie theaters (everyone in the industry has one) and some catering and booze. Maybe a popcorn machine.

Jeff and I got dressed to go, our outfits on brand and off base, and got into our Honda minivan. Jeff was dressed like a ninety-year-old man on vacation in Havana with his Hawaiian shirt, chinos, and sailing loafers, and I looked like a Hasidic wife in my midcalf denim skirt and flowy blouse with sandals. We drove to the location in Santa Monica. We gave the valet our keys and walked in. The venue was a bar right on the cusp of being hip that had been rented out and rearranged for the evening. There were probably fifty-plus young production staff, all of whom turned to look at us. I heard whispers. "That's Jeff and Jenny!" It was as though they were watching us on a screen at that very moment, like we weren't flesh and blood. We weren't real, but somehow they still knew us. I'd witnessed my mom in this situation a thousand times, but I was always adjacent and protective. It caught me off guard.

At my request, Jeff went straight to the bar to get us drinks. I wiggled my way through tables and chairs and stares looking for a familiar face and found Jake. He was schmoozing a bit and knew more of these people than I did. I hid behind him until I could find my next refuge.

Jeff found me and I found my drink in his hand and we found our clan hunkered in the safety of a booth, while strangers milled about saying our names. Then the lights went down, and the show started playing on the five giant monitors that had been carted in for this party. The opening credits came on, animated and humiliating. The cartoon was of my mom hogging the spotlight Jeff was holding on a boom before he dropped it, making him look like an idiot within ten seconds. I watched him watch. It was painful.

The rest of the show was three weeks of real work and real pitches to several places, which the team had edited to make it look like Jeff and Jake were buffoons who knew nothing. A keen eye, or some experience in Hollywood, and you can see how ridiculously pieced together it all was. In one scene, I am wearing three different outfits. That's because they took any footage they had of my being annoyed with my mom and pieced them together to make me look like a spoiled bitch.

At the end of the episode, everyone started mingling again. People I didn't know came up to tell me how much they loved the show. It was horrifying, and we wanted to leave. My mom was fed up. The tension between her and R.J. was obvious. She got up to leave, too. None of us had had time to process where we stood on any of it, so we were still being cordial as we wove our way toward the front door. That's when R.J. stopped us. I couldn't look at his face. I slipped my fingers through Jeff's to remind him that we could just keep walking. R.J. was oblivious to our frustrations.

"Hey, guys! What'd you think?!" R.J. asked Jeff.

"Well . . ." Jeff paused a dramatic Hollywood pause. A critic's pause. The pause of a person who is going to talk for an hour about all the intellectual properties of each and every second of the show. Or so it seemed.

"I think you're an asshole," Jeff said so matter-of-factly that R.J. could do nothing but laugh. He threw his head back and guffawed in such a way that I could see the soft insides of his skull.

When his head came forward again you could see he was expecting Jeff to laugh, too. Which he didn't.

"No. Seriously. You're an asshole." Jeff said nothing else, waiting for R.J. to have a moment of awareness about why we were so mad. There was none.

"Hey, I got you on TV, didn't I?!" R.J. said, as if this was some sort of a gift for which we owed him gratitude. We both stared blankly at him.

At this point we both knew it was useless to expect this person to see our point of view, so I tugged at Jeff and we left. At the valet, the man who brought us our car couldn't figure out how to get the minivan doors open. It occurred to me that he'd probably never seen one before. We climbed back in and drove home. We talked about leaving LA and fantasized about where we would go and what we would do.

"I want to go somewhere beautiful with no people."

The show premiered on TV a few days later, and Jeff was horrified. I told him not to worry, no one was going to watch it. We decided not to watch it again, so instead we went to sit in our cute little backyard. Through the slats in the fence between us and our neighbors, we could see the glow of the five-foot TV they had. I rocked back and forth to get a zoetrope going to see what they were watching. I choked. There was Jeff's head talking right there. Right in our neighborhood, our own backyard. He spent the next hour pacing and the next few days brooding, feeling betrayed and upset. I felt bad for dragging him into the mess of my world. I wanted nothing more at the moment than to get him and Eitan out. I wanted to go buy a tiny house in the suburbs of Denver and waitress while Jeff worked his way up to manager at Sears or something. I owed them the quiet invisibility of a real-person life.

Thankfully, the show was canceled almost immediately, partly due to ratings and partly because my mom had to have an emergency hysterectomy that made her unavailable to film. She joked later that she had gotten the surgery just to get out of the show's contract.

A few months later, on vacation in Maui, where we had started going once a year as a family, Jeff and I decided to try for another kid. It took precisely three days of my being off the Pill before I was pregnant, this time with Cosmo. I went on the mini-Pill after having him because it's breastfeeding-friendly, and then I stayed on it because it didn't make me feel insane or like my skin was made of jalapeños and maggots. Although it is almost as effective as the regular Pill, there is a slightly higher chance that it might fail. Remember this—this is important.

Fifteen months after Cosmo was born, we were on vacation in Colorado and I was grouchy and bitchy and barked at Jeff when he went for a walk, leaving me at the hotel with the boys. "You're on vacation from your *home, not your kids.*" My mom asked me why I was so mad. I told her I didn't know and joked that I was probably pregnant. Instead of laughing, she said, "I hope not! Jeff is not gonna stick around for that!" Two days later, everyone got the stomach flu except me. I wondered why my immune system had spared me and could only think of one reason. I fought for my turn in the bathroom and took a pregnancy test. His name is Otis.

Back home, our house renovations were dragging on. I ended up living in our eighteen-foot travel trailer while Jeff refinished the floors. The fumes were too strong for me and my morning sickness and our two little kids. The only available spot to park the trailer was downwind of the reclamation plant in El Segundo, and I dry-heaved constantly from the smell. I had to stay inside with the AC on at all times, but I ended up preferring the simple and close proximity of the trailer and the fact that you could be taking a piss and handing out string cheese at the same time. I could be lying in bed *and* cooking dinner. It was like a giant functional playpen in which we all could fit. I started craving a quiet, simple place I could cave up in and really watch my kids grow without the observer effect of the public eye that seemed, like Sauron, always to find us.

We had just finally moved back into our house when Jeff told me that he had talked to my mom about finding her a summer house in Hawaii. Our family had spent every summer there since Buck was born, and now she wanted a place of her own. Jeff went out to the Big Island alone to look at properties and stayed a few weeks. One day he called my mom and said, "I found *it.*" She bought the forty-acre macadamia nut farm sight unseen. Now all it needed was a caretaker. Or five. When my mom asked if we wanted to do it, it wasn't a hard decision.

Just like people dream of coming to Hollywood to make it big, I dreamed of leaving it for something small. I dreamed of no one knowing my name. I dreamed of being invisible. I wanted a simple life free from the complications of success. Though I was provided with several opportunities because of my connections, I have subconsciously avoided success because I associate success with money, and I have a horrible relationship with money. I am scared of it. I am scared of what comes along with it. I realize that I associate money with upheaval, betrayal, and fucked-up power dynamics. I would like to have respect for money as a means of doing good. I want a life of purpose beyond the accumulation of wealth, but I also want to eat and have health care. I am sure there is a balance, and I hope to find it someday.

I'd like to remove the pressure from Jeff and the sense of obligation to my mom, who bought me a house and paid for my kids' schooling. I suppose there are ways to have money that don't make you complicit in Big Ponzi. I'll research it.

I wanted out of this consumeristic trap, and, the more I thought about it, the more I figured that the best way for me to do that would be to use my privilege to spend time relearning all the things we forgot during the industrial revolution. Trade, barter, weaving, cooking, tanning, growing—the things you trade money for—what if I could do them all? I love DIY books and shows. I can't get enough. I want to work on something until I've mastered it, and then I want to work on something else.

Back when we first moved to LA, Jake and I were playing G.I. Joes in the backyard under our avocado tree when we noticed our neighbor climb a ladder on her side, sneak her arm over onto ours, and steal some fruits off a branch. She would steal our kumquats, plums, oranges, lemons—everything that we had in our yard. I couldn't begin to imagine what she was going to do with these fruits.

My brain sputtered when it dawned on me: She was *eating* the foods she took off our trees! Food grows on trees! Up until then, there was a distinction between the fruit in our yard, whose sole purpose seemed to be falling onto the ground, and the edible fruit from the grocery market that had been vetted by the FDA and therefore was legal, in my mind, to consume. I had to know in some regard that the food in grocery stores came from somewhere, but until that moment, I thought . . . well, I don't know what I thought. I had never acknowledged anything outside of a store or restaurant as food, but now it was everywhere. This epiphany was a game changer for a girl with a padlocked fridge. Immediately after this epiphany, I had a lot of questions. My dad, probably growing irritated with answering my queries, bought me a *Farmers' Almanac* from the local convenience store. I read it over and over. I was fascinated by the weather patterns, moon phases, seasons, and planting and reaping schedules. Everything was a beautiful symbiotic cycle. Death was the fertilizer for life and life was the food for death. A single seed contained an infinity of seeds. Everything relied on the moon. This was *ultimate witchcraft,* and I wanted to know everything about it! But there hadn't been time then.

Now that I was a free adult, there was time. I bought all the Peterson Field Guides and read them over and over. There was a book called *Eat the Weeds* that was fascinating to me. Jeff didn't seem especially interested in plants until one day when we had to re-stucco our house and had to pull up a bunch of roses. He carefully potted them, even though our neighbor told him they were as good as dead, and cared for them until they could be put back in their place. At one point, the roses started to die, and I told Jeff we would just get more, but instead he talked to the roses and told them to live and . . . they did. I remember Jeff coming inside and bragging about how good the replanted bushes looked and saying all he wanted to do was be a gardener. We talked about having a sustainable farm and how to do it and felt excited. I loved the ocean and being warm, and I loved Hawaii and the Hawaiian people. I would miss my friends and family, but we weren't getting out of the house much these days and would probably see them more once we had an enticing place for them to visit.

We had been thinking about moving to other places on the mainland that were more kid-centric. We have a lot of family in Utah, and I did enjoy not being stared at or told, "You have your hands full!" every time I went to the store when visiting.

The downside of Utah for me was the religiousness. Although I would be accepted by the Church of Latter-day Saints (LDS) for my breeding skills, that warm welcome wouldn't last beyond a single conversation with me. Once, at a local park, a woman asked, "Are you LDS?" and when my immediate impulse was to say, "No, I'm just DTF," I knew a conservative place might not be the best fit socially.

We accepted my mom's offer and put our house on the market. When we were signing the final paperwork, Jeff told me I looked "super-hot" and was "glowing." The real estate agent thought that was so romantic and sweet, but I knew better. There was only one reason I would glow.

The blood left my face. I took a pregnancy test that afternoon. It was positive. I cried. I was terrified and overwhelmed. I called Jessica, and she reminded me that I was always happy about being pregnant after the initial shock wore off. She was right. I refused to tell my mom, though, based on her previous reactions. I made Jeff do it.

I thought maybe this would be *the girl*, since it seemed to have been an immaculate conception. I swear we did not have sex that month. At the sonogram office, the tech said, "It's a boy!" And Jeff and I were like, "Wow, okay." The tech was shocked at our lack of enthusiasm and called us out. I told him I was very happy that the baby seemed healthy, it was just that we had three boys at home. He almost dropped his sonogram wand along with his jaw. I giggled at his reaction at first, but he really just *couldn't* get over it. I asked him if he'd never seen a person with four kids before.

"Not your age. Not white."

Time to get out of there.

We moved to Hawaii on December 17, 2008, a day before our ninth wedding anniversary. I was three months pregnant.

They say about Hawaii that you'd better have your shit together, because it will put a microscope on everything and, if you're not ready, it'll break you. It speeds up karma and escalates conflicts and magnifies insecurities. It tests you to see if you deserve to be here. Maybe it's the lack of distractions, as everything is rural and closes at eight, the internet is slow and sporadic, and the cell service works only part of the time. Maybe it's the heightened accountability, since everyone knows everyone and everything about everyone. You can't get away with anything.

It only took eight days for me to be homeless. Our plan to live at the farm fell through when my mom decided to move to Hawaii a few days after us. We had to move out, but we didn't have anywhere to go or enough money for a deposit for first and last months' rent. I wanted to undo everything and go back home to Los Angeles. I wanted my sister and my friends and an In-N-Out Burger binge.

We lived in a hotel for two weeks trying to figure out what to do next, hiding half our kids in the bathroom any time an employee came to our room because only four guests were allowed. The two older boys shared a full bed while Jeff and I shared the other full bed with Otis. I cried at the drop of a hat. I was sad and scared for our future. In a few months we would have another mouth to feed. I didn't know what to do.

Jeff ended up finding a small plantation house for rent out in the middle of nowhere, and we left the hotel and moved in with nothing but a suitcase each. Luckily, it was furnished and had a collection of plates and silverware that looked to be looted from a Salvation Army. We used our beach towels for blankets until my visiting sister jokingly said someone was going to call CPS. All our money was tied up in the sale of our house, and we had to do what we could to skate by for now. We used a credit card to buy two twin mattresses and two comforters from Costco. Although the situation was not ideal, the view out of the kitchen window was insane. The house sat on the border of Bishop Estate, a land trust that was used as pasture only. It was rolling green hills sprinkled with slow-moving cattle all the way from our house to the ocean a couple miles away. Past that was the vast sea empty of all activity apart from one Matson barge every few days. Because of the strange shape of the lot, you couldn't see anything else. It was stunning. The house itself was shantylike: wooden single-walled construction with plank floors. Termites had eaten holes in various places, and I could see the dirt underneath the platform on which the house was built. It made for a nice breeze, though.

Once we were settled in, the landlord came by. I opened the door with three kids around my ankles and my belly falling out of the dirty tank top I was stuffed into. She needed to talk to me about her plans to sell the house. She wanted us to show it a few times a week for her and laid down the rules of what that meant. She would contact us as far in advance as she could to let us know buyers were coming. I agreed initially, but after three days in a row of two-hour showings with only twenty minutes' notice, the view stopped being so spectacular and we moved again.

We found another old plantation home tucked off the main highway and rented it. I hit bottom in this house on a day when I woke up and my kids were hungry and I had nothing in the kitchen, no gas to go to the store, and no money for food. I decided I would go out into that big yard and scavenge for some things to eat. I tried to pretend it would be fun, but I was struggling not to lose my mind. When I opened the door, there was a pile of bananas, papayas, and avocados on my steps. No one was around, and Jeff had left early that morning. Maybe he had picked all this and left it? But there was no way. We didn't have the tools to reach any of these things. I gathered everything up and went inside and fed my kids.

The next morning, the same thing happened, then twice more that week until I caught an older man in my front yard one day and said hi. I asked him if he was the one leaving the fruit and he said yes. He had noticed that I had "a lot of *keiki*" (the Hawaiian word for kids) and figured I could use extra. I bit my tongue so I wouldn't cry and thanked him. I wanted to tell him how much of a help it was, but I couldn't do that without tearing up, so we just chatted instead. He lived across the street and had a farm and always had extra produce. His name was Teddy, and I love him still.

When summer came, we went back to Los Angeles to have the baby. We moved into our travel trailer that we kept stored in California and hooked it up at the RV park in Long Beach, where my dad and Becca had been living as full-timers for years after traveling the United States. They settled in this area to be near us when Eitan was born and only occasionally went on the road afterward. We spent the next few weeks hanging out with the grandparents, going to the nearby attractions like the Queen Mary and the Aquarium of the Pacific, or swimming and scootering at the RV park. My OB was pressuring me for an induction as I seemed to just keep being pregnant, so I agreed to come in on July 5, after the onslaught of people who had blown their fingers off on Independence Day had cleared.

The night of July 2, 2009, I woke Jeff up and told him to go get my dad. I was in labor. My dad walked over to watch the older boys so we could go to the hospital, and Buster was born the next day. The first time I saw him, I was completely in love, as always, but also sad, thinking he would be my last baby. I was going to enjoy every minute of him. I watched some fireworks from the hospital window as I recovered, and then took him home to the trailer, where I stuck him in a mini bassinet by the window to help with his minor jaundice. Bringing Buster home to a trailer felt like his birthright. We stayed for the rest of the summer and returned to Hawaii in early August for school.

My mom stayed in Los Angeles, and Jeff went back to work on the farm. That meant that the kids and I went back to work, too. There was too much for Jeff to do alone. The six of us spent all of our time either working on or exploring the land, learning about plants and animals and life and nature, going to the beach, driving around the island, throwing footballs in parks, lying in the sun in a dogpile, eating sand-covered *lilikoi* that I'd cut open with the pocketknife I kept in my bra, while screaming, "DON'T HIT YOUR BROTHER!" These will forever be my favorite years, even if they were some of the hardest.

In March 2010, the house we had put on the market in Manhattan Beach *finally* sold. The escrow ended just as the summer began, and so we packed up again and moved back into the trailer that we kept in Long Beach. We'd spend a few months moving our furniture and belongings out of the house and into storage and visiting with family and friends before returning to Hawaii for school.

My brother, Jake, came to visit us in the RV park. He was still working at the small studio in El Segundo and living nearby with his new wife. He told us our mom was pursuing a reality show on the farm. Jeff and I were the last to hear about it. They wanted the kids and us to be on it.

We were caught off guard. We had defected from Hollywood intentionally and wanted nothing more to do with it. We wanted to be alone on a volcano, far from any entertainment executives or producers. We wanted to look like shit and wear dirty clothes and have filthy kids and just *be*, but Hollywood was going to come for us again like an impossible-to-kill villain, and this time I didn't think we'd have the strength to survive it.

18.

Parallel Reality

Jeff and I were both opposed to being involved with the show and extended our stay on the mainland until we could be sure the production wouldn't affect us, but two weeks later there was no escape. We had to return to Hawaii for the kids' school year.

My problem with the new reality show was not that it was being made on the farm, but it was being made *about* the farm. It was going to be called *Roseanne's Nuts*, and it was supposed to document the production of macadamia nuts for retail sale. There was no way Jeff and I would be able to both avoid the reality show *and* continue to work. We would either have to be involved, or we'd have to back completely out of all our plans, which would essentially leave Jeff jobless.

Jake told me he really wanted me and Jeff and the kids to participate since it was all of our dynamics together that were interesting, and I knew he was right. Seeing my mom with my kids is still the funniest thing in the world. She truly *sees* each and every one of them, the good and the bad, and playfully jibes at them. She gives them a forum to speak freely, which always ends in hilarity. She challenges them to think. She teaches them how to laugh at themselves.

I didn't want to take this experience from any of them. I decided I was being stubborn and agreed to be on the show a couple times—with the stipulation that I would have final say in anything that my kids were involved in.

My mom wanted my dad and stepmom to come out to be on the show, too. The idea didn't come out of nowhere. Both of them had worked on and off for my mom in some capacity for years. So they stored their RV and moved to Hawaii, too. Jake came also, but flew back and forth every few days because he shared custody of his two cats with his now-ex-wife, and he refused to be an absentee father to them. Buck came out to Hawaii to attend high school. We were all one big happy family again. Even Jessica moved to Hawaii, although she refused to have anything to do with the show. She was just coming to be with me and my kids, looking for a new life after her own divorce.

Buck started boarding at a private school in the nearest town. They had a day school program, too, but they had no spots open on such short notice, so Buck lived in a dorm. What was my Jewish mother's solution to this? To buy a house directly across the street and make him walk home for dinner every night. She split her time between the farm and this house, depending on Buck's schedule.

It was common for me to go over there and see my mom and dad and brother talking on the porch. I would think about how normal that looked from the outside, but how my mom's boyfriend and my dad's wife were also nearby, while my brother's dad was in Nevada. *That's* a good storyline, I thought. Maybe I'll mention it to the producer.

I agreed to be in two episodes, one about homeschooling (which I was doing now after a very bad two weeks at our public school) and one for Mother's Day.

For the homeschooling episode, they asked me to drop my kids off for the day . . . um, no? I sat in the tent watching the TV screens to let them know not to fuck with me, but they somehow (intentionally, they would admit later) coerced me a hundred feet away to do interviews for the "bumpers." They cut these in in between scenes and before and after commercial breaks to help tell the story. When I returned to get my kids, they were all hyped up and wanted to tell me everything they had done for the couple hours I had been busy.

"We shot water guns at Granny! And we exploded some of her stuff!

And we buried a dead lizard! And, and, and . . . !" It all sounded like an average day with Granny, so I didn't think much about it. Later, I was sitting there with Cosmo, and I asked him about the water guns. I realized ours were at our house and wondered how they got here.

"They weren't ours, they were the crew's," Cosmo said, confusing me further. I let him keep talking.

"They had a big plastic bag full of them, and they told us all to take one and go inside and shoot Granny."

"You shot water guns *inside* Granny's house?!"

Cosmo gleefully confirmed this.

My mom has amazing taste in art, and her walls and tables and shelves are covered in stunning originals. My kids would never do something like that unencouraged. I was pissed. I tried to talk to the producers and explain to them that these were real kids with real relationships and real consequences. They didn't seem to care. There was no risk in it for them, and the crazier things got, the better it was for ratings.

The Mother's Day episode came next. Historically, the rule for that holiday is All Children Must Leave Mom Alone. She is on duty all other days of the year and insists on having twenty-four whole hours to herself. We are not even supposed to call her. I wanted the producers to work with that. Not only was it true, but it was darkly hilarious.

The producers had a better idea, though. They wanted me, an out-of-shape, lactating mother of four, to take my mom, a sixty-year-old woman who begged to be left alone on this day, *surfing*. I was emailed a call sheet the night before with instructions on what I was supposed to do. I would show up at my mom's house with a bouquet of flowers, pick her up, and drive her to a surfing spot an hour away. We would endure some lessons, then head home. Our conversations both ways would be recorded in the car.

Whatever. I showed up at my mom's house with the bouquet of flowers and revealed that I was taking her—surprise!—surfing! Like she had always wanted!

I have never hated myself more.

If you go back and watch those episodes now, you can see the rage in my eyes. You do it, I can't. I was doing my best to focus that rage in a proactive way, trying to keep the main part of my attention on the farm. I knew this show would be short-lived and that we could return to the grand plan of sustainable living again, so we kept moving in that direction. It wasn't long before filming was over. I don't remember what happened exactly. Was it canceled? Just not picked up for a second season? I suppose I could google it, but no thanks. I was just glad it was over.

18B.

Character Limits

Of all the pre-Trump things I miss most, I'd say Twitter is in the top five. It still exists, technically, but it went from being listed in the App Store under entertainment to being listed under news, and it's now a confusing mess of both—no . . . neither.

I miss when it just fell into a few basic subcategories, like Motivational Twitter, Self-Promotion Twitter, Horny Twitter, Joke Twitter, and, my personal favorite, Weird Twitter. Although there were crossovers, most people on it identified mainly with one of the above.

Joke Twitter and Weird Twitter had some things in common, like being funny sometimes, but they were very different. JT was mainly used by stand-up comics and wannabe TV writers. Their tweets were carefully curated, and the amount of positive feedback they got (likes and retweets) was closely monitored using a second app called Favstar, which no longer exists.

Favstar let you track the interactions your tweet received, and it also let you give one award a day to another tweeter, so naturally cliques and alliances formed. Grammar was extremely important for this sect, and if you messed up, you would get private messages and even text messages at times to let you know so you could fix it. There was no edit feature, so fixing meant you had to delete the tweet, correct it, and repost it, losing all your previous likes and retweets. It was a sacrifice, but one that needed to be made. There was legit internet fame at stake.

Weird Twitter was messy on purpose. Grammar was out the window. Most blurbs were stream of consciousness or actual attempts to connect to other people. Irony was big and ridiculousness was even bigger. Sometimes you would read a WT tweet and think about it for years. It was as if the *Thinking Man* statue were perched on the toilet. It was my favorite.

All these things still exist, but the main point of Twitter is to have a community that shares your beliefs. With a long enough timeline, you will eventually disagree with everyone about something, so those communities seem to be shrinking and going from echo chambers to vacuums. I miss them. They were there for me when I moved to an island where I knew no one, when I was a stay-at-home mom with no adults to talk to, when I was crippled with anxiety and agoraphobic, when I didn't have time to sit and write more than the 140-character limit. It gave me a place to express myself.

Although my mom was also on Twitter, a lot of people didn't know we were related, so I had a bit of creative autonomy for the first time. Although most of my tweets were just reporting funny things my kids said, some were more than that. I started gaining "followers" and getting to talk to people the way you talk to strangers at the bar: deeply and concisely and with no obligation. It was very therapeutic.

Some of my tweets were about my mom:

- My mom put a banana in the juicer.
- Please don't tell me that my mom basically raised you unless you were in mental institutions for five years and/or weighed 300 lbs.
- I know everyone's reality is strange, but I think mine takes the cake right now. Tom Arnold is trying to take the president down

with a reality show about pee and my mom is on Hannity. And I just bought a bag of meat outside of Starbucks.

- We were at a nice restaurant once and the waiter kept saying everything was organic and my mom said, "You know what else is organic? Shit."
- Yesterday, my mom's phone rang and she got a disgusted look on her face and said, "Ugh. I hate that people think they can just call me."
- I can actually *feel* emails from my mom come through.

Some were more general and philosophical:
- Please be sure to let me know if the way I live my life is in total accordance with your beliefs.
- My favorite human trait is mistaking subjective experience for absolute truth and holding other people accountable to that illusion.
- I wonder if caterpillars know they're gonna fly someday or they just start building a cocoon and are like "why am I doing this?"
- Your soulmate married someone else while you were reading *The Secret*.

Some were just straight from my life:
- I went on a date at 13 with the only other Jew from Fat Camp. We saw George Michael. His mom was really into it. I cried in the bathroom.
- My dad made an X-rated country album when I was locked up in a mental home for ruining my mom's wedding to Tom Arnold.
- All I wanted to be when I was a girl was a woman, and now as a woman, all I'm supposed to want to be is a girl? (pulls mom-jeans up higher)
- A pair of underwear flew out the ankle of my jeans as I walked my kid into his first day of middle school. They weren't mine.

- "I'll watch your baby for job interviews and therapy, but not for psychic readings or affairs." —me drawing healthy boundaries with friends

Many were about death:
- "Mom! I don't want to die when I'm old!" "Oh, sweetie . . . you can die at any age, really."
- Me gracefully handling 500 things that would each individually destroy the strongest people I know: "I'm okay." Me stubbing my toe: dies of heartbreak from the betrayal of being a soul forcibly stuffed into a rapidly decaying body made out of pain receptors and 90,000 miles of nerves.
- We feel victimized by death, but it's our most unconditional and transformative relationship.
- Conquer your fear of death with immersion therapy.
- "You can't live your whole life with skin. It dies. You have to live some without it." —4yo on death

I tweeted plenty about parenting:
- My 12yo was winning Monopoly so I shook the board, told him to wait for FEMA's help, then took all his railroads under Eminent Domain.
- I have been dying in childbirth for sixteen years.
- Until you wake up to a young child's silhouette blankly staring at you in the darkness, you know nothing of fear.
- What's one trillion times more insufferable than your teen angst? Your teen's angst.
- Just realized that my idea of success as a parent is my kids hating me without hating themselves.

- Told the kids "shucks" is the worst possible offense because it is half "shit" and half "fuck," and now I'm not scared to go in public anymore.

Most of my top tweets are things my kids said:
- Me trying to start a movie on Netflix

    My 11yo—not that one mom. It's inappropriate.

    Me—How do you know?

    11—I watched it.
- My 9yo was right about something I was wrong about, so he turned around and told me to "suck on the butt of knowledge."
- "Dad puts you on a timeout and takes your video games away, but Mom peels you like an artichoke, taking one leaf off at a time until she gets all the way down to the heart, and then she eats it."
- I just heard my 9yo mutter "oh thank god" when my husband read about being forgiven for the sins of the past year tonight for Rosh Hashanah.
- "Hey! Dat guy hab da same pants as me!" My 3yo looking at a picture of himself.
- I was arguing with my husband and my son screamed, "Yay! Two Christmases!" from the other room.
- I just asked my 8yo to quit yelling and he said, "I'm NOT yelling. This is my voice and all my life I've been whispering. Now I'm free!"

A few were about marriage:
- I don't tweet about my husband that much because I like him.
- My husband keeps saying, "I'm not gonna play your little games" like that's not Step 1 of playing my little games.

- My husband asked me if I was jealous of his exes and I said yes because they're your exes.
- My husband was complaining that I was excluding him from my online life, so I gently took his hand in mine and used his finger to scroll.
- My husband told me to calm down and it worked!
- I told my husband I was gonna be out of town for our anniversary and my 10yo walked over to him and said, "Dump her."
- My husband calls my phone my boyfriend like it's not him who is the side piece.
- My husband in 1999: Wow. What books have you been reading? You're paranoid!
- My husband 2017: I have passports, iodine, and a gold bar in my Kevlar spacesuit.
- I trust my husband in strip clubs more than I trust him in Home Depot.
- I synced mine and my husband's calendars on iCloud and he keeps adding event alerts like "take off bra."

Some tweets were about letting myself go:
- My sister who just had a baby told me she was going to "just give in and let herself go" and then showed up in the exact same outfit as me.
- My kitten thinks my armpit hair is its mom.
- If I ever apologize for the state of my dress or house or car or hair or anything, I am lying.
- I washed my hair and the whole town noticed.
- I might only use 10% of my brain, but I use 110% of my stomach.

Many were about my anxiety:

- I just realized that I pick my friends by who I don't mind having an anxiety attack in front of.
- Having an anxiety disorder is like talking a person down from a really bad trip while also being that person.
- Most of my anxiety comes from the misunderstanding that reality is real.
- Sorry you couldn't talk me out of my anxiety disorder with your impenetrable logic but I "appreciate" the effort.

Some were anecdotes about my life:

- My life is half killing time and half apologizing for being late.
- I just remembered earlier today when a PTA mom asked me if I was a bath or shower person and I said "neither." I hate when it gets quiet at night.

And here are some of my nonsensical personal favorites:

- Who named them kegels and not puss ups
- dang r u 9/11 cuz my bush wants to do u
- I love bidets, the car wash of the ass

I will be forever grateful for Twitter, may it rest in peace.

19.

Don't Eat Your Pets and Don't Pet Your Eats

Now that the reality show was over, we could get back to our original mission. My mom had tried to create her Xanadu before in Iowa with Tom Arnold, but that place was in ruins now. There is a video on YouTube where someone walks around the overgrowth-covered cement slab where their home was supposed to be. This time, we could do it right. We could build her Xanadu.

We got beehives to pollinate the macadamia nut trees and goats and sheep to keep the grass down. We got chickens for pest control and manure. We built a beautiful garden and a huge greenhouse. We grew and preserved and pickled and dried veggies and fruits. We harvested honey. We collected a dozen eggs a day. I found a tame and beautiful milking goat named Ruth and learned to make cheese and yogurt.

At this point we weren't buying much from the store. Our goal with the farm was a whole week of everything we ate coming from our own land. Imagine my ancestors hearing me say that out loud. "She wants *what*?! That lucky bitch has antibiotics and McDonald's! What is she doing?"

Around this time, Jeff and I were talking to a local guy who was doing some mechanic work on one of our dozers and he said, "You guys come over here and talk about sustainability and farming, permaculture and raising animals like you *just* invented it all, but we've been here for generations and that's how we live and have lived." I was humbled and, to be honest, jealous that the chain of information passed down to him uninterrupted.

This same guy invited Jeff to help him and some friends clean a pig they had hunted. He had never been a part of anything like that before. He went and came home smelling like blood and burned hair. He had eaten all sorts of animal parts he'd never tried before, like eyeball and brain, and he talked to me about how cool it was to be part of that. He explained it to me in detail. It was an initiation of sorts.

We talked about that part of farming. The death part. The killing part. We were trying to decide how self-sufficient we wanted to be. Could we kill our own animals? We were both grappling with that and trying to find a place where we felt at peace. How can we eat meat but not raise or kill it? That felt cowardly at worst and disconnected at best. Should we just be vegan so we didn't have to deal with this question at all?

Our cowboy friend suggested we get our kids involved in 4H. Eitan was the only one old enough, and he hated sports, so I figured this was his best bet at a social life as a homeschooler. This would be a good experience for him. He would become more responsible, and he would have a better understanding of, and respect for, life. He'd learn the ins and outs of raising an animal and could then be more involved in the farm labor. Our kids didn't love the hard work associated with this way of life, but we hoped they'd look back and be grateful. I signed him up.

We went to a local pig farm to pick out a sheep to take home to raise. All the other kids knew what they were looking for. They inspected hooves and the way the lamb walked, what its head looked like, its teeth. Eitan felt out of place as I kept trying to get him involved. I whispered, "Just go pick the cutest one," so he did. She was a fluffier-than-standard-looking lamb with a sweet face, and he named her Chunk.

There were several 4H meetings a month. You left your animal at home but brought your notebook and log. One day there was a potluck meeting where we were supposed to bring a piece of his sheep's poop to dissect and make sure the animal was healthy. I didn't get the memo so I only brought cookies.

I sat in the parking lot wrangling the other kids inside my van for two hours until the meeting was over. Eitan looked like he felt so out of place, and I wondered if I was being ridiculous making him do this. He walked to the van with his head down and got in. I asked him how it was.

"Well, the only thing worse than being at a table with a group of kids holding bags of shit is being the only kid who forgot to bring his bag of shit. Don't worry, Mom. Someone lent me some of their shit." He emphasized the word *shit* each time he said it. I laughed and thought that it was definitely ridiculous to make him carry around bags of shit, but we couldn't back out now. We had the sheep. We were in too deep.

Our neighbor was a sheep farmer who had done 4H as a kid, and he offered his advice. Cob. Fatten Chunk up on two weeks of cob (a mix of corn and grain and molasses that animals love the way we love Taco Bell) before the auction. Auction? we wondered. We must sell our tame animals for breeding stock at the end.

It was Memorial Day, 2012, and also my thirty-sixth birthday, and I was content to sleep in until three p.m. I didn't have to get up to take the kids to school. I had big plans to do nothing. We screamed down to the kids to do their daily chores, and I let myself fall back asleep. Eitan was in charge of chickens because it was the most involved job. Cosmo would feed the cats and dogs; Otis would fill the water troughs; and Buster would help with anything extra. Buster loved the animals more than his brothers did. He'd climb the fence and hang out in the shelter with the goats. I have a picture of him in rubber boots in the baby goat shelter with his pacifier in his mouth. So far, most of our farm experiences had been extremely pleasant and rewarding. But today, the pendulum was swinging the other way. We were about to get a taste of what farming really is.

"MOM! MOM! Something's wrong with Chunk!" I woke up to Eitan yelling.

We could see the pasture on our one-acre homestead from our

bedroom window. I jumped up and looked out the window to see Chunk lying on her side, motionless, Eitan beside her.

"Fuck," I mumbled.

Jeff jumped up, we ran out to the pasture, the little kids in tow, and found her breathing heavily and looking like she had eaten a wrecking ball. The vet was closed for the holiday, so I opened one of my seven thousand farming books to what I thought the problem was—bloat, which was serious but fixable if caught early. I ran and got vegetable oil to defoam her insides and poured it down her throat.

We didn't have the right medical supplies. All the stores were closed. The closest place was an hour away, and they wouldn't have much more than what we had. The one thing we did have was ammo. I wanted that to be the second-to-last option, the last being watching Chunk writhe in pain until she died.

I left a message for the vet. We knew everyone was off duty and weren't really expecting a callback, but it turned out she lived two houses up from us and made an exception. She came to our house and into the pasture and studied the sheep for a minute. It was indeed bloat, and we needed to intubate. This meant pushing a three-foot-long hose through her mouth and into her stomach to drain the bile out. We moved her onto the hill so her head was lower than her body, and we siphoned her like a gas tank. I can't remember what we used to start the flow, where the suction came from. Maybe I just don't want to remember.

After we finished draining the bile, the vet took a long hollow needle out of her bag. It looked like what you'd use to fill a football the size of a car. She showed me how to palpate for the rumen, the first compartment in the four-part stomach, and how to tell the difference between another organ and the full balloon of gas right next to it.

She took the needle and pushed it into the sheep's rumen, and immediately, gas started hissing out. It took minutes for this cartoonish sound to end as the pressure was slowly released, and then it sputtered to a stop with a squirt of bile, which hit Eitan's leg like the impotent last shot in a water gun. He locked eyes with me and said nothing.

Here is where I thought that maybe I had made a mistake. Maybe I *shouldn't* have packed up and moved onto an active volcano in the middle of the Pacific Ocean.

Maybe teaching my kids about sustainable living was really just teaching them that living isn't sustainable.

It was a cruel lesson that generations of industry had made unnecessary. There seemed to be no place for it unless you were trying to break someone and turn them into a sociopathic cult member.

Maybe I should have stayed in Los Angeles in the entertainment industry and just enjoyed my nepotism-gained jobs. I could be stuffing my face with a pantry full of Joe's O's, with access to retail stores and whatever ethnic food I was craving that day. Up until now, my only regret was leaving behind friends and family, but now I regretted everything.

With the pressure off of her lungs, Chunk started wiggling about a little. She looked more comfortable and seemed like she was improving, so we all relaxed. We sat in the grass in the pasture and watched her slow recovery. Our hard work, diligence, and luck had paid off. The vet bill wouldn't be in vain. Eitan's famous grief eye bags were fading. My birthday was saved. I could now go return the numerous texts I'd received saying, "We hope you're having a great birthday and your family is spoiling you!" I'm always tempted to return those texts with the truth, or a video of me lying next to a pile of gore while the kids whine at one another in the background and ask for food, but it would come across as so rude. Instead, I answer those well wishes with a simple "Thank you." Chunk got up and walked around, though clumsily, and we all breathed a sigh of relief.

That's precisely when she went into a series of seizures that took about fifteen minutes to kill her. We sat with her and petted her and whispered, "It's okay," as she vacated her wooly body. The shock of the last few hours was too much for her, and, to be honest, we all understood.

We found out a few days later that the auction at the end of the project wasn't for farmers to buy good, tame breeding animals, it was to buy meat. Eitan would've had to have Chunk butchered for the highest bidder, and then would have to inspect and grade the carcass at the local slaughterhouse.

We were sad Chunk was gone but were grateful to skip this final step. Chunk had a decent life and the wonderful privilege of gorging herself to death on sweet, sweet corn snacks. We should all be so lucky, really.

I made Eitan go to the auction for a sense of completion, and he won first place in the "meat cuts" quiz, so at least something came out of it.

When Eitan was born, I did his astrological chart with my sister, and after studying all its aspects, we both said, "Welp. Sniper or chef." This seemed a step in the right direction. I was bragging to my sister about his win when he overheard and confessed that he had cheated by copying from another kid's quiz. I have always asked my kids to be honest above all else, but really, he could have just let me have that one.

20.

I Hate Costco

In line at Costco, the lady behind me grabbed my shoulders, looked me right in the eyes, and asked me if she could hug me. I was clearly on the verge of tears and looked like I hadn't slept or showered in a week. I had just stopped in the Tupperware aisle to send my three older boys on missions to different areas of the store to gather supplies so I could clean up the diarrhea their youngest brother had just sprayed our full cart with.

I dispatched Eitan to grab a box of size-four diapers and a box of wipes, figuring that, at eleven, his arms had the largest capacity. Cosmo was asked to get three plastic produce bags from the roll by the meats, and Otis was instructed to pick out a size-two pajama set from the clothing section and grab a towel on his way back. I had to stay put so as not to leave a trail. As a courtesy, I used my body to block any gore from people walking down the aisles.

When the supply runs were over, I laid the towel on the floor between my cart and the shelving and carefully took my two-year-old, Buster, out of the cart and put him on the towel. I had the other kids circle the cart as a privacy block and I stripped him very carefully. Like a surgeon to her nurses, I shouted out what I needed next: Plastic bag! The kids handed me one. I carefully rolled up the shit-covered clothes and tied them inside. Wipes! I cleaned him from his head to his toes as pulling his soiled clothes over his head had spread fecal matter everywhere. Plastic bag! I tied up the diaper and all the dirty wipes inside. Diaper! Eitan tore into the box and handed me one. While I was putting it on, I asked Otis to take the tags off the outfit and hand it to me. I got Buster dressed again and sat him on a lower shelf so I could clean the seat in the cart and then I put him back in and cleaned my arms and the floor, then used the third bag to tie up those wipes and the rotisserie chicken that was below him that was also tainted.

I handed each kid a bag to throw away, gathered the tags from the new outfit and towel, put them in my pocket to pay for later, finished my shopping, and then went to the front to get in line. I'm sure I looked like a mess. I was too disheveled to try to hide my feelings at all, and when this stranger asked me if she could hug me, I threw my arms around her without even answering.

During the long, warm embrace I melted into her and whispered into her ear, "I hate Costco."

"You're doing great," this stranger said. I thanked her and went to my car, packed it full of kids and groceries, climbed into the driver's seat, put a movie on the DVD player, gave my boys each a set of headphones, and started bawling. I sat there until I felt better and realized that I needed to change my tampon. I would have to take all four kids with me as I couldn't leave them in the car, and by the time I had them all ready to go, the metal entrance to Costco was being rolled down and locked. I improvised and then opened the Twitter app on my phone and wrote a tweet about what had just happened.

I had originally started an account to communicate with everyone I had left behind when I moved to Hawaii. It was basic mommy blogger stuff about what I had for breakfast or what cute things my kids had said. When the second reality show started taping, the production company suggested I use my account to promote the show and myself, which I reluctantly did a few times, but it was naturally metamorphosing into my lifeline. I understood now why my mom had looked for work outside the home. I felt like I was disappearing as an individual. My dream of becoming a mother had materialized, and what naturally came next was the dream of having a self again. I needed something of my own to keep me a whole person and not just a mom or a wife.

I didn't have many friends or family members on the island. I didn't have a therapist or a free hour of time to spend with one. My kids went where I went, and I rarely finished a sentence when speaking to another adult. I had always kept journals, always written. I have blogs all over the place. I needed to write, but I did not have time. I could, however, eke out 140 characters here and there without worrying about grammar and punctuation, and because I could, I did. It was a very simplistic strategy, and a very effective one, too.

Since I was always a passenger in the car shuttling kids here and there and driving hours for a Costco or Target run, or lying next to kids in bed at night waiting for them to fall asleep, I had time to spend making invisible friends and fine-tuning my writing skills.

I was always on my phone. Besides my Twitter career, I handled all of our family's social obligations, bills, appointments, and other responsibilities using my iPhone. Jeff and the kids would get irritated that I was distracted and would make passive-aggressive comments to me about it, and the day came when I'd had enough. We were watching a family movie together, which is our favorite group activity. It was something Disney that I had seen a hundred times, and, although I was being utilized as a beanbag by all five of them, I was still managing to read an article about hoof care for goats. Jeff turned to me and said something about how I should get off my phone and watch the movie with the family and then the kids all chimed in because that's what they do.

"Yeah, Mom. Get off your phone and watch the movie!" they said, one after another, not leaving any space for me to defend myself.

I lost my shit.

"I HAVE SEEN THIS MOVIE ONE THOUSAND TIMES AND I AM KEEPING IN TOUCH WITH BOTH OUR FAMILIES, PAYING ALL OUR BILLS, WATCHING THE NEWS, LEARNING HOW TO GROW AND PRESERVE FOOD, MANAGING OUR ENTIRE LIVES, AND STAYING SANE. I AM LYING HERE TOUCHING EVERY ONE OF YOU. I AM COMPLETELY PRESENT. I AM JUST STARING AT A DIFFERENT SCREEN. DOES THAT FUCKING MATTER?

SAY ONE MORE FUCKING THING ABOUT MY BEING ON THIS PHONE AND I WILL LEAVE!"

Jeff made a comment about how I wouldn't be so mad if he wasn't right, which pissed me off more because he was wrong. I needed my phone. I needed the tiny seconds of autonomy with which it provided me. I needed a distraction from all my anxiety about who might have scarlet fever and who might've eaten bug spray or who had hit whom. I needed to hear my own thoughts to see if I still recognized my own voice. I needed to talk to people who didn't want me to wipe their butts or make them food. How could Jeff not see that?

"You do it all, then!" I threw my phone across the room and screamed, "THERE! EVERYBODY HAPPY NOW?" Then the kids all cried, and Jeff looked at me disappointedly, so then I cried and stormed out.

That was the most pissed off I'd felt in a long time, the most taken for granted. The most misunderstood, misjudged. The most like a piece of property that everyone was entitled to but me. Although I had thrown a fit like a toddler, I had also realized how badly I needed a space for myself, like Twitter. I acknowledged a sense of duty to myself that I had only experienced for my kids and husband until now. I was creating something, and no one was going to stop me. Even if it was just a silly app on which I said things like, "dang r u 9/11 cuz my bush wants 2 do u," for stars and cartoon trophies, it was mine.

It took some time for Jeff to understand the importance of what I was doing on this one tiny device, the fact that I was my own teacher, accountant, therapist, nurse, horticulturist, head chef, business manager, college professor, guru, and everything else. He eventually left me alone about it, so I stayed married to him.

Twitter would become even more important to me as time went on.

A few weeks after the Costco incident, I was playing Cards Against Humanity with Doug and Angela, my brother-in-law and sister-in-law, who were visiting for two weeks from Los Angeles. We were drinking and having the best time, but for some reason, I felt anxious. Anxiety wasn't new for me, but having that anxiety build into a full-blown panic attack was.

There was a sense of dread and doom sitting in my gut that got worse as the night went on. Everyone went to sleep but me. I sat on the floor of my bathroom trying to calm myself, but I couldn't. Five hours in, I woke Jeff up. My heart was racing, and I was positive I was dying. I asked him to sit with me and he did. As the sun came up, I was feeling a little better, but an emotional and mental darkness lingered with my hangover and then just wouldn't go away.

Doug and Angela got on a plane to go home that day. I came out of my room long enough to say goodbye to them, and then I went back inside and didn't leave for days. It was as if someone had zipped me upside down in a sleeping bag as a cruel prank. Days turned into weeks, and weeks into months, and it didn't get better. I would leave the house only if Jeff was with me. I couldn't go inside a store unless he came, too. I couldn't talk to anyone without being on the verge of tears or a panic attack. I would hyperventilate and almost faint if Jeff left me in line at the register, which is for some reason his favorite activity. I couldn't take or make phone calls, pay bills, or think clear thoughts. I didn't sleep through the night anymore. I would wake up with my heart racing and chest burning and lie there waiting for it to get so bad that I might have to wake Jeff up to take me to the emergency room (which he never actually had to do) or talk me down. The very act of having him awake and near me would soothe me enough that I would sometimes fall back asleep.

Every time this happened, I would feel more helpless and the heaviness would be compounded. I felt guilty for being a burden, for disturbing his sleep, for needing attention and reassurance 24/7. I was embarrassed and apologetic, which was even more embarrassing. It was cyclical and never-ending.

It just kept getting worse, and I didn't even know what "it" was. I had no logical reason to feel this way. I decided to go back to Los Angeles alone and consult some doctors to see if what I was feeling had any physical cause. Jeff was working about twelve hours a day at this point, and I was home alone with the kids, or at least some of them, all day. I was less and less able to engage with them and mostly just lay near them while they engaged with one another. I'd break up fights and stop accidents, but beyond that, I had nothing to give.

I flew to the mainland for a month by myself, having the worst series of panic attacks I'd ever had on the six-hour flight. I had a panic attack as I approached the airport in Kailua-Kona, one in the security line, one in my seat for takeoff, two midflight, one upon landing, one waiting on the tarmac to deplane, one waiting in the line to deplane, one waiting for a ride to my mom's empty house, where I would stay, one in the car on the five-minute drive, and one when I reached the house. I had another that night as I tried to sleep. Another in the middle of the night. Another in the morning. When the sun came up, I moved to the couch and lay there for the entire day trying to rest. I slept there that night, getting up only to pee, and started seeing doctors the next day. Jeff had been making all my medical appointments from Hawaii. His skill in finding the absolute best doctors available is unparalleled. He would tell me where I needed to be and when, and I would show up.

I saw seven or eight different specialists. After having every medical test possible, an Ativan prescription, MRIs, and CT scans, I found an endocrinologist who actually listened to me and came up with a proactive diagnostic regimen. He had me use a glucometer for two weeks to track my blood sugar levels. I had already had them tested several times with no sign of any issues, so I figured it wouldn't reveal much.

With previous tests, my levels were always normal. With this testing method, I could see that the normal highs and lows were happening in fifteen-minute cycles when they should have been taking three hours. That quick of a drop would set off my adrenal system in a way that would actually cause a fight-or-flight reaction.

It was called reactive hypoglycemia and was common for people who had had gastric bypass surgery, as I had. Drinking alcohol (like I had that night with my brother-in-law and sister-in-law) was a trigger. Once the cycle was set off, my hormone levels would jump all over the place, and that would cause psychological symptoms. The chemical fluctuations would cause their own hangover the next day, whereby my nervous system would be on constant lookout for an attack, and then anything would set it off. The cycle would repeat itself over and over. Cool.

The more understanding and awareness I had about it, the more I was able to see the physical reactions objectively and separate my psyche from my body, but I was still anxious and having frequent panic attacks.

I flew back home, this time on Ativan, with my new diagnosis. I hoped that the awareness of the physiological aspect of my apprehension would make it easier to manage, but there was a whole other component that this illness had unleashed in me. It opened a Pandora's box of latent anxiety and repressed trauma that I'd thought I had moved past.

One day, Buck asked me for a ride to his girlfriend's house, and, halfway there, I had to pull over. I couldn't breathe. I thought I was going to die, and, worse yet, I was going to die while driving, and then Buck and all my kids would die with me. The weight of the responsibilities on my plate, the number of people who relied on me, how many dynamics I was at the center of, how pivotal my existence was to everyone else's, was Too Big. I went home and refused to drive again. I refused to do anything that put me, as unstable as I was, in charge of anything.

Nothing tasted good, so I stopped eating anything but almonds. I lost thirty pounds, at which everyone was quick to compliment me and ask me how I was doing it. "Thanks!" I said. "I'm dying," which no one thought was as funny as I did. It was funny, but I wasn't joking.

I was afraid to be alone with my kids even in the safety of our house. I was afraid I couldn't take care of them. I was sure I was going to drop dead at any second, leaving them to fend for themselves, or lose my weakened grasp on reality and start speaking in tongues in front of them. I couldn't sleep for more than an hour at a time, and my dreams were terrifying. Waking up every morning felt like an assault. I struggled to take full breaths, and my physical symptoms were increasing.

I couldn't handle any stimulation. I couldn't watch a movie or even listen to music.

One day, I went into my kids' room. They each had their own room, but slept only in one, and I lay down on the floor. I told them to shut the door and stay in this room so I could watch them without moving. They all sat playing quietly for hours while I tried to hide that I was weeping by burying my face in their giant teddy bear. I had learned to cry out of one eye, and to cry from the most hidden corner of it. I would funnel all the angst into my own hair or sleeve and the kids were none the wiser. I got so good at this that I could smile and have a pleasant conversation at the same time. I had been in decline for so long, I couldn't imagine ever regaining a decent quality of life, let alone giving my kids one. The thought of taking them to their soccer games or having their friends over for a birthday party was daunting beyond belief. I was starting to feel as though they would be better off without me, and Jeff would, too.

This was the point when I knew that I couldn't pull myself out of this pit alone. I woke up one morning and I thought, Either I will let myself die of atrophy and starvation in this bed, or I will get up. I was surprised to find myself outside on my lanai a few minutes later begging the universe for help. If I could stand up, then I could go outside. If I could go outside, I could get help.

I decided to get a therapist. I had never, as an adult, actively sought help for myself. I had been reluctant to do that because I had had so many bad experiences with therapy in my youth. I realized that, by the time I hit adulthood, I had already spent a third of my life in therapy of one kind or another. I didn't want to waste another minute on introspection. I had thought out every detail of everything I'd ever done. I had analyzed, reanalyzed, and overanalyzed it all. Was the tattoo I wanted of a smashed fly because it would be funny and interactive, or was it because I subconsciously thought I was a piece of shit? Was that poem I wrote about advertisements for cream on TV not about consumerism but really about how fat I was? Did I cut my arm for attention or was it because I wanted to root myself in the physical world through pain, like pinching myself to wake up? I just wanted to live my life now. I could think about it later, like in my winter years, when I might write a book about it.

I had come out of my teens and gone into adulthood fast and furiously, trying to outrun my trauma, which I guess . . . didn't work? Weird. Maybe it was time to deal with it instead.

A few sessions into treatment, I had summarized my life story sufficiently for my therapist to get an idea of who I was and where I was coming from. I told her about my youth and teens. I told her about the anxiety I was feeling. I told her how it was making it impossible to live. I told her about my psychic sensitivities, my food sensitivities, my aversions to certain textures, how I hated love songs. I told her everything I could think to tell her because I wanted a diagnosis of some sort. A syndrome or something. A reason to feel the way I was feeling. Nothing explained this.

"This is ridiculous! I have a loving husband and four healthy sons, and I live in the most beautiful place I've ever seen and with pet goats. It's my dream life. It makes no sense. I must have some sort of chemical imbalance!"

And that's when she asked, "Did it ever occur to you that you should feel this way?"

Wait. What does that even mean?

She told me I had PTSD.

"From what?" I asked, but as I said the words, I realized I knew the answer. I had been making jokes for years about having it, but I never let it sink in that I actually did. It made sense, but also I felt ridiculous about it. Poor me for having people take my picture against my will when everyone was starving and being murdered. And they didn't seem to be as much of a mess as me! Poor me for having a famous, rich mommy. Poor me for having been sent to a bunch of cushy placements instead of being thrown out on the street like most people would have been . . . but I guess it was time to admit that my experiences were not just funny anecdotes I'd collected. They were real and painful things that I'd lived through, and they were going to destroy me if I didn't look at the fact that I had been victimized.

I don't want to be called a victim because I don't want to be called a survivor. I hate that. It implies that the suffering is over, and I know better. Don't call me a survivor until I'm dead.

I traced my current state of mind back to that night playing cards with my in-laws, and I realized that we had been talking earlier that evening about how all of our kids were growing up so fast. I remembered looking across the room at Eitan. He had just turned fourteen. He was technically a teenager but clearly was still a child. Eitan still slept with stuffed animals on his bed, even if they were all Tim Burton characters. He still slept on the floor of one of his brothers' rooms when he was scared, still asked me to tickle his arm to soothe him, still needed to be reminded to shower.

As I gazed at him, it hit me like a train that, at his age, I had already been separated from my family for a year. I had already been subjected to body searches, had taken personality inventory testing like the MMPI, had my showers overseen by nursing staff, and spent scared, sleepless nights alone in solitary confinement.

Eitan was still losing his baby molars, for fuck's sake.

I continued seeing this therapist, meeting my dad in the parking lot so we could switch cars and he could take my minivan full of kids to do something fun for an hour. They'd come back with their laps full of Happy Meals and stories about geocaching adventures in graveyards, and I'd drive them home with a headache from crying, hoping that I was getting better.

After around six months of this, my therapist ended up having a health scare and deciding that the medical care in Hawaii was too much of a risk for her, so she moved to Texas. I told everyone she quit, because that was a much funnier story. I was very grateful for the time I had with her, but I had a lot more work to do. I could find another therapist and start over, or I could DIY it like I did everything else.

I googled "immersion therapy." I made a pact with myself that I was going to go into all the terrifying places that made me want to flee, and I was going to sit there until I was calm and could leave a victor. Each win would make me stronger, and at some point, I might be able to be alone in public again. I was going to reclaim myself and my life one step at a time. First stop: Costco.

Costco was the perfect place for me to experiment because it was full of people with no boundaries, giant overstimulating product labels, free-sample pushers demanding conversation, fluorescent lights, and long, long lines. It couldn't have been more on point if it were a simulation.

On my last few trips to Costco, I had clung to my patient husband's side, scolding him and hysterically whisper-begging him to not get too far ahead of me. This next trip, I informed him, I was going to walk away from him. Maybe I'd just go a few feet. Maybe a whole aisle over. He was acting nonchalant about it, but I could tell he was looking at me out the side of his eye like you do the first time you let your kid cross the street without holding your hand. I asked him to please just keep the ringer of his cell phone on so I could call for a rescue if I needed it. I knew I would be paralyzed if I started to panic, and I wouldn't be able to do anything but relay my coordinates and wait to be found. He agreed and did exactly that. I felt like a big old burden, but that was even more incentive for me to try to beat this.

I had to call his phone a few times per trip. It felt as if it took him an hour to come find me, but in reality it was only seconds. I'd catch my breath and follow him until I was calm and then I'd try again. I'd like to say that it took me only a few visits to Costco, Target, the grocery store, etc., to be able to shop like the average housewife, but it took more than a year. It was embarrassing and I was low-key disgusted with myself. I pitied Jeff for being cursed with loving me. I somehow found strength to let all those feelings push me harder instead of burying me deeper. That was the real victory. It was this tiny shift in perception that rippled out and changed everything. Once I had that algorithm down, it didn't matter how long of an equation I had to solve. I slowly dragged myself out of the pit, one cell at a time.

That was five years ago. I still struggle with anxiety, though it rarely escalates into a full-blown panic attack anymore. I've gained another level of resilience that can't be touched. I thought I would never have a good quality of life again, and now here I am, getting out of bed in the morning, showering, eating things that are not almonds, talking to people, spending time alone, handling being human. I started working with my close friend Iris at her little country market in town, and every day it got a tiny bit easier.

There came a day where I went shopping alone without even checking once for my bottle of Ativan. I hadn't taken one in years, but I kept it on me as a security blanket. Maybe it was time for me to let go of this crutch and see how I handled life without it. When I got home, I rifled through my purse and dug the container out. The contents had turned to powder. The expiration date was half a decade ago. I disposed of it and replaced it with a bulk-size bottle of gummy vitamins and six ChapSticks from my now-favorite place in the world: Costco.

20B.

Going Ballistic

In January 2018, I flew back to Los Angeles with Cosmo for a tonsillectomy. I scheduled it to coincide with my sister Jessica's trip to take her three-year-old daughter, Maisie, to have surgery to have her tear ducts opened. Living in Hawaii has its price, like a lack of specialized medical care and affordable milk, and most of our doctor appointments require a three-thousand-mile commute. I was still afraid to fly alone and test my theory that I didn't need Ativan to function. Airplanes and airports seemed to be my biggest trigger, along with leaving my other kids and Jeff without me on an island that I might not be able to get back to, were there some kind of unforeseeable event like an atomic war. Irrational, right? Just wait.

Jessica might not have been the best choice for a flight companion as she is known for curling into a fetal position and hyperventilating at the slightest bit of turbulence, and, of course, on our flight to Los Angeles, there was turbulence. Jessica somehow managed to remain calm enough to keep the plane from being turned around, but just barely. When we landed, we rented a car and drove to my mom's house to stay with her. She wanted to be at the kids' appointments and help with their aftercare.

Jessica has always had the Pentland anxiety like the rest of us, but it's been worse since Eitan was born. Ever since his cleft palate surgery at ten months old (and an allergic reaction he had at nine months old that sent us to the emergency room), she's been a wreck. She used to finger swipe his throat every time he so much as hiccupped. One time she took a chunk of his uvula out with her too-long pinky nail. She makes my kids hold her hand any time they are within a block of a street. She cut their food into pea-size bites until they were tweens. She doesn't let them out of her sight. She makes an excellent babysitter for these reasons, though.

Her "aunt-xiety" pales in comparison to the mom version. She spent tens of thousands of dollars and several years of time to conceive her one and only child, and none of us will ever have a break from her neuroses ever again. When I make fun of her for it, she says, "Well, I only have *one*," which implies that the more kids a person has, the less it would bother them to lose one. I'm pretty sure it doesn't work like that.

I tease her about how she won't let her husband, Rich, take their daughter to the beach without her. She wants to be there to make sure he is holding Maisie's hand as she puts her feet in the water, even if she's wearing a floatie. She cuts Maisie's food into crumbs. She had a tiny breathing monitor called a Snuza that Maisie had to wear any time she slept for the entire first year of her life. She's not a helicopter mom, though. She allows her to roam mentally, spiritually, and socially, just not physically. I get it. I was like this for a while until I had more kids than hands and no choice but to surrender. It was a huge relief that Maisie's tear duct surgery took only minutes and had zero recovery.

Cosmo's procedure was slightly more complicated. My mom came to his appointment with me and did her comedy magic to keep his spirits up as he lay on the gurney waiting to go in. Once he was wheeled away, she got quiet and sat next to me in the waiting room palming her pocket prayer book until it was over. As soon as the doctor came out to tell us that everything had gone well, she perked back up. We were both relieved. Now, we just had to stay in Los Angeles for two weeks to watch for bleeding.

Cosmo's recovery was slower and more painful than expected, but since he got to miss school and lie on a couch playing video games all day and night, he didn't complain. The stressful parts of this visit were over and we could just enjoy our time here as if it were a vacation.

A week into Cosmo's recovery, I was playing dolls with Maisie in the office adjacent to the living room, where Jessica was arguing with someone on Facebook, probably about the benefits of communism. Maisie likes to play adult dolls, not baby dolls. Barbie is always springing it on Ken that she's pregnant, and Ken (me, I never get to be Barbie) has to get flustered and scramble for baby supplies. These pregnancies last only a few minutes each, so she can play this game over and over and over. I'm here for it.

While we were playing, I got a text on my phone. I glanced at it out of habit and put my phone back down. Wait. That couldn't possibly have said what I thought it did. My anxiety must be skewing the text. I picked it up again and stared at it.

EMERGENCY ALERT
BALLISTIC MISSILE THREAT INBOUND TO HAWAII. SEEK
IMMEDIATE SHELTER. THIS IS NOT A DRILL.

Maisie bounced a Barbie on my leg to win my attention back, and I just stared at her. I debated whether or not to tell Jessica. Because Maisie was here with her, she might be able to handle it, but the nephews . . . Her nephews were there. My kids. MY KIDS. OH MY GOD, I KNEW IF I LEFT THIS IS WHAT WOULD HAPPEN. I KNEW IT. I DIDN'T HAVE *ANXIETY*, I HAD THE PENTLAND CURSE, WHICH IS EXACTLY LIKE ANXIETY BUT WITH MANIFESTATION POWERS.

I couldn't remember how to dial a phone but eventually got my fingers to work enough to call Jeff. He answered, and I could hear a growing murmur in the background.

"JEFF! WHAT IS HAPPENING?!" I struggled to hear what he was saying. Was he telling the kids to get in the garage? Was he loading them up into the ferro-cement catchment tank buried in the garden? Was there a stampede approaching? He told me to hold on.

"Two eggs over easy on brown rice with extra-crispy bacon . . ." Oh my God, he was ordering breakfast! He was getting food. He must not have seen the text. That meant he wasn't helping our kids. He wasn't even with them. He was going to die at a fast-food restaurant. I kept calling his name, but he had put the phone at his side. I was about to hang up and call my dad when he finally came back on the line.

"Jeff, there's a missile! Where are the kids?!"

"The kids are asleep. Grandpa is with them. I'm out grabbing food. I saw that text on my phone," he said, "but I don't think it's real. I didn't hear it on my radio." For the last few years, he had been a volunteer firefighter, which meant he had to carry an official radio at all times. He assured me that, if it was real, he would've heard something from civil defense. I hoped he was right but didn't believe it, given my exceptional luck. The message *was from* civil defense. Why would they waste time radioing anyone? That's what the text was for.

I hung up and called my dad. He sleeps with the news station on all night and then carries his iPhone with a news station on all day. He answered in a panic and asked me if I'd seen the warning. I said I had and was scared but that Jeff didn't seem to think there was any cause for concern. I asked him if my kids had seen it. He told me that they were sleeping. I asked him if he was going to wake them up.

"I figured I should just let them sleep," he said. My heart sank so deeply that I couldn't talk. I'd never felt more horrifically sad than I did in that moment, thinking of their peaceful, sleeping faces lit up by an explosion, being rained down on with shrapnel without me there to tell them it was okay.

Although I longed to hear my kids' voices for possibly the last time, this seemed the kindest scenario. "Okay," I said, and hung up.

Iris was calling me on the other line. She and her husband, Griffin, were underneath their living room couch. Griffin had flipped it and put the kids under it while waiting for Iris to speed home from work. She was panicked, too, and Iris doesn't panic. Even when she should. She once dropped a freezer on her toe and almost severed it and then calmly walked to my car so I could drive her to the ER with a trail of thick blood and meat behind her.

I scrolled through every news site I could to try to figure out what was going on. Most TV stations had a ticker saying there was an incoming missile, but Hawaiian residents were speculating that it was a false alarm because the siren system hadn't gone off. Helicopter footage showed college students and drivers panicking and running, but there was no evidence of an incoming projectile. People were shown looking up in the sky, but nothing was there. There was nowhere to go to get clarity.

I thought about how, if I lost my kids, I couldn't go on. As I waited for definitive answers, I considered what the logical next steps were for me, but I wasn't exactly thinking straight. If my family died, I was going to have to mercy-kill myself. Then I remembered that Cosmo was with me, and I thought about how I'd have to stay alive for him. Or else murder/suicide us both. I was calmly mulling over all scenarios when I found a tweet from Congresswoman Tulsi Gabbard saying the alert was an accident. I quadruple-checked and called Jeff and could hear him eating his breakfast.

"I can't believe you're eating and not trying to speed to our kids," I said.

"Well, if there was a missile coming, I couldn't get there in time. Plus, they're asleep and your dad is there. I'm hungry." I sort of wanted him to bite his cheek really hard or get a gross, slimy bite of runny egg white, but also, I appreciated his ability to stay calm until he knew there was a real threat. I called my dad to decompress, and we went over and over the last hour processing everything. I asked him to have my kids call me when they woke up. He agreed and we hung up.

I stood up, woozy from the cyclone I'd just endured, and found Jessica in the living room. She was just now seeing the news, after it was already proven to be a false alarm.

"Did you see some idiot set off a fake missile alert in Hawaii?!" she asked me, relatively calmly.

"Yeah," I said, and then stared off into space for the next three days.

21.

The Tag

At the end of May 2018, Eitan graduated high school. It wasn't the graduation I had been imagining for years, his neck laden with lei while his entire extended family rallied around him, congratulating him. I imagined he would move to the mainland and attend a fancy culinary school and eventually open a restaurant that I could eat at for free. I had a vision for him. For us.

Just a year earlier, he had been debate captain and junior class president. His grades were decent. His headmaster, who was also the debate coach, loved him. He had great friends and a girlfriend and was well liked and happy.

Well, for the first few months, anyway. Halfway through the year, a teacher with whom he had been having trouble ever since he had cc'd her on an email to the headmaster accusing her of infringing on his freedom of speech for not letting him make fart jokes in the talent show a couple years earlier, asked him what he wanted to do with his life. "I want to be a writer," he said. She cackled and told him that was ridiculous. "You can't make a living doing that."

That one single interaction was enough to discourage him completely. It didn't matter that he had won first place in both of the all-ages spoken-word competitions he had entered that year, or that his stories were often picked to be on display at that school, or that his tuition was being paid by a writer; his confidence was destroyed. His grades fell, and by the end of the year, he was failing everything. His attitude was standoffish, and he started arguing about every little thing. All of our interactions ended in a fight, during which he would practice his debate skills and Jeff and I would yell.

As parents, we tried all the things we had learned in our youth. Demanding respect. Threatening eviction. Forcible drug testing. Spying. Tough love. Punishments. None of it was working. We were in over our heads.

I woke up one night to a phone call from the police saying Eitan had been in an accident. Impossible. He was asleep in the living room. I was sure it was a prank but got up to check that he was home anyway. I was in a dream state as I walked the long hallway to where he slept, but when I got there, he was nowhere to be found. I started trembling. The officer was talking to someone in the background, and I couldn't hear well enough to tell what they were saying. Oh God. Was he talking to a paramedic?! My knees buckled. I repeated, "Is he okay?! Is he okay?!" over and over, trying to hear an answer over my own panicked breath.

"He's okay, but the car isn't," the officer said. I went outside to see if our other vehicle was there. I'd need a way to get to him. My car was there in the driveway, but my mom's was not. We had been staying at her place for a few weeks while construction was being done on my house. She was in Los Angeles, but her Ford should've been there. It dawned on me that Eitan must've taken and crashed her car, the matriarch's car, his dad's boss's car—the only thing worse than crashing mine.

Thankfully, he wasn't hurt. We picked him up and drove him home. I was in shock at having seen the damaged vehicle and having the cop explain to me that Eitan would've flown off a cliff and landed square on top of the Mormon church if not for the telephone pole he'd hit. I was shivering with adrenaline. Jeff was silent: the absolute worst of all Dad Reactions. When we pulled up in our driveway, Eitan got out and ran away, and for the next few months he stayed with friends, scared to come home and face consequences.

I was devastated and sad, and Jeff was angry and disappointed. We both felt like we were failing our kid. Jeff had had a fairly protected childhood. He was allowed to watch only movies from the forties or fifties and TV shows from the seventies, in which the problems were small and always solved immediately. Life was literally black and white for him. There was a right way and a wrong way to do everything. I mean *everything*. Laundry. Driving. Shopping. Relationships. One of our biggest arguments early in our marriage was over the way I made mac and cheese: the wrong way, according to him. You see, I put several ingredients in—mustard powder, garlic, pepper, Gouda, and milk—whereas the *correct* way is boiling macaroni noodles and then melting cheddar over them. Can you put puke emojis in books? (Doesn't mean I don't eat seven portions when he makes it.) Jeff was a nurture-over-nature type and thought he just needed to double down on consequences and provide some good tough love to regain control of the situation.

I grew up in comedy clubs and mental institutions. The teens I knew were selling their bodies for drugs or places to stay. They smoked and drank and had promiscuous sex. They stole cars often, not just once, and got into high-speed chases with police officers. They made homemade explosives. They snorted coke off dicks and made alcohol out of cafeteria apple juice. I wasn't as worried about Eitan's behavior as Jeff was. I thought of it as a phase that would end and I just wanted it to be over as soon as possible. I missed him.

I missed peeking into his room at night to see his round alabaster face sleeping. I would put six plates on the table for every meal out of habit and then lose my appetite when I realized there were only five of us to feed. I noticed his laundry wasn't in the rotation and missed folding his ridiculous *Breaking Bad* and Tupac T-shirts. I told Eitan he needed to come home and he refused. He didn't want to deal with Jeff's strict parenting, and Jeff had no plans to ease up.

I tried the middleman peacekeeper role for a minute, and, when that didn't bring him home, I called the police. When they informed me that they couldn't do anything since Eitan was sixteen, I was stupefied. How could that be? He was still a minor! I paid my taxes! Fuck the police and such.

I had a realization in that moment. I couldn't force Eitan to be part of my life. I had taken that for granted as his mother. I'd just assumed he would have some kind of genetic inability to leave. I was wrong. That golden rope of light that tied him to me like a phantom umbilical cord could not be used as a lasso or leash. My priorities began changing in ways I could have never predicted. Safe and happy kids became more important than compliant and even present ones.

I would have to figure out another way to indenture—I mean . . . connect with—him. I would have to be open and mutable. I couldn't just be his mom anymore, I had to be his ally.

How can you be an ally for your kid without enabling or excusing him? I was at a complete loss. I didn't know how to do that, and I definitely didn't know how to do that and stay married. In desperation, I googled "Wilderness Survival troubled teen" and looked to see if a non-punitive version existed.

In that moment, I thought about my parents and what their lives were like during *my* teens.

In the span of five years, my dad had quit the job at the post office for which he had worked his ass off; moved several times; started, succeeded at, and quit doing stand-up; become a stay-at-home dad; landed a writing job on a number one sitcom; learned how to navigate all the legal and social aspects of Hollywood; endured a bitter public divorce; lost his job on a number one sitcom; fought an endless custody battle; co-parented with an abusive addict; and turned in desperation to professionals who might not have had the best suggestions.

During those same years, my mom had started a new career, landed a number one show, endured a bitter public divorce and then gotten remarried to an addict, found a long-lost child, starred in a number one sitcom, starred in a movie, wrote two books, produced a second sitcom, starred in a TV movie, done cameos in other projects, fought for her life daily in the press and at work, fought several lawsuits and court cases, completed a million interviews, sobered up a drug addict, started intense therapy that would cause a huge rift in her extended family, had a bunch of plastic surgery, started her own production company, opened a restaurant, started building a house—all while shouldering the responsibility of thousands of people that relied on her work to live.

I would have crumpled, if not died. There is zero shame in admitting that I could not have handled that. I feel only gratitude and awe now for what my parents endured on my behalf. They truly did the best they could.

I thought about what I could do differently than what they did, and my answer was "listen." My voice was so often lost amid the professionals' voices, the public's commentary, or else my own screaming. I wanted to hear my kids. I hoped that would be enough and that one day they would forgive Jeff and me for not knowing what we were doing and would think, They did the best that they could.

Jeff was less than thrilled with my new approach to parenting, and we started fighting about our fundamental beliefs. They had been compatible for raising boys, but now we were raising a man. We had to meet in the middle somewhere, but that was a very broad middle. We couldn't see eye to eye, and it got so bad that we lived apart for two weeks before we started therapy together.

Listen, if your parents get divorced when you're a teen, it actually *is* your fault, no matter what anyone tells you. Just kidding.

With the help of a therapist, Jeff and I were communicating a lot better. We were mostly on the same page now. I mean, we were *always* on the same page with regard to our goal of having happy kids, we just didn't agree on how to get there. We had to learn to compromise, not just with each other but with our expectations of our kids.

The compromise started with allowing Eitan to drop out of the private school he had been attending since sixth grade in order to go back to the homeschool program we had done years before. He could continue to work his job at a pizzeria, pay back Granny for the car he'd trashed, and still graduate high school.

I pushed for him to get a GED, thinking the sooner he was done, the better, but Jeff really wanted him to finish his schooling and not quit, and when Eitan was presented with those options, he chose to get his high school diploma.

To me, that meant he was thinking about his future, and that was wonderful to see. Nothing compares to the thrill of witnessing your teen doing something in his own best interest.

The homeschool was mainly online and serviced the entire island chain, so graduation was to take place on the island of Oahu, a forty-minute flight away. The school provided two plane tickets, one for the student and one for a support. Naturally it had to be me.

Though I received a call the day before the ceremony saying that Eitan was behind and would need to finish his work in the next two weeks to get his actual diploma, the school wanted him to attend the celebration. They would give him a blank portfolio at the ceremony that he could fill with his certificate later.

The day of his graduation, we woke up at five a.m. and drove an hour to the airport. In the security line, I went to write a tweet about how I was boarding a plane without Ativan and I saw that my mom was trending. I casually checked her page, saw her infamous tweet about Valerie Jarrett, and wondered what it meant as I boarded the plane. When the plane landed, I went to tweet about how I had survived the flight and saw my in-box full of DMs and all my friends tweeting about my mom. I tried to understand what had happened, but it wasn't making any sense in the few seconds I had in between deplaning and hailing a taxi. By the time we got in the cab to the venue, I saw that her *Roseanne* reboot had been canceled.

I wasn't totally surprised. Her internet-trolling, name-calling, conspiracy-theory-based tweets were upsetting to people, and even though her public relations staff and the network suggested she stay off Twitter, she kept at it. She doesn't like being told what to do, in case we haven't already established that.

I could tell she wasn't truly invested in the new *Roseanne* show. Most of her time was spent studying Judaism or watching true-crime programs, and this new attempt at staying relevant in an industry she didn't much care for seemed more of a burden than a joy. She had sounded exhausted and underwhelmed any time we had talked on the phone recently.

I tried to follow the story in the cab, but Eitan said, "Are you really going to be on Twitter all day?" I could see he needed to be the center of my attention. I told him that there was something happening with Granny and it appeared her show had been canceled after a tweet that was perceived as racist. I apologized and vowed not to look at my phone any more that day. I told him we would go have a nice mommy-son lunch and he should pick anywhere he wanted. He picked sushi, so we googled and found a place with good reviews within walking distance of the graduation ceremony.

I tried not to think about opening Twitter while we made our way to the restaurant. Whatever was happening would, I assumed, resolve and blow over.

We went inside and were seated. We were the only ones there since they had just opened for the day. It was quiet and calm, with several small resin water fountains trickling around us. We hadn't really connected in a while, and it was exciting to be talking about Eitan's goals. He seemed truly invested in himself and his future. That felt really hopeful, and I was proud of him.

We talked about the twists and turns of the last couple years, about what had started the spiral of his losing interest and giving up. I asked him if he had any immediate goals for after graduation, and he said he wanted to go back to Los Angeles, work in a restaurant, and take writing classes. I was happy to hear that he hadn't been totally discouraged from his dream of writing.

There was a sense of urgency on my part because I felt like this was my last chance to teach him something. Everything from here on out he would learn on his own. I struggled to think of a way to instill a final value. A perfect tool. One that could save him from anything and everything.

"We come from a long line of writers. Your great-great-grandma and great-grandma are both writers; your grandparents and your aunts and uncles all write. This is how we survive. I have gotten through every terrible situation I've ever been in by assuring myself that whatever was going on would make a great story someday. The more ridiculous a situation, the funnier it would be down the line."

Just then, a fifty-year-old man and his twenty-year-old date came in and sat two tables over. He wore a gaudy Hawaiian-print shirt and talked loud enough that Eitan and I could barely hear each other. I tried to pace my words so they would fall on his breaths. It was just one more distraction pulling our attention away from this important moment in both our lives.

I centered my thoughts and asked Eitan how soon he wanted to move to LA, and as he opened his mouth to answer, the guy said,

"DID YOU HEAR ABOUT ROSEANNE BARR? THEY CANCELED HER SHOW TODAY. YEAH. TURNS OUT SHE'S A RACIST AND CALLED A BLACK WOMAN AN APE! YOU CAN'T SAY THOSE THINGS IN PUBLIC THESE DAYS!"

What?! No fucking way. This wasn't the Roseanne I knew, and I *knew* Roseanne, so I opened Twitter to try to understand. All I saw was one tweet after another calling her a racist. EVERYONE. Even corporations were chiming in. Her friends, coworkers, former neighbors, Tom Arnold, everyone. I wanted to jump in, to explain what I knew. I could sense the outpouring of hurt and I wanted to stop it in its tracks, but reminded myself again of my current mission—being present for my son—and so I redirected my attention to him.

When I looked up from my phone, I saw Eitan's flared nostrils and knew he was on the verge of a reaction. Although he didn't know specifics, he knew that her show had been canceled and that she was trending for a tweet she had written. I didn't want him to fall in the trap of angrily defending himself to someone who was just mindlessly repeating gossip, so I tried to cut him off. "Eh. Nope. Ignore. He doesn't know—" I was too late. Eitan was already barking over his shoulder, "THAT'S MY GRANNY YOU'RE TALKING OUT YOUR ASS ABOUT!"

The guy turned around and stared at us staring back at him. He hadn't heard what Eitan had said, he just knew that my son had yelled in his direction. There was no way to explain in any easy terms what was going on, so we all just continued staring at one another until he turned back around, ready to talk incessantly again. The waiter and waitress ran over to us and asked if we were okay. Had something happened? Did we want them to do anything? I considered explaining the situation, but thought about how ridiculous everything would sound.

"My son here has had quite the two years and is attempting to graduate with a blank diploma from a homeschool program he hasn't actually completed yet, but the Pentland Curse that follows our family has made it so a major family crisis is happening at the exact same time, and . . . are you guys familiar with Twitter?"

I asked for a to-go box instead and shrugged at Eitan, preparing to give him that one final gift that would guarantee his survival.

I said, "Well, if this isn't one for *your* book, I don't know what is . . ."

22.

It's a Wrap

As part of my self-administered therapy, I decided to welcome any opportunity that presented itself to me, so when my friend Lisa asked me if I was ready to write a book, I was forced to say yes.

I figured it couldn't be that hard. I could write a book. All I had to do was type the words that had been running through my head for the last forty years. It would be cathartic, if nothing else. I signed a contract so I couldn't renege, then organized my life so that I had time every day to write. That meant Iris wouldn't have as much help at the store, though, and Jeff would have to pick up my slack at home. He was already working ten hours a day, six days a week, on average. Those two things alone made me want to say no, but I couldn't. I had promised myself, and I knew the stakes of chickening out. I knew how fast and far I could and would regress, and that was terrifying to me. I knew it was time.

As soon as I began to type words onto the screen, my life started to unravel. I don't know what I expected. I must've thought my Pentland Curse was in remission, when in truth it just lay dormant long enough for me to sign a contract, as is the nature of the disease. The next year would be difficult for many reasons, but the main reason was Jeff losing his job working for my mom because of the financial strain the loss of her show caused. Immediately after, Jeff had a nervous breakdown to rival my own.

He was feeling as anxious and lost as I had been feeling just a few years before, and so I tried to help him through it. I booked him on a solo trip to his favorite place in California—the Monterey Bay Aquarium. He could be outside the chaos of our very loud home and get centered.

I could continue to write my book, work at the store, and watch the kids while he went on the trip. No problem.

Two weeks before he was scheduled to get on the plane, I was at work when a customer came in doused with an obscene amount of perfume. I made a comment when she left, but no one else had smelled it. I panicked and sent Eitan to the local grocery store to buy me a pregnancy test. I told him it would be less embarrassing for him since I knew everyone in town (Chapter 7: Buying Mother's EPT, for his book).

The test was negative, but the one I took a day later was not.

I didn't want to tell Jeff I was pregnant because I felt as though the stress of it would break him forever. We had recently started fostering a dog, and he was the most perfect pup on Earth, but Jeff asked me not to adopt him because there was no way he could handle one more thing on his plate. I adopted the dog. How could I tell him just a week later that I was also having a baby? "I got the kids a dog! And I got the dog a kid!" There was no way.

I kept the pregnancy from him as an act of mercy. I would tell him after his trip—or never. I could just come home from an errand one day with a baby and be like, "Look what I got." I had a lot of muumuus that could hide a growing belly.

Unfortunately, I ended up telling Iris, who told her husband and one of the employees, and then I told my sister, who told her four-year-old. I told my closest friends and also some strangers. Within a few days, everyone but Jeff knew, which forced my hand so that I had to tell him.

When the time seemed right, or as right as it could, I made a joke about possibly being pregnant, just to gauge the room. He guffawed and said, "*That* would be the worst thing ever." Well, now I was definitely not going to tell him. Plan Show Up with Baby One Day was back in effect. Then he said, "Well, not the worst thing. But it would be horrible timing for you and the book." Okay, maybe I would tell him. Then he said, "I like having babies with you, though." And so I thought for a second and said, "Good, because . . . guess what?"

Naturally he didn't believe me because I had told him I was pregnant and then said I was kidding a few times now. I sent him to the same store to buy another pregnancy test and took it in front of him. He was in shock, but something in him seemed happy for the first time in a year. I was relieved.

Even though he had a glimmer of joy, he was still extremely apprehensive about a baby because he was now unemployed and in the middle of a complete restructuring of self. I reasoned with him that this must be the daughter he had always seen himself having. It had to be some sort of divine intervention because there had been virtually zero chance of my getting pregnant based on my cycle that month and my age. Not zero enough, I guess. When my chromosomal testing came back the next month, so did the gender. A healthy baby . . . boy.

Well, I was definitely not telling him this news. I panicked and fled my house when Jeff got home that day. I just needed a minute. I ran to Iris at the store and told her with tears streaming down my face. She threw her head back and chortled. She had done that when I told her I was pregnant, too. Even though she delighted in my misery, she was a good sounding board, and I was calm enough now to break the news to Jeff.

We were both in disbelief, but with every test that came back okay and every ultrasound that showed a healthy baby, we were growing more and more accepting.

Jeff went on his trip, which we had to put on a credit card as we had no expendable cash. The day before he left, he accidentally caught the dog's tail in the door and the dog had to have stitches. It cost four hundred dollars, so Jeff wanted to cancel his travels to save money. I assured him it would be okay, and he went.

Three days later, the dog's tail got infected and he had to go for surgery to remove the tip. While I was loading our pup up to take to the vet, Cosmo came in the house screaming. He had fallen off his skateboard and cut his knee on a rock. I couldn't tell how bad it was until he took his pants off, and then I almost fainted. I hadn't eaten in a solid month because of morning sickness, and I certainly was not strong of stomach at the moment. I told everyone to get in the car to go to the ER. It needed stitches. Cosmo, Otis, Buster, and I all piled into the van and went to watch Mo's knee get scrubbed clean and stitched. Another four hundred dollars. Jeff called me to say hi while I was at the ER, and all I said was, "Fine. It's all fine. Just making dinner. I love you." I'd fill him in when he returned.

The next morning the vet called to yell at me for skipping my appointment the night before without calling. I apologized and told her what happened, and she was completely defused and gently rescheduled me with pity in her voice, but that didn't stop her from charging another three hundred dollars for the amputation.

I kept telling myself that everything would be fine and I managed to keep it together until Jeff got home. I downplayed how chaotic it was with him away. For the first time in a long time, he seemed hopeful.

We could overcome nervous breakdowns and unemployment, dog adoptions and unexpected geriatric pregnancies, financial strain and medical emergencies. We could handle it.

I could write my book with my right hand while football-holding a breastfeeding infant with my left while Jeff recovered from a nervous breakdown and searched for jobs.

Then, when I was four months pregnant, COVID hit.

Okay. Fine.

I could finish my book with my right hand while football-holding a breastfeeding infant with my left while Jeff recovered from a nervous breakdown and searched for jobs *during a pandemic*.

On July 28, we had a perfectly healthy baby boy named Ezra. He fits so well, it seems that he was always here. Eitan came home for a few days to watch his brothers while I was in the hospital and never left. Though I feel for him and his entire generation, who were just about to spread their wings and fly when we got locked down, I can't pretend that I don't love having my whole family together.

A month after I had Ezra, Jeff told me he was going to go to school for a year for a certificate in neuro-linguistic programming and hypnotherapy. When? I asked. Next year? When I'm done with the book? No, he answered. Now.

OKAY, THEN. I CAN FINISH MY BOOK WITH MY RIGHT HAND WHILE FOOTBALL-HOLDING A NURSING INFANT WITH MY LEFT WHILE HOMESCHOOLING THREE KIDS AND WATCHING MY HUSBAND RECOVER FROM A NERVOUS BREAKDOWN WHILE HE STARTS SCHOOLING FOR A NEW CAREER DURING A PANDEMIC.

I just did.

Acknowledgments

Thank you, Jeff, for taking care of our kids so I could lock myself away to work. Thank you for being my biggest ally and my best friend. Thank you for laughing at all my jokes, even the silent ones that no one else gets. I love you for all eternity. Thank you for all the babies and thank you for no more babies.

Eitan, I'm so proud of you. You're such a hardworking man and so deep and wise. You are the best big brother. Thank you for coming home and helping out. Thank you for your wordplay, openness, and your love. Thank you for humoring me when I send "The moon is in Scorpio for three days so be extra careful" texts. I love you.

Mo, thank you for you drive-by advice, your wisdom, your depth, your genuineness, and your concern for the underdog. Thank you for making sense when no one else does. Chungus Amongus. Chicken butt. Hey, guess what? I love you.

Otis, thank you for showing me that I'm still capable of being shocked, that I haven't heard it all yet. Thank you for your sensitivity, your secret desire to help people, your quick mind, and your ability to make me choke-laugh. I love you like my own son.

Buster, thank you for being my helper, for your problem-solving skills, your trustworthiness, your innocence, and your terrible jokes. I love you so much.

Ezra, thank you for sneaking your way into our lives, for gluing us all together in love, for reminding us of what is important and what isn't. Thank you for your precocious slapstick, your joyous laugh and toothless smile, and for reminding us how quickly the car can go from spotless to covered in purée in a matter of milliseconds.

To all the kids in my life—Maisie, Ari, Sasha, Alani, Sadie, Olive, Evie, Jordan, Livia, Cooper, Milo, Letta, Eliza, Josie, Kawena (you were a kid when I met you, so. . .), I love you all. Thank you for letting me be a part of your lives in any capacity, for making me laugh, and letting me live my childhood over again through you. I live to watch you all grow into resilient, hilarious, wild destroyers of The Patriarchy.

To my extended family, I love you all and am grateful for any time I get to spend with you.

Thank you, Mom, for teaching me how to laugh my way through anything. Thank you for being more than a mother. I am eternally grateful for all I have learned from you.

Dad, thank you for your sense of humor, for your worry and concern, for teaching me how to be graceful and forgiving, and for remembering all the times and dates of all my major life events so I could write this book.

Becca, thank you for always being there for me and the kids and for taking photos and videos of all the precious memories that would've been lost without you.

Jessica, thank you for being the most interesting character in my book and life, for loving my kids like they were your own, for laughing with me always, and for being my other half.

Jake, thank you for letting me talk about your fat rolls, potty-training you, and your JFK obsession. Thank you for teaching my kids a whole other level of disgusting and inappropriate humor. Thank you for my Gemini moon niece. I can't wait to hear her first snarky comment.

Brandi, thank you for your unique perspective, your dedication to saving the world, your optimism, your sense of humor, and your ability to exist in several realities at once.

Buck, thank you for activating my amygdala and teaching me how to love unconditionally even if you're not aware that you did that. Thank you for being the easiest toddler to nanny and for your hilarious Instagram stories. You're Super Saiyan.

Bubbe, thank you for always seeing the good in me, for fighting for me, laughing with me, and overfeeding me. Thank you for letting me live vicariously through your dating life. Thank you for saving the box of tea I bought you when I was eleven until now and thank you for being the only phone number that hasn't changed.

Grandma Mary Alice, thank you for brushing knots out of my hair and for helping me in my darkest hour.

Beckie, I am so glad you approached me at RMA to tell me you liked my shoes, even if you had no eyebrows. That moment felt fated and now I know why. I will always be here for you.

Jen, I'm so sorry I didn't write about you in this book but technically I did because this is in the book, so now you can't throw that in my face anymore. Can you imagine if I did write about you, though? Think about that . . . What would I say? So many stories to choose from . . .

Iris, thank you for making me laugh like no one else can and for making the End Times a fun adventure. Same for you, Griffin.

Maneli, thank you for understanding me. I love you.

Lisa Gabriele, thank you for wanting to hear my story enough for me to want to tell it.

Eve, thank you for talking me down and for being removed enough from American pop culture to be the perfect amount of helpful.

Christy, Sarah, and Hayley, thanks for patiently walking me through the book-writing process.

Thank you, Jess Zimmerman and DVS, for your perfect insights, advice, and encouraging words.

Thank you, Twitter friends, for the stars, hearts, and camaraderie.

Thank you to the secret Butt App that started as boobs and then morphed into a perfect, safe little community where I could work some shit out.

About the Author

JENNY PENTLAND is a writer, mother, and goat farmer. Pentland is the daughter of Roseanne Barr and inspiration for "Becky" and "Darlene" on *Roseanne*—though their TV lives were a picnic by comparison. She and her family live in Hawaii.